Paul Martin was educated at Cambridge University, where he read Natural Sciences and took a PhD in behavioural biology, and at Stanford University, California, where he was Harkness Fellow in the Department of Psychiatry and Behavioral Sciences. He lectured and researched in behavioural biology at Cambridge University, and was a Fellow of Wolfson College, before leaving academia to pursue other interests including science writing. His previous books include *The Sickening Mind* and *Counting Sheep*.

Visit www.AuthorTracker.co.uk for exclusive information on your favourite HarperCollins authors.

From the reviews of *Making Happy People*:

'Cogently argued . . . Drawing on all the latest scientific research, Martin is able to conclude his jaunty book with a list of ten tips. How gratifying it is that common sense is at last vindicated by science. Now we must act upon it. Paul Martin proves himself a man of kindness and blithe optimism whose delightful diktats would be of benefit to us all'

ALEXANDER WAUGH, *Mail on Sunday*

'Well written, accurate and engaging . . . Martin is at his best when discussing how the education system so often fails to equip children to lead happy lives, and how it might be changed to remedy this deficit. He makes a powerful case . . . His book should be required reading for anyone working in education policy'　　　DYLAN EVANS, *Nature*

'Paul Martin discusses how we can bring up our children to be happy, and why we should. There is something almost shockingly nice about these arguments' NATASHA WALTER, *Guardian*

'Happiness, as Martin continually reminds us, is always within our reach. It is not to be found in material wealth or celebrity, but in our relationships and a healthy enthusiasm for life itself'

GINNY CLARK, *Glasgow Herald*

D0431574

'Martin writes clearly. He asserts that people are not always motivated by financial incentives, and that in some cases financial incentives actually reduce motivation rather than increase it'
ANTHONY DANIELS, *Daily Telegraph*

'A fascinating book that provokes thought and appreciative interest. Martin's quest to promote an ideal of human happiness where the success of close personal relationships is as important as material success is to be applauded. His clear, scientific and humane opinion on a subject heretofore governed by self-help gurus and descendants of Dr Spock is very welcome. Martin wisely uses the ideas of thinkers, scientists and authors, both contemporary and ancient, to make the science and psychology more accessible and relevant . . . Intriguing'
ELIZABETH MCGUANE, *Sunday Business Post*

'[Martin's] core ambition is to shift the direction of public policy away from crude economic indicators of progress to more sophisticated measures, involving "well-being" and "quality of life" . . . On the way, there will have to be some humanistic reforms of education – well argued by Martin, with an expert justification of the power of play' PAT KANE, *Independent*

'Paul Martin, in his new book, writes sagely. Happiness, as Aristotle first pointed out, is our ultimate goal in life'
MARY ANN SIEGHART, *The Times*

'This isn't a self-help book, though, as Martin himself says, it could well be helpful. Well laid out and clearly written'
MELANIE MCGRATH, *Evening Standard*

'The nature of happiness, Martin argues, may be debatable, but the recent upsurge of research now suggests that, far from being intangible, it is a skill that can be learned. His book tells parents and teachers how they can best generate the circumstances that will create truly happy children' JIM GILCHRIST, *Scotsman*

PAUL MARTIN

Making Happy People

The Nature of Happiness and its Origins in Childhood

HARPER PERENNIAL

London, New York, Toronto and Sydney

Harper Perennial
An imprint of HarperCollins*Publishers*
77–85 Fulham Palace Road
Hammersmith
London w6 8jb

www.harperperennial.co.uk

This edition published by Harper Perennial 2006
2

First published in Great Britain by Fourth Estate 2005

A catalogue record for this book
is available from the British Library

isbn-13 978-0-00-712707-8
isbn-10 0-00-712707-3

Typeset in PostScript Sabon by
Rowland Phototypesetting Ltd, Bury St Edmunds, Suffolk

Printed in Great Britain by Clays Ltd, St Ives plc

For Harriet, whose idea this was

Contents

Contents

Acknowledgements

I am very grateful to Gillon Aitken, Emma Barrett, Nic Coombs, Philip Gwyn Jones, Harriet Martin, Kristina Murrin, Edward Pointsman, John Sants and Patsy Wilkinson for their kind help and advice.

· ONE

First things

The biggest issue

This is the story of something we all want for ourselves and for our children, but which few of us are sure how to get. It is about the conditions that give rise to happy children who will grow up to become happy adults. Along the way, we will consider how happiness develops during the lifetime of each individual, and hence how parents and schools can help to make happy people.

Happiness is a notoriously elusive aspect of human existence, whose nature and origins have been debated throughout history. But one point on which almost everyone agrees is that happiness is a uniquely desirable commodity. In every culture where researchers have posed the question, the majority of people say they regard happiness as their ultimate goal in life. Most people rate happiness above money (even if privately many of them behave as though money really were their primary goal). According to research, many Americans believe that happy people are morally superior to unhappy people and more likely to go to heaven. America even enshrines the inalienable right to 'life, liberty and the pursuit of happiness' in its constitution.

The idea that happiness is the ultimate goal in life is reinforced by a simple argument which was set out more than two thousand years ago by the Greek philosopher Aristotle. He pointed out that no one ever seeks happiness as a means to something else. With the sole exception of happiness, everything we humans desire can be regarded as a means to some higher end – and that higher end is usually happiness. People chase after money, power, material possessions, beauty or fame because they believe – often mistakenly – that these will bring them happiness. But no one ever seeks happiness in the belief that it will bring them some even higher benefit. Therefore, Aristotle concluded, happiness must be the ultimate goal.[1]

But what exactly *is* happiness, and how do you achieve it – if not for yourself, then at least for your children? Why are some people consistently much happier than others? Is it genetically encoded, or can you buy it? Why is happiness virtually ignored by the education system, economists and governments, as though it were irrelevant or faintly embarrassing? We all say we want children to be happy, but why is so little actually done to pursue this aim? How can parents and teachers help children to maximise their chances of being happy people, both in childhood and throughout adult life?

These are big questions that do not invite simple answers. The novelist Michael Frayn wrote that happiness is the sun at the centre of our conceptual planetary system, and is just as hard to look at directly. Fortunately, we now have science to help us. Within the fairly recent past, scientists have begun to gaze at happiness and they are formulating tentative answers to questions about its nature and causes. As we shall see, a fair amount can now be said about happiness that is based on verifiable evidence rather than folklore or opinion. Even so, plenty of popular myths persist, and we should knock these on the head before going any further.

One of the silliest myths is that actively pursuing happiness is the best way to lose it. According to fortune-cookie philosophy, happiness is like a cat: it will never come if you summon it, whereas if you ignore it you will soon find it jumping into your lap. So, if only we would stop thinking about it, happiness would spontaneously blossom within us. This notion seems to be widely believed, in that many people behave in their daily lives as though happiness cannot be actively cultivated. But it is wrong. There are plenty of things we can all do to make ourselves and our children happier – and the starting point is knowledge. Someone who has a basic understanding of the nature and causes of happiness is much better equipped to become happier and to help others become happier. Knowledge is power.

A related myth is that happiness is essentially a matter of blind chance, and we must wait for it to creep up on us. Indeed, the word itself reflects this notion: 'happy' is derived from the Old Norse word *happ*, meaning luck or good fortune. The scientific evidence points to a very different conclusion, however. Happiness does not just fall randomly out of the blue: we can discover where happiness comes from and we can encourage it.

A more up-to-date piece of folklore, which has a seductive whiff of pseudoscience about it, asserts that happiness is all in the genes. According to this version of reality, the setting of your personal 'happiness thermostat' was fixed at the moment you were conceived. Thus, if you were unlucky enough to draw the short genetic straw, then trying to make yourself happier would be as futile as trying to make yourself taller.

Again the science tells a different story. Genes do of course play crucial roles in the development of any human characteristic, and happiness is no exception. It is also true that a person's overall level of happiness will tend to remain fairly stable over quite long periods of time. But there is no such thing as a 'gene for happiness', and no meaningful sense in which anyone's happiness is fixed for life by their inherited DNA. Happiness resides in the mind, and we all have the capacity to make ourselves and our children happier (or unhappier) than we are now. As we shall see later, the basic building blocks of happiness are shaped by our experiences, attitudes and ways of thinking. Parents and schools therefore have a big impact on children's chances of being happy people, and for reasons that have nothing directly to do with genes. The single biggest influence on happiness is something we all have the scope to influence for better or for worse – namely, our relationships with other people.

Far from supporting the idea that happiness is hard-wired in our genes, scientific research increasingly suggests that happiness is more akin to a skill that can be learned. Graphic evidence for this has come from recent investigations by neuroscientists into the effects of meditation on brain function. Carefully controlled experiments have revealed that certain forms of meditation consistently produce changes in brain activity which are separately known to be associated with feelings of happiness and freedom from anxiety.[2] People can learn to change the way their brains work and hence how happy they feel. When it comes to fortune-cookie philosophy, Abraham Lincoln was closer to the truth when he remarked that most people are about as happy as they make up their minds to be.

One of the most pernicious of all the common myths is that happiness is provided by wealth or celebrity. Although most people claim that happiness is their ultimate goal, they often behave very differently in their everyday lives. In practice, many of us expend much of our time and effort on acquiring wealth, social recognition, or both, in the belief that these will bring us enduring happiness. The reality, as revealed by a mass of research, is that they will not.

Money, fame and new possessions can make us feel better for a while – but not much better, and not for long. The gloss soon wears off. Winning the lottery, appearing on reality TV or buying a new car is not a reliable route to lasting happiness. Meanwhile, the quest for wealth, success and social recognition often distorts people's lives and makes them unhappy, especially if it gets in the way of things that really *do* matter, such as close personal relationships. As we shall see later, excessive materialism is a pervasive cause of unhappiness.

When it comes to children, parents sometimes pay lip service to happiness. If asked, most would agree that what they want above all else for their children is happiness. But, just as with their own happiness, parents do not always behave as if they really mean what they say. Their everyday concerns typically focus on tangible issues like their children's performance at school and prospects of getting a good job. Few parents make their children's happiness an explicit objective, and the education system certainly does not: there are as yet no national league tables for happiness. In real life, the quest for demonstrable success generally overshadows the quest for happiness.

Fortunately, parents do not need to choose between wanting their children to be happy and wanting them to succeed at school or get good jobs, because there is no real conflict between these goals – quite the reverse, in fact. Happiness and success go hand in hand. Research has demonstrated that happy people are on average mentally and physically healthier, more successful in the classroom and at work, more creative, more popular, more sociable, longer lived, and less likely to become criminals or drug addicts. In short, happy children make better students and better employees. We shall look at some of the evidence for this later.

So, even the pushiest of parents – those who care only about their children's tangible achievements and regard the quest for happiness as woolly-minded self-indulgence – should nonetheless make happiness their top priority. In this case, you really can have your cake and eat it. The added bonus is that raising happy children who develop into happy adults will also benefit society as a whole, for all the reasons listed above. Wanting your child to be happy is not even selfish. Helping children to become happy people should be an explicit and praiseworthy goal of parenting and education.

About this book
The story comes in three parts. First, we will consider what happiness is and why it really matters. Defining happiness at the outset is obviously crucial, because although the word is bandied about in everyday conversation, its meaning is rarely clear. 'Happiness' signifies different things to different people.

To preview the next chapter, I will argue that happiness consists of a combination of three distinct elements: pleasure (the emotional sensation of feeling good in the here and now), the absence of displeasure (freedom from unpleasant sensations such as anxiety or pain) and satisfaction (judging, on reflection, that your life is good). Thus happiness depends both on feeling (pleasure) and thinking (satisfaction). We will then look at the many different ways in which happiness is good for us, such as making us physically healthier and more likely to succeed in our chosen aims.

Having looked at the nature and benefits of happiness, we will examine the main factors that influence its development during each individual's lifetime. We will consider, for example, how happiness is affected by personal relationships, work, genes, health, intelligence, marriage, money, education, religion and physical attractiveness. Some of these influences, notably personal relationships, turn out to be very important whereas others, notably wealth, have surprisingly little enduring impact.

The final part of the book discusses how parenting and education can help or hinder the development of happiness in children. We will see how different styles of parenting behaviour affect children's long-term prospects for happiness and well-being. We will also imagine what an education system might look like if it paid more attention to happiness. One conclusion here is that a preoccupation with short-term, measurable attainment can do more harm than good. Education must obviously provide children with far more than just qualifications if they are going to be happy, successful people for the rest of their lives.

This is not a self-help book in the conventional sense, although I hope you will find it helpful. Vast numbers of books have been written on the subject of happiness, but I would like to think this one is different for a number of reasons. For a start, it approaches happiness in terms of development – that is, how happiness emerges and changes during the lifetime of the individual, from conception to death. Often the best way to understand a complex aspect of human nature is to see how it is assembled during the early years of life, and how it changes over time in response to experience. Most self-help books on happiness are only about adults, or only about children, and they focus on one slice of a person's life, usually the here and now. But a fuller understanding can only come from thinking about the whole lifespan. Happiness is not an afterthought to be grafted on when we have grown up: its foundations are laid in childhood.

Childhood, however, is not merely a preparation for adulthood, and there would be no excuse for subjecting children to prolonged unhappiness on the grounds that it might make them happier or more successful as adults. Forcing children to neglect their friends and hobbies in order to study hard at subjects they dislike might pave the way to well-paid careers, but at what cost? Such strategies often backfire before the hallowed goal is ever reached. Conversely, keeping young children 'happy' (or, at least, docile) by indulging their every whim is not difficult, but children who are spoiled in this way sometimes turn into unpleasant adolescents and unhappy adults. Happiness is for life: it should start at the beginning and continue through to the end. The aim should be to raise happy children who develop into happy adults.

Old age matters as well. Thanks to improvements in living conditions and healthcare, the populations of wealthy nations are living longer and spending a larger proportion of their lives as elderly people. Laying solid foundations for lifelong happiness will therefore be even more important for future generations than it is for ours. Fortunately, the ingredients that contribute to successful aging are, by and large, the same ones that promote happiness earlier in life.

Some self-help books on happiness or parenting appear to be based on remarkably little evidence, relying on anecdotes and appeals to 'common sense' rather than verifiable data. The novelist Ian McEwan was barely exaggerating when he wrote that there is 'no richer field of speculation assertively dressed as fact than childcare'. In my opinion, it is a good idea to be sceptical of any argument that relies mainly on appeals to 'common sense', because 'common sense' often turns out to be wrong. (Albert Einstein famously defined common sense as the collection of prejudices we acquire by the age of eighteen.) I have tried as far as possible to base my arguments on published scientific evidence rather than 'common sense' or personal opinion – although I have not shied away from expressing my opinions as well. Many of the scientific papers and books from which I have drawn this evidence are listed in the References section at the back.

A substantial body of objective research evidence is now available to cast light on a subject that was once the preserve of philosophers, theologians and gurus. Over the past decade or so, many scientific investigations have been conducted into the nature, causes, consequences and origins of happiness.

Within psychology, in particular, there has been a revolution in thinking. During the second half of the twentieth century, psychology focused almost exclusively on what goes *wrong* with people's minds, largely ignoring all the things that usually go *right*. For instance, between 1967 and 1994 the main academic psychology journals published nearly 90,000 papers about depression, anxiety or anger, but barely 5,000 that even mentioned happiness, satisfaction or joy.[3] The negative outnumbered the positive by 18 to 1. Since then, however, there has been an explosion of interest among psychologists in positive states of mind such as happiness, optimal experience and satisfaction with life. A whole new field of study has emerged, which its practitioners refer to as positive psychology.

Positive psychology is concerned with well-being rather than with disease, with how people flourish rather than how they become ill. Its ultimate aim is to make lives happier and healthier, and to help individuals realise the highest possible levels of human potential. In a much more limited way, that is also the aspiration of this book. You do not have to be an unhappy adult, or the parent of an unhappy child, to benefit from knowing more about the nature and causes of happiness.

TWO

What is happiness?

What is the highest of all the goods that action can achieve?
The great majority of mankind agree that it is happiness
... but with regard to what happiness is, they differ.
ARISTOTLE (384–322 BC), *The Nicomachean Ethics*

Heart and head

During a visit to France many years ago, the former British
Prime Minister Harold Macmillan asked Madame de
Gaulle, wife of the French president, what she was most
looking forward to when her hard-working husband
retired. To Macmillan's surprise and embarrassment,
Madame de Gaulle replied, 'A penis.' Only later did it
dawn on him that what she had actually said was 'Happiness.' Most of us recognise a penis when we see one, but
we might feel less confident if asked to define happiness.
Ask two parents what they mean by the word and you will
get two different answers; ask two philosophers and you
will probably get at least five.

Debating definitions is usually a tedious exercise beloved
of pedants, but in this case it really does matter. After

11

all, I have already suggested that happiness is the most important thing in life. On a practical level, implicit but faulty beliefs about the nature of happiness have a pervasive influence on almost every sphere of human activity, ranging from government economic policies to religion, from education to therapy, and from how we raise our children to how we conduct our daily lives. So, before burrowing into the causes of happiness and their practical implications, we should first decide what happiness *is*.

For a start, happiness is a distinct state in its own right, and not merely the absence of sadness or depression. You can be happy and sad at the same time, if you think about it. Imagine, for example, how you might feel (or felt) on your last day at school, or when your youngest child leaves home for college, or when you leave a job you have enjoyed for an even better one. Your feelings might be a complex mixture of pride, satisfaction, excitement, anxiety, sorrow and anticipation. Happiness is more than just the absence of unhappiness in much the same way that health is more than just the absence of disease.[1]

Happiness also means more than just feeling good in the here and now. Like any other fundamental aspect of human nature, happiness is too complex to reduce to a single dimension or a simple formula. So, what *is* it? Rather than dance round the issue, I will set out a definition that is as simple as I can make it, but which should nonetheless be recognisable to most scientists and philosophers who make a professional study of the subject. In short, happiness is a mental state composed of three distinct elements:

- *Pleasure*: the presence of pleasant, positive moods or emotions such as pleasure, contentment, joy, elation, ecstasy or affection.[2]

12

- *Absence of displeasure*: the absence of unpleasant, negative moods or emotions such as sadness, anxiety, fear, anger, guilt, envy or shame.
- *Satisfaction*: judging, on reflection, that you are satisfied with your life in general and with at least some specific aspects of your life (for example, your personal relationships, career or physical abilities).

Thus happiness is a combination of experiencing pleasure, not experiencing displeasure and being satisfied with your life. The relative proportions of pleasure, absence of displeasure and satisfaction can vary enormously, although you need at least a little of all three to be truly happy. Happiness therefore comes in many shapes, colours and flavours, comprising different combinations of satisfaction, pleasure and displeasure. Furthermore, any one combination of the three can be attained in many different ways: each person has their own unique blend as a result of their own unique life history and experiences.

Some psychologists and philosophers argue that there is a fourth dimension to happiness, which they variously refer to as 'meaning', 'purpose' or 'virtue'. This embodies the sense that for a life to be truly happy it must have some deeper purpose or meaning beyond pleasure or satisfaction. For some people, this fourth dimension means religion (a subject we shall return to in chapter 6). However, the concept that true happiness requires a deeper purpose or meaning goes back at least as far as the philosophers of ancient Greece, for whom it did not necessarily have religious connotations.[3] This is complex philosophical territory. Suffice it (I hope) to say that my threefold definition of happiness, and especially the element of satisfaction, is meant to be interpreted in the broadest possible sense, to encompass this fourth dimension. Great satisfaction, and hence great happiness, clearly can be derived from believing that your life has some deeper purpose or meaning, whatever that is.

The more straightforward distinction between pleasure and the absence of displeasure also has deep roots running back to ancient Greece. The philosopher Epicurus, among others, argued that avoiding pain and displeasure is a crucial element of happiness.[4] The seventeenth-century poet John Dryden captured the thought in these lines: 'For all the happiness mankind can gain / Is not in pleasure, but in rest from pain'. Early Buddhist teachings express a similar view when they advocate the avoidance of suffering, and depict the ultimate state of nirvana as one in which all suffering has ended.

Modern research has confirmed that pleasure and displeasure are distinct states, not just opposite ends of the same spectrum. Perhaps surprisingly, the amount of pleasure we experience is found to be relatively independent of how much displeasure we experience, at least when measured over reasonably long periods of time. You can have a lot, or a little, of one or both in your life. A heroin addict might have a life packed with intense pleasure and intense displeasure, whereas a routine-bound suburban drone might have little of either. Given a magic wand, you would probably choose to have a generous serving of pleasure, with occasional homeopathic doses of displeasure to heighten the contrast.

Pleasure and displeasure even have different brain mechanisms. A chemical messenger substance called dopamine is released by the brain in response to food, sex, drugs and other pleasurable stimuli, and for this reason dopamine is sometimes referred to as the brain's 'pleasure chemical'.[5]

Pleasure also stimulates the release in the brain of natural opiate substances called encephalins and endorphins. An imbalance in a different chemical messenger, called serotonin, plays a central role in unpleasant states such as anxiety and depression. Prozac and certain other antidepressant drugs work by inhibiting the re-uptake of serotonin in the brain and thereby boosting its level.

Pleasure and displeasure can become more closely intertwined in people suffering from severe depression. As well as experiencing intense displeasure, some depressives lose the capacity to feel pleasure – a condition known as anhedonia. They become unable to enjoy experiences that would normally raise their mood, which is one reason why it can be extremely difficult for them to emerge out of their depression.

Even more crucial to an understanding of happiness is the distinction between pleasure/displeasure and satisfaction. Pleasure and displeasure differ from satisfaction in two fundamental ways. First, pleasure and displeasure reflect how you *feel*, whereas satisfaction reflects how you *think* about your life.[6] Satisfaction can come from achieving long-term goals, and it extends the concept of happiness to include the fulfilment of mental as well as physical appetites. 'No man is happy', wrote the Roman philosopher Marcus Aurelius, 'who does not think himself so.'

The second big difference between pleasure/displeasure and satisfaction concerns time frames. Pleasure and displeasure are rooted in the present: they are about how you feel *now*. Satisfaction is rooted in the past, as you look back on your life. A Greek scholar called Solon, who lived around 600 BC, expressed this retrospective aspect of satisfaction in a strong (if not wildly overstated) form when he wrote that no man could be described as happy until he was dead. The distinction between pleasure/displeasure and satisfaction means you can be happy without having to be one of those smiley people who appear to be permanently bubbling over with bliss. Some of us are just not very jolly most of the time, but that does not necessarily mean we are unhappy. Happiness comes in many forms, not all of which are built on immediate delight.

Happiness, then, depends both on feeling (pleasure and displeasure) and thinking (satisfaction); it involves both the heart and the head. This has important practical implications. It means, for example, that you can be satisfied, and therefore happy, without necessarily experiencing much immediate pleasure. We all have to put up with occasional bouts of displeasure in order to achieve satisfaction, because most satisfying activities involve effort and some entail outright pain. Most of us would feel satisfied (and therefore happy) about, say, comforting a crying baby or a sick relative, even though the experience might not be particularly pleasant at the time. Our happiness would derive from a deeper sense of satisfaction at having done something good. Similarly, I am told that training hard for a competitive sport can be highly satisfying despite at times being painful.

The eminent American scientist Martin Seligman, who is one of the founders of positive psychology, has neatly encapsulated the three elements of happiness into what he calls the Pleasant Life and the Good Life. As its name implies, the Pleasant Life is one built primarily on pleasure and the absence of displeasure. This is the materialistic vision of hedonism, fuelled by lashings of raunchy sex, prolific shopping, exquisite food, recreational drugs, designer clothes, or whatever presses your button.[7] The underlying attitude is characterised by an overriding

16

concern for the self, a drive for immediate gratification of physical needs, and a belief that material possessions produce happiness. The outward sign of someone living the Pleasant Life is a big smile.

In contrast, Seligman's Good Life is one built mainly upon satisfaction. Someone living the Good Life derives much of their happiness from engaging in worthwhile activities like work, parenting or study, and attaining goals that mean something to them. They may not always be grinning with joy, because they sometimes do things that are difficult or unpleasant, but they nonetheless feel good about the life they are living.[8] If all is going really well, you could have a life that is both Pleasant and Good. A Good Life rich in satisfaction may also be a Pleasant Life. Someone who has a loving partner, close friends, an interesting job and a stimulating social life may have experiences that are both satisfying and pleasurable. There is no rule against having both.

More than pleasure

Equating happiness with pleasure has been a common error throughout history. Across the centuries, various sages, politicians and gurus have preached that the ultimate aim in life should be the pursuit of pleasure and the avoidance of pain.[9]

In eighteenth- and nineteenth-century Britain, for example, Jeremy Bentham and like-minded utilitarian philosophers championed a world view that made happiness synonymous with pleasure. Bentham, whose stuffed remains are still on display in University College, London, regarded pleasure as the ultimate arbiter of right and wrong, and argued that playing pub games was just as good as composing a symphony if it produced the same

17

amount of pleasure. He famously asserted that 'the greatest happiness of the greatest number' should be the supreme criterion for morals and legislation. Bentham even tried to devise objective methods for measuring the greatest happiness of the greatest number using his 'felicific calculus', but the task was beyond him.

Twenty-first-century attitudes are not vastly different, in that many people are still inclined to focus on pleasure rather than satisfaction when thinking about happiness. This mindset, which evaluates happiness in terms of feelings rather than thoughts, lies at the heart of our consumerist 'me' culture, and it starts early in life. Young children readily discover the immediate fix that comes from a pleasurable experience like eating chocolate or watching TV. Satisfaction is more elusive, since it requires thinking, effort and a certain amount of patience. Children can all too easily develop a lifelong habit of relying on short-term pleasures rather than learning to attain satisfaction. As we shall see later, a child's ability to resist the desire for instant gratification, in return for greater benefits at a later time, is a good predictor of subsequent happiness and success.

Now, there is certainly nothing wrong with pleasure: personally, I am in favour of having as much as I can get. One of the simplest and most reliable ways of making yourself feel better, at least for a while, is to do something you enjoy. For many people, listening to music is a reliable way of eliciting powerful sensations of pleasure and relaxation. Research using brain-scanning techniques has revealed that pleasurable responses to music are mediated by the same regions of the brain that respond to other pleasurable stimuli including sex, food and recreational drugs.[10] Listening to music can also ease anxiety and induce a physiological relaxation response, which is why music therapy has been used successfully for many years to help patients suffering from painful medical conditions.

But, as I have said, there is more to happiness than pleasure. William James, who was one of the founders of modern psychology, put it like this: 'If merely "feeling good" could decide, then drunkenness would be the supremely valid human experience.' It's good to feel – but it's also good to think. After all, thinking is one of the hallmarks of being human. A life built on pleasure alone can be empty and one-dimensional – a life for grazing animals, as Aristotle scathingly described it. Taken to excess, the Pleasant Life can be self-destructive and un-happy. Elvis Presley and the Marquis de Sade reportedly lived lives rich in pleasurable sensations and the gratifica-tion of physical appetites, but not everyone would regard their later years as enviably happy in the broader sense. At the other end of the spectrum, saintly figures have lived lives rich in self-sacrifice and satisfaction but rather short on pleasure. There is something to be said for a happy life built on generous measures of both.

How is happiness measured?
Throughout this book I will be referring to evidence drawn from published scientific research into the nature and causes of happiness. Some of this work is cited in the References section at the end. However, you might be wondering how scientists could possibly *know* all these things. After all, happiness is an essentially private experi-ence. And if you ask someone how happy they are, can you trust their answer? Investigating happiness is not a trivial problem. Fortunately (or I could not have written this book) psychologists have devised an array of proven

and reasonably reliable techniques for measuring happiness, which they have been studiously deploying for many years.

How, then, do psychologists go about measuring happiness? In most cases they do it simply by asking direct questions to suitably selected samples of people. A number of special questionnaires (or 'scales', as they are known in the trade) have been developed for this purpose. Some are designed specifically to assess pleasure, displeasure or satisfaction with life, while others are intended to assess happiness in the round. The simplest versions use a single question, such as 'How satisfied are you with your life in general?' The respondent answers on a scale of, say, one to ten. More sophisticated versions use many different questions (or 'items') which are designed to probe specific aspects of pleasure, displeasure or satisfaction. For example, the Oxford Happiness Inventory contains 29 different items, and for each item the respondent must select one of four statements that best describe how they have been feeling over the past several weeks – for example, 'I do not feel happy/I feel fairly happy/I am very happy/I am incredibly happy'.

Asking people directly is not the only way of gauging their happiness. Other techniques have also been devised. These include conducting one-to-one interviews, asking partners, friends or close relatives to assess the individual's happiness, and measuring levels of various hormones and neurotransmitter chemicals such as dopamine, serotonin, cortisol and endorphins. Another widely used technique is known as experience sampling or mood sampling. In this case, the subjects carry a notebook or miniature electronic recorder around with them and make a note of their current experience, activity, mood or level of happiness at various times throughout their normal day, whenever they receive a prompt from a pager or timer.

Memory can also cast light on happiness. Studies have found that happy people find it easier than unhappy people to remember good events in their lives and to forget bad events. Unhappy people are typically faster at recalling unpleasant memories than pleasant memories. This seems to be partly because happy people actually experience more positive events than unhappy people, and partly because they are more likely to interpret any event in a positive way.

Happiness – or, rather, positive mood – can also be gauged by recording how much time people spend smiling. However, only certain types of smile indicate genuine jollity. Experiments have revealed that the so-called Duchenne smile, which involves smiling with the eyes as well as the mouth, is a true indicator of positive mood, whereas a mouth-only smile is not. The non-Duchenne smile is the contrived, have-a-nice-day smile of the fake who feels they should appear happy even when they are not. Researchers have found that people can sense whether a stranger is smiling or frowning from the sound of their voice alone, without seeing their face. In fact, you can judge whether someone is smiling just from hearing them whisper.

A good mood even has a distinctive smell. Scientists have discovered that people can judge whether someone is in a positive mood from their body odour alone. In one experiment, men and women were made to feel either cheerful or frightened by showing them funny or scary films, while their armpit odours were collected on gauze pads. A week later, the researchers presented these gauze pads to complete strangers and asked them to decide which ones had come from people in a jolly mood and which from frightened people. They were able do this – not perfectly, but well above chance levels. This ability to divine mood from smell is not as remarkable as it might seem. We humans are primates, and zoologists have known for decades that other species of primates communicate information about their emotional states, particularly fear, through smell.

One reason for placing a degree of trust in psychologists' measurements of happiness is that these very different techniques produce results that are broadly in accord with each other. Thus, people who report feeling in a good mood and satisfied with their lives are also likely to be judged happy by their friends, to have a lot of objectively positive experiences, to smile more, to have lower levels of stress hormones in their bloodstream, and to find it easier to remember nice events. They probably smell jolly as well. Another reason for believing that measurements of happiness are meaningful is that they relate consistently to other indicators of well-being. Measures of happiness are reasonably good predictors of people's mental health, the state of their personal relationships and family life, their success at work or in the classroom, their physical health and even how long they live. (We will be exploring these connections between happiness, health and other aspects of well-being in the next chapter.)

One day it should be possible to judge how happy someone is by analysing the patterns of electrical activity in their brain. Scientists have made some progress in this direction, but the technology is still far from mature. Techniques such as PET (positron emission tomography) brain scanning have revealed that particular moods or emotions are consistently accompanied by distinctive patterns of electrical and chemical activity in various regions of the brain.[11]

The brain activity patterns associated with happiness and sadness are quite different from one another, reinforcing the view that they are distinct mental states. A recent series of brain-scanning studies has shown that happiness is particularly associated with heightened electrical activity in an area on the left side of the brain known as the dorsal-superior region of the left prefrontal cortex. Individuals who routinely display higher levels of activity in this brain area are found to be better at regulating their emotions and faster at recovering emotionally from unpleasant experiences.

It may not be too many years before measurements of brain activity provide a new window on happiness. Meanwhile, scientists are able to assess happiness in meaningful ways, and are beginning to unravel its causes and consequences.

THREE

Why does happiness matter?

When we are happy we are always good, but when we are good we are not always happy.

OSCAR WILDE, *The Picture of Dorian Gray* (1890)

Happiness breeds success

Happiness may be the supreme goal, but what seems to dominate many people's lives on a daily basis is the quest for material success. If you are a young person grinding your way through the qualification mill of school, or an adult slogging away at a demanding job, then you might feel that the pathway to happiness and the pathway to success lead in opposite directions. To be successful, it seems, you must choose hard work over cosy pastimes like schmoozing with friends. To be happy, on the other hand, you should downshift and follow your heart. The siren of happiness beckons you to do more of what you fancy, but the taskmaster of success demands that you keep striving. For parents, this dilemma can seem to apply to their children as well. Should they be pressurising their children to study harder or should they just allow them to relax and be happy?

24

The encouraging steer from science is that happiness and success are not mutually exclusive, nor even in competition with one another. The supposed dichotomy between happiness and success is false. In fact, happiness and success are natural bedfellows.

Happiness breeds success. The evidence from research shows that happy people are generally more successful in material terms than unhappy people. On average, they do better in their careers and earn more money; they are also healthier and live longer. Now, you might suspect that rich, successful people are happier simply because their success and wealth make them happy. But that is not even half the story. The relationship between happiness and success works even more strongly in the other direction: in other words, happiness breeds success more than success breeds happiness.

Happiness and success are intertwined because the key personal qualities that promote success are mostly the same ones that promote happiness. Success is linked with happiness, both in school and the adult workplace, because success and happiness are built from many of the same basic ingredients. These include social and communication skills, emotional literacy, freedom from excessive anxiety, motivation, resilience, optimism, self-esteem, an ability to think clearly, wisdom and physical health. If you have these qualities in abundance you are well equipped to be both happy and successful.

Happiness starts contributing to success early in life. Numerous studies have confirmed that happier children perform better at school than less happy children, other things being equal. For example, children who feel good about themselves demonstrate greater abilities in reading, spelling and maths, and are judged by their teachers to be more popular, more cooperative and more persistent in the classroom. Happy children are also more resilient and better able to handle life's knocks. Conversely, unhappy children typically achieve less at school and are more likely to seek relief from chemicals: unhappiness, low self-esteem and anxiety are major risk factors for drug abuse and alcoholism in young people as well as adults.

One of the many reasons why happy children tend to do better in school is because happiness boosts mental performance. Children (and adults) are faster at learning and faster at performing mental tasks when they are in a happy mood than when they are feeling low. Experiments have demonstrated, for example, that children are up to 50 per cent faster at solving mental arithmetic problems when they are in a good mood.

Happiness and success continue to be intertwined in adult life. Happy people are typically more energetic, more sociable, more creative and more decisive than unhappy people. They feel more in control of their lives and are more optimistic. These characteristics help them to achieve and succeed in whatever they are doing. Unhappy people, on the other hand, are more inclined to be passive, intro-spective and indecisive – characteristics that can get in the way of achievement, both in the workplace and elsewhere.

One crucial ingredient of both happiness and success is the ability to form and maintain personal relationships. Few jobs can be done really well by someone who cannot get on with other people. Another key ingredient is emo-tional literacy, which means being able to understand and respond appropriately to your own emotions and other people's emotions. Again, it is hard to excel in most jobs if you are incapable of reading or dealing effectively with common emotions like anger, jealousy or anxiety.

A basic level of social and emotional competence is essential for success in school or the workplace, as well as for happiness. Indeed, research suggests that social skills and emotional literacy have a bigger influence on work performance and career success than specific academic skills or intelligence (in the narrow, IQ, sense of the word). Knowing someone's score on a conventional IQ test would enable you to make a relatively weak prediction about their future career success (provided their IQ was within the normal range). Other attributes such as social skills, emotional literacy, motivation, communication skills and resilience are usually far more significant in the long term.

Creativity is another area where happiness is a powerful ally. Living, as we do, in a knowledge economy means that the ability to think creatively has become increasingly important in the world of work. More and more jobs depend on being able to generate original ideas and solve problems in ways that cannot be reduced to simple procedures. (Of course, even in the Stone Age, humans needed to innovate in order to survive and thrive, so there is nothing really new about this.) Numerous scientific studies have shown that happiness helps to stimulate creativity and problem-solving. For instance, in one experiment volunteers were given a candle, a box of matches and a box of drawing pins, and were challenged to attach the candle to the wall so that the wax would not drip on the floor. The creative solution was to empty the matchbox, pin it to the wall and use it as a candle-holder. The experimenters found that people were much more likely to solve the problem if they had first been put in a good mood by watching a funny film. Happiness (or, at least, a jolly mood) helped them to think creatively.

Being happy systematically changes the way we view the

27

world. When we are feeling low we tend to take a narrower and more defensive view: we concentrate on what is going wrong and search for solutions. When we are feeling happy, however, our thinking tends to become more expansive, more open-ended and more constructive. Instead of dwelling on specific problems, we look for new ways of doing things.

Psychologists have discovered that people think more in terms of the big picture when they are in a happy mood, whereas they are inclined to focus on detail when feeling sad. In one study, volunteers were shown a drawing and were later asked to reproduce it from memory. Those who were feeling happy were better at reproducing the general effect of the drawing, whereas those who felt less happy tended to concentrate on specific details of the drawing and were worse at capturing its overall effect. The drawings produced by happy people were more recognisable and more like the original. (Incidentally, the connection between happiness and big-picture thinking implies that you might be better off tackling some tasks when you are *not* feeling especially joyful. Tasks that require a focus on detail and a defensive approach to problem-solving, such as filling in tax forms, buying a car or taking an exam, are probably better done when you are feeling a little restrained.)

Converging evidence that we see the world in a more open-minded way when we are happy has led the American psychologist Barbara Fredrickson to develop her 'broaden-and-build' theory of positive emotions. Fredrickson argues that positive emotions like feeling happy have evolved over the course of human evolutionary history because they help individuals to survive and reproduce. And they do this by broadening our repertoire of thoughts and actions. Feeling joyful or happy makes us more playful, more curious, more creative, more sociable and more reflective. This widening of perspective enables us to build up our physical, mental, emotional and social resources when the going is good. We can later draw upon these resources if faced with an opportunity or a threat. For instance, a happy person will tend to be more sociable and outgoing, which in turn will strengthen their personal relationships. When the going gets rough, these relationships might be crucial to their well-being. By broadening our range of thoughts and actions, Fredrickson argues, positive emotions make us more resilient and better able to cope with adversity.

An obvious parallel can be drawn here between happiness and play. Children and young animals of many other species spend a lot of their time engaged in seemingly pointless activity known as play. A hallmark of play, as opposed to 'serious' behaviour, is that it appears to have no immediate benefits. In fact, play does have important benefits, but these are mostly long-term. By playing, the individual acquires valuable skills and experiences, and develops their physical, social and mental skills. Play is about building foundations for the future. We shall return to play later.

As well as being good for parents and good for children, happiness is good for organisations and for society as a whole. On average, happy employees perform better at their jobs, have lower levels of absenteeism, and are less likely to quit than unhappy employees. Studies have found that happy workers are typically more satisfied with their jobs, more productive and more persistent. They aim for higher goals and earn more money. In fact, the general level of personal happiness among employees is a better predictor of good performance and low staff turnover than how satisfied they specifically feel about their jobs. In the long term, happiness is a stronger motivator than money.

The clear implication of all this is that any enlightened organisation should regard improving the happiness of its employees as a legitimate and important business objective. Organisations could seek to do this in various ways – for example, by enabling individuals to maintain a better work–life balance, developing their skills, making them feel valued, and helping them to maintain good physical and mental health. The dreary reality is that few organisations think in this way. Happiness receives no mention in most companies' strategic plans or annual objectives.

Outside school or the workplace, happiness continues to work its spell in myriad ways. If, like most people, you believe that being popular and having lots of friends is an indicator of success, then happiness is what you should be chasing, both for yourself and your children. One of the most consistent characteristics of happy people is that they get on well with others. Research confirms that happy people are generally more sociable, more empathetic, more cooperative, more generous, more energetic and more competent in their dealings with others. Happiness and sociability go hand in hand. One of the recurring themes in this book is that personal relationships are of central importance to happiness.

Research has also shown that we have a higher quantity and quality of social interactions when we are happy. For instance, experiments have demonstrated that people become measurably more sociable and outgoing when they are put in a good mood (by showing them an amusing film, for example). Happy people find social encounters more satisfying, they adopt a less cautious social style, and they are more inclined to be cooperative and generous. What is more, this link between sociability and happiness works both ways: sociable people become happier and happy people become more sociable, creating a virtuous circle. On the flip side, unhappiness can erode social relationships. Individuals suffering from low mood or mild depression are apt to behave in ways that elicit negative responses, which in turn adds to their unhappiness.

The mutually reinforcing connection between unhappiness and social isolation is illustrated by Moaning Myrtle, the doleful ghost in J. K. Rowling's *Harry Potter and the Chamber of Secrets*. Myrtle, who haunts the girls' toilets in Hogwarts School, has turned her social isolation into a self-reinforcing state by indulging in extremes of self-pity. Myrtle is glum because everyone avoids her, and everyone avoids her because she is glum. In her rare social encounters, Myrtle instantly assumes the worst and accuses her interlocutor of making fun of her. Without provocation she moans about people calling her rude names behind her back. Being down in the dumps can result in a downward spiral.

Happiness is good for your health
Another compelling reason for paying more systematic attention to our own happiness and our children's happiness is that happy people are physically healthier and live longer. Being happy is seriously good for your health.

Abundant scientific evidence shows that happy people live longer than unhappy people, other things being equal. This correlation between happiness and longevity was illustrated by the 'nun study', in which scientists analysed handwritten autobiographies written many years earlier by a group of very elderly Catholic nuns. The results showed that those individuals who had expressed the most positive emotions when they were in their early twenties were significantly more likely to be alive six decades later. The nuns whose youthful writings had revealed the sunniest outlook lived several years longer on average.

The most extreme and obvious manifestation of the link between happiness and lifespan is suicide, which one writer described as the sincerest form of criticism that a life can receive. The suicide rate among young people in the UK has increased markedly over the past 20–30 years, especially among males. Indeed, suicide is now the most common cause of death among young men, accounting for more than a fifth of all deaths in males aged 15–24. And as you would expect, unhappy people are statistically much more likely than happy people to kill themselves, other things being equal. One large investigation in Finland, for example, found that very unhappy people were seven times more likely to commit suicide over the following 20 years than those who rated themselves as very happy.

For every person who actually commits suicide there are many more who think about doing it. In fact, cases of harbouring suicidal thoughts outnumber actual suicides by around 400 to 1. The largest survey of its kind in the UK found that 1 in every 25 men and women had contemplated suicide at some point during the preceding year. In another demonstration of how crucial personal relationships are to happiness, the same study found that people were much less likely to have considered suicide if they were married or cohabiting, or if they felt they had good social support from friends and relatives.

More generally, low mood and depression remain serious and widespread problems. A few years ago a large study discovered that one out of every six adults in Britain was suffering from some form of depression or anxiety (so-called neurotic disorders).[1] Mental health problems of this sort account for a third of all days lost from work in the UK due to ill health, and a fifth of all visits to GPs. Depression can produce serious impairments in social and physical functioning that are as disabling as many physical illnesses. The World Health Organization has estimated that by the year 2020 depression will be the second biggest cause of disability in the world, after cardiovascular disease. Depression is not just an adult problem either. On the contrary, it is surprisingly prevalent and underdiagnosed among children, in whom the symptoms can be hard to spot. A major study found that 4 per cent of 5–15-year-olds in Britain were suffering from an emotional disorder involving anxiety or depression.

So, being happy can make a big difference to your chances of survival, especially if you are a young man who might otherwise be at risk of committing suicide. However, a longer life is not the only dividend – happy people also enjoy better physical health while they are alive. Numerous studies have found that happy people typically score better than unhappy people both in terms of how they perceive their own health ('subjective health') and how their health is judged by doctors ('objective health'). For example, happy people tend to have lower blood pressure. Some recent research, which tracked more than 22,000 Finnish twins over an 11-year period, found that those who were dissatisfied with their life were much more likely to be unable to work in later years because of mental or physical health problems.

One way in which happiness promotes physical health is by providing a buffer against stress. Several of the key building blocks of happiness, including personal relationships, optimism, wisdom and humour, help to protect us from the stressful effects of adversity. Happy people, with the support of friends and family, are able to take more knocks. Happiness assists health in other ways as well. There is good evidence, for example, that happy people tend to have healthier lifestyles. Among other things, they are statistically less likely than unhappy people to smoke, abuse alcohol, eat badly or be physically inactive. This probably has something to do with their personal relationships.

The fact that happiness promotes physical health should come as no surprise, given what scientists know about the intimate links between mental and emotional states and physical health. You are probably familiar with the idea that negative states of mind such as stress, anxiety and depression can contribute to physical illness. For example, there is abundant evidence that prolonged psychological stress can increase vulnerability to bacterial and viral infections by impairing the functioning of the immune system. Prolonged stress can also increase the risk of heart disease and stroke. Well, the converse is also true: positive states of mind can make us healthier.

Scientists have been unearthing more and more links between positive mental states and measurable benefits to physical health. In particular, experimental studies have uncovered evidence that happiness is associated with better functioning of the immune system. In one experiment, individuals who naturally tended to respond more positively to depressing or potentially threatening experiences were found to display a stronger immune response when their immune system was challenged by giving them an influenza vaccination. The implication of such findings is that positive psychological and emotional states bolster the body's immune defences. Recent research has even shown that beneficial changes in immune function can be produced by meditation. Carefully controlled experiments have demonstrated that a widely used form of meditation can elicit a significant rise in the number of antibodies produced in response to a vaccination. (However, the most noticeable long-term effect of meditation, according to its practitioners, is happiness.)

Is there anything *bad* about happiness?

So far, then, we have seen that happy people are typically more successful at school and at work, have better social lives, are more creative, live longer, and enjoy better health. And, of course, they are happy, which is arguably the most important thing of all. But despite all these powerful attractions, the state of happiness has not always enjoyed an entirely untainted image. Over the years it has been vilified on various grounds, including claims that it leads to complacency, immorality, self-delusion and even death.

One ancient belief is that pursuing happiness puts us on a path to self-destruction. In their quest for happiness, it is said, people indulge in excesses that are bad for them and bad for others. This notion stems from a basic confusion between happiness and pleasure. There are good reasons for being cautious about the shallow pursuit of pleasure, which does have the potential to be stultifying or self-destructive. But pleasure is not the same as happiness, and a life built on the pursuit of pleasure alone is unlikely to be truly happy.

Another commonplace criticism is that happiness is a form of self-deluding fantasy which blinds us to the awful realities of life or, at the very least, makes us complacent. According to some cynics, the world is such a ghastly place that the only way for intelligent people to be happy is to cut themselves off from reality and live in a fog of self-delusion. When the French President Charles de Gaulle was once asked if he was a happy man, he replied: 'What sort of fool do you take me for?' Aldous Huxley famously explored this idea in his 1932 novel *Brave New World* – a chilling futuristic vision of an all-powerful state in which the masses are kept under control with a drug called *soma*, which banishes all unhappiness. Liberal quantities of *soma* ensure that everyone is content, well behaved and free from any disruptively original or subversive thoughts. If anyone should feel a tinge of dissatisfaction or anxiety, they are told to take a gram of *soma*, which is said to have 'all the advantages of Christianity and alcohol' but none of their defects. Only one character in Huxley's novel, the Savage, is recognisably human – and he claims the right to be unhappy.

A seemingly more technical assault on happiness was mounted in an academic paper published in the respectable *Journal of Medical Ethics* in 1992. The paper's author, psychologist Richard Bentall, proposed that happiness should formally be classified as a psychiatric disorder, to be known as 'major affective disorder, pleasant type'. In support of his thesis, Bentall pointed out that happiness fits the key criteria that psychiatrists use to diagnose mental illness: it is statistically abnormal, consists of a discrete cluster of symptoms, is associated with distinctive patterns of brain activity, and involves distortions in thinking and memory. Happy people, Bentall argued, are impulsive and irrational; they have an unrealistically rosy view of themselves and the world, they find it harder to remember bad experiences, and they overestimate their ability to control events. In other words, they are deluded. Furthermore, their happiness lures them into irrational and damaging behaviour: happy people overindulge in food and alcohol, and become obese.

Happily, Bentall's paper was a spoof. The real target of his satire was not happiness, but sloppy thinking in psychiatric diagnosis. In reality, there is no reason to believe that happy people are deluded, irrational or living in a fantasy world. Research has found that even very happy people – those fortunate individuals who are consistently much happier than most of the rest of us – still display appropriate emotional responses to the vagaries of life. They may be very happy most of the time, but they do nonetheless experience occasional low moods in response to real disappointments or setbacks. Even very happy people do not live in a state of continuous bliss, cut off from the realities of life.

If anything, the evidence suggests that happiness gives people a better grip on reality. Studies have shown that happy people with a positive outlook on life are better at attending to relevant information, including negative or threatening information. In one set of experiments, volunteers were exposed to potentially worrying information about health, such as evidence of links between caffeine consumption and fibrocystic breast disease. Those individuals who were feeling happy at the time they received this worrying information were more receptive to it, better at remembering it, and more objective in the way they assessed it. Being in a happy, positive frame of mind did not blind them to reality, even when faced with news they might prefer not to hear.

Happy people also appear better able to cope with practical problems because they know when to change tack or give up. This was highlighted by an experiment in which volunteers were confronted with a series of mental tasks,

some of which (unbeknown to them) were literally impossible to solve. Individuals who had a positive, optimistic
outlook and a belief in their own ability to control events
proved to be significantly better at disengaging from the
unsolvable tasks and switching to other tasks that were
solvable. The implication is that happy people are more
realistic about what they can and cannot achieve.

So the notion that happiness is a form of delusion has
little solid basis in fact, and even less to commend it as a
philosophy of life. The world might well be a ghastly place,
but being unhappy will not make it any better. Happiness
does not turn us into 'contented cows' – on the contrary,
we would all be better off if there were a few more happy
people around.

Another dubious piece of folklore asserts that you have
to be unhappy to be creative. Happiness encourages intellectual mediocrity, it is claimed, and creative geniuses are
usually tortured souls. This romantic belief runs counter
to the evidence, which I outlined earlier, that happiness
boosts creativity; it is hard to find credible support for the
'tortured genius' hypothesis, even in the form of historical
anecdotes.

In sum, then, happy people feel better, achieve more,
create more, enjoy better health and live longer than unhappy people. They make better employees, better friends,
better partners and better parents. They are also less likely
to turn to drink, drugs or crime. In a world of happier
people there would be less illness, less depression, less
crime and shorter queues in doctors' surgeries. There is
nothing feeble or self-indulgent about wanting to make
ourselves and our children happier. The only ones who
might lose out would be psychotherapists, pharmaceutical
companies, drug dealers and the writers of self-help books.

Is there anything good about *un*happiness?
Happiness has a lot to recommend it and little to be wary of; the more, the better. What about *un*happiness and its key ingredient, displeasure? Is there anything good to say about unpleasant emotions like sadness or anxiety? Biology casts some unexpected light on this issue. The capacity to experience displeasure is actually an immensely valuable asset. Being sad or anxious may feel horrible, but under the right circumstances it can be good for you. How could this be?

The human mind, like the human body, is the product of millions of years of biological evolution. The process of evolution through natural selection has given rise to immensely elaborate physical structures such as eyes, lungs and kidneys, which look as though they have been exquisitely designed for a particular purpose. The brain is also a product of biological evolution, and similar reasoning can be applied to the 'design features' of mental and emotional faculties, including the capacity to feel joyful or sad.

Emotions guide our behaviour, and they are crucial for our ability to function in the real world. They immediately point us in roughly the right direction, before we can begin to fine-tune our judgments using the more conventional instruments of conscious thought, logic and reasoning. Individuals suffering from certain types of brain damage that specifically impair emotional faculties can end up incapable of coping with everyday life, even though their intelligence and cognitive abilities remain intact. Even a simple decision like whether to have tea or coffee can become cripplingly difficult if the only thing you have to rely on is pure logic and rational analysis. The emotionless Mr Spock of *Star Trek* would have been useless.

Sadness, anxiety and other disagreeable emotions can be

thought of as the mental equivalents of physical capacities like pain and fever. Being able to feel pain is essential for survival because it stops us doing things that would damage our bodies. Very rarely, individuals are born who lack the capacity to feel pain: they invariably die from injuries or infection before they reach middle age. In a similar way, fever is unpleasant but beneficial. Fever is one of the body's defence mechanisms for fighting infection. The rise in temperature makes your body a less hospitable place for the invading bacteria or viruses and thereby speeds recovery.

Unpleasant emotions help to protect us in an analogous way. Feeling frightened is immensely beneficial if it stops you being eaten by a lion, and feeling anxious can pay dividends if it stops you ambling down a dark alley where muggers lurk. The American scientist Lewis Thomas described worrying as the most natural and spontaneous of human functions, and argued that we should all learn to do it better.

We are born with the capacity to experience fear, anxiety, sadness and other unpleasant emotions because they helped our ancestors to survive and reproduce (and hence to become our ancestors).[2] Someone who was permanently joyful, regardless of their actual circumstances, would be at risk of ignoring real threats to their well-being. Biology tells us that there is nothing natural or biologically optimal about feeling happy all the time. As the philosopher Arthur Schopenhauer put it: 'There is only one inborn error, and that is the notion that we exist in order to be happy.'

If anything, negative emotions are *more* important in biological terms than positive emotions like pleasure or joy, because they help to keep us alive. Many different things can go wrong in life, threatening our well-being or safety, whereas relatively few things are needed to make a life good. This could explain why the number of distinctly different negative emotions far outweighs the number of different positive emotions. The repertoire of negative emotions includes numerous specific fears and phobias, anger, sadness, depression, anxiety, jealousy, hatred, rage, boredom, and so on, whereas there are relatively few variations on the theme of pleasure, joy and contentment.

The protective functions of negative emotions also help to explain why they are often more vivid and more compelling than positive emotions, and why negative emotions usually override positive emotions. A feeling of relaxed contentment can be swept away in an instant by sudden fear, anger or sadness, but the reverse seldom happens. Our minds are 'designed' to be more responsive to negative events precisely because these are the ones most likely to threaten our well-being.

Sadness usually occurs in response to some loss or setback, and it encourages us to behave differently. We seek to change whatever is making us sad, or we withdraw so that we are no longer exposed to it. If things are going really badly, the best option may be to give up and withdraw rather than carry on and waste time or cause further damage. And because sadness is unpleasant, we try in future to avoid situations that experience suggests might make us sad. Sadness does not feel nice, but it sometimes helps us to do the right things. Pursuing this logic still further, the writer Gwyneth Lewis has argued that even severe depression can have its hidden benefits. In her autobiographical account of her own struggles with depression, Lewis explores the idea that it forces the sufferer to reappraise their life. 'Depression', she wrote, 'is a lie detector of last resort. By knocking you out for a while, it allows you to ditch the out-of-date ideas by which you've been living and to grasp a more accurate description of the terrain.'

Much of the sadness we all sometimes feel is social in origin; it arises from our relationships with other people. To understand why people feel happy or sad, contented or anxious, it is usually necessary to understand their personal relationships. We shall return to this theme later.

The idea that unpleasant emotions are biological defence mechanisms, akin to pain and fever, has some non-obvious implications. Numbing the pain of an injured joint can increase the risk of inflicting further damage on that joint. Similarly, taking drugs to suppress a fever can actually impede recovery from infection. We feel better, but our defences are impaired. By the same logic, blocking negative emotions with anti-anxiety drugs, tranquillizers or antidepressants might carry risks as well as benefits. It would be interesting to know, for example, whether people who routinely take antidepressants or tranquillizers have more accidents or make more bad decisions. There are reasons to think they might. For example, controlled experiments have shown that the tranquillizer diazepam (trade name Valium), which is used to treat anxiety, impairs the ability to recognise facial expressions of anger and fear. Someone who has taken diazepam is prone to mistake fear for surprise, and disgust for anger. You can imagine how this perceptual distortion, combined with the lack of anxiety, might affect their ability to respond appropriately in an aggressive social situation or an encounter with a nervous mugger.

Routinely suppressing anxiety might also have unforeseen consequences on a grander scale. In early 2000, the American psychiatrist and leading Darwinian thinker Randolph Nesse published a superbly prescient article called 'Is the market on Prozac?' In it, Nesse asked whether the extraordinary boom in world stock markets, which was then still in full flood, might be attributable not just to the dot-com revolution, but also to the fact that a substantial proportion of investors, brokers and dealers were taking psychoactive drugs. Was it possible, wondered Nesse, that their natural caution and anxiety were being chemically suppressed, leading to irrational optimism, overconfidence and unsustainable rises in stock values? A few months later, the vastly overinflated dot-com bubble burst. A little fear or anxiety is not such a bad thing.

FOUR

Where does happiness come from?

There is nothing either good or bad, but thinking makes it so.

WILLIAM SHAKESPEARE, *Hamlet* (1601)

Happiness is (mostly) in the mind

Why are some people consistently happier than others? Why do we all feel happier at some times than others? Historically, there have been two contrasting schools of thought as to what makes a happy person happy. According to one view, happiness is largely a consequence of what happens to us. It depends on how many pleasant or unpleasant experiences we have, whether we succeed in satisfying our desires, how people behave towards us, how much money we earn, and so on. Set against this is the belief, common to many ancient philosophies and religions, that happiness is essentially a product of how we perceive and construe the world around us – in other words, that happiness is all in the mind and has little to do with external events.

These two very different perspectives on the causes of

happiness imply two very different approaches to achieving it. If happiness reflects the world around us, then we should seek to make ourselves happy by changing the world to match our desires – for example, by acquiring pleasurable experiences, possessions, wealth, fame or power. A belief in the ability of material possessions and pleasurable experiences to create happiness is one of the driving forces behind our consumerist culture. If, on the other hand, happiness is all down to our beliefs and attitudes, then we should be able to find it by altering our perception; nothing in the world around us need change.

The alluring idea that happiness is all in the mind has a long history. More than two thousand years ago Aristotle argued that happiness depends not on the external world but on how we perceive it. And because happiness depends on how we think, it can be cultivated. In similar vein, the Greek Stoic philosopher Epictetus, who was born in the first century AD, championed a lofty indifference to the hardships and imperfections of life. 'What upsets people', he wrote, 'is not things themselves, but their judgments about the things.' Epictetus argued that the path to happiness lies in wanting what you have rather than having what you want. Many other ancient schools of thought, including the Yogi, Taoist, Zen and Buddhist traditions, similarly hold that happiness depends on freeing the mind from the malign influence of external events. Strong echoes of this time-honoured view can be found in contemporary self-help books which advise that happiness comes from positive thinking or learning to love ourselves more.

Everyday experience, however, suggests that the reality is less clear cut. Events and circumstances obviously do have some bearing on personal happiness. Most of us would feel better after eating a delicious meal, having fantastic sex, being successful at work or winning a large sum of money. Equally, we might feel downcast if we had just lost all our money, suffered a major career setback, or if a close friend had suddenly died. But events clearly cannot account for more than part of the story, because individuals can respond very differently to identical circumstances. An event that casts one person into gloom might seem trivial to another and a source of amusement to someone else.

Many people manage to be reasonably happy (in the broad sense as defined in chapter 2) despite living in dreadful circumstances. Even severe illness, disability or poverty does not inevitably condemn someone to lasting unhappiness. Research has shown that people living in conditions of extreme poverty in developing nations are sometimes considerably happier than might be expected given their grim physical circumstances. One study of slum-dwellers in Calcutta found that they derived considerable happiness from their relationships with other people. Personal relationships make a huge contribution to personal happiness, but they have little to do with wealth or material possessions. You do not have to be rich to have supportive friends and a loving family.

Similarly, many people with severe illnesses or disabilities are found to be only slightly less happy than averagely healthy people, once they have come to terms with their condition. For instance, one American study found that more than 80 per cent of people who were paralysed in all four limbs considered their lives to be average or above average in terms of happiness, and more than 90 per cent of them were glad to be alive. Another study, which assessed paralysis victims years after their injury, found that those who were receiving good social support from family and friends were about as happy as anyone else. Objectively bad events or circumstances do not automatically condemn us to persistent unhappiness, and good events do not automatically create lasting bliss. The truth is that happiness depends both on what happens to us and how we perceive those events.

The characteristic style in which you interact with the world around you, including other people, is known as your personality. And your personality has a major influence on your happiness for two basic reasons: first, because it shapes your lifestyle and experiences; and second, because it affects how you perceive those experiences.

The experiences you have during the course of your life do not just randomly happen to you: they are to some extent your own creations and depend on your personality. Someone who is highly sociable, outgoing and adventurous is likely to live their life differently from someone who is shy, timid and conservative. Personality also affects how we perceive and construe our experiences. As well as having a larger number of positive experiences, happy people tend to interpret those experiences more positively. For their part, unhappy people have an unfortunate habit of interpreting objectively similar experiences in less positive ways, thereby reinforcing their doleful view of the world and prolonging their unhappiness.

Research suggests that personality has a stronger influence on the emotional elements of happiness (namely, pleasure and displeasure) than it does on the thinking element (satisfaction). Someone may have the sort of personality that makes them feel low much of the time, perhaps because they are shy and anxious. Nonetheless, they may still derive considerable satisfaction from their work and family life, leaving them reasonably happy overall. Personality traits typically remain stable over time, which helps to explain why an individual's overall level of happiness will also tend to be moderately stable.

The characteristics of happy people

We have seen, then, that happiness is a reflection both of who we are and what happens to us. But which particular aspects of personality and circumstances make the biggest differences to happiness? Some are more important than others. As we saw in chapter 2, happiness comes in many forms, comprising different blends of pleasure, displeasure and satisfaction, and each blend can be achieved in many different ways. Nonetheless, some patterns can be discerned among the complexities. Happy people usually have most or all of the following characteristics in common.

1. Connectedness

Probably the single most important and consistent characteristic of happy people is that they are connected to other people by personal relationships. Happy children typically have secure and loving relationships with their parents, get on well with other children, and have one or more good friends. For their part, happy adults typically have one or more close relationships with a partner, relatives or friends, plus a range of shallower relationships with friends, acquaintances and colleagues.

One of the main themes of this book is that personal relationships are central to happiness; we shall be exploring this further in the next chapter. The support, confidence and emotional security that come from close personal relationships form the bedrock of happiness, especially for children. And when it comes to relationships, quality is more important than quantity. One close relationship with a partner, parent or friend may be sufficient to sustain happiness, in a way that hundreds of casual acquaintanceships rarely achieve.

To have any relationships at all, of course, a person must have some basic willingness and ability to interact with other people. The more someone is naturally drawn to the company of others, the more relationships they are likely to have and the greater their scope to form close relationships. That is one reason why socialites tend to be happier than recluses. The philosopher Bertrand Russell hit the nail on the head when he wrote that to like many people spontaneously and without effort is perhaps the greatest of all sources of personal happiness. Over the years, research has consistently found that sociable people are, on average, happier than those who find company difficult or unattractive. For example, a long-term study of everyone born in the UK in one particular week in March 1958 found that those who were more sociable during their teens were significantly happier when assessed again in their mid-thirties.

Much of the psychological research in this area has focused on a personality characteristic known as extroversion, which is essentially an indirect measure of sociability. Extroverts are friendly, outgoing, sociable, warm and active. They have a natural tendency to enjoy social situations and social activities such as parties, games and team sports.[1] Numerous studies have uncovered links between extroversion and happiness throughout the lifespan, including in old age.

By the same token, shy people – those who consistently feel anxious, self-conscious and reticent in social situations – tend to score low on measures of happiness. Shyness can be a real problem, both for adults and children. On average, shy children are lonelier, have lower self-esteem and suffer from more anxiety than sociable children. Very shy adults are found to be unhappier even than people suffering from anxiety or mood disorders. Not *all* shy people are unhappy, however. A significant minority of 'happy introverts' are happy despite not being gregarious.

Sociability and happiness form a virtuous circle: sociable people become happier because they are more connected, and happiness, in turn, makes us more sociable, as we saw in the previous chapter. Happy people spend more of their time engaging with other people and have a larger number of social interactions.

2. *Social and emotional competence*

A second almost universal characteristic of happy people is having at least moderate levels of social and emotional competence. To be happy, you need basic social skills to form and maintain personal relationships, together with the emotional literacy to understand and deal effectively with your own feelings and other people's.

A socially and emotionally competent adult or child can read and interpret the feelings that underlie other people's actions and expressions. They can work out whether another person is angry, sad, jealous or afraid, and then respond appropriately. Such skills are subtle but crucial, and not everyone is richly endowed with them. Aristotle put it like this: 'Anyone can be angry – that is easy. But to be angry with the right person, to the right degree, at the right time, for the right purpose, and in the right way – that is not easy.'

Individuals with poor social skills are, not surprisingly, at greater risk of being socially isolated, with potentially damaging consequences for their happiness and health. Children and adults who lack emotional literacy find it hard to manage their own feelings or to understand other people's feelings. They consequently have more problems coping with anger and aggression, among other things. Studies of school children have found that those who are poor at understanding and managing emotions are more likely to become violent. Responding aggressively may be the only tactic in their repertoire for dealing with everyday situations of conflict.

Socially and emotionally competent people are better equipped to succeed in the classroom and in the adult world of work. They tend to be better motivated, more persistent, more focused and less easily diverted by upsets or squabbles. Social and emotional competence is a stronger predictor of children's future success than narrow measures such as exam grades. It even reduces the long-term risk of drug abuse: studies have found that teenagers with good social skills are significantly less likely to be using drugs when they are in their thirties.

3. Freedom from excessive anxiety

We saw in chapter 2 that happiness is a mixture of three basic elements: pleasure, the absence of displeasure, and satisfaction. Being prey to frequent unpleasant emotions can erode happiness. And the unpleasant emotion that probably does most to erode happiness among the largest number of people is anxiety – that nagging sense that something might go wrong. Research confirms that anxious individuals who frequently worry about themselves or their loved ones tend to be less happy. Conversely, happy people typically experience low levels of anxiety and are less inclined to feel anxious in any given situation.

In addition to being an everyday source of displeasure, anxiety erodes happiness in other ways. Someone who continually feels anxious will find it harder to focus on whatever they are doing, or to pay full attention to their personal relationships. Anxiety fosters a distracted self-consciousness that eats away at other sources of happiness.

Some people are consistently more prone than others to be anxious, worried and emotionally changeable; they are inclined to fret even when objectively there is little to fret about. Psychologists describe these natural-born worriers as neurotic. Not surprisingly, individuals who score high on measures of neuroticism are found to be less happy. Indeed, neuroticism is one of the stronger predictors of unhappiness.

4. *Communication skills*
The ability to exchange information and feelings with other people is crucial for happiness and success. You are unlikely to maintain good relationships with partner, friends, relatives, parents, children or colleagues if you are unable to communicate effectively with them or if you keep inadvertently sending them the wrong messages. Moreover, education is a social activity, and virtually every job involves interacting with other people. Poor communication skills can therefore be a real impediment to success at school and in the workplace.

Happy people are generally good at making themselves understood, both emotionally and rationally, and good at listening to other people. (Communication is of course a two-way process, although you would not think so from the way some people behave: perhaps you know someone who is permanently jammed on transmit.) Good communicators are capable of communicating through all the available channels, using speech, facial expressions, gestures, body language and the written word, as appropriate.

Adequate communication skills may not be a sufficient condition for happiness, but they are certainly necessary.

5. Engagement in meaningful activity

We humans are by nature problem-solvers. We are generally happier when actively engaged in some reasonably challenging task, rather than passively witnessing other people's experiences on a TV screen. Happy people spend at least some of their time engaged in meaningful and satisfying activities. Happy children socialise, play games or learn in the classroom; happy adults throw themselves into their jobs, hobbies, sports or voluntary work. The precise nature of the activity seems to be unimportant, provided it is reasonably demanding and worthwhile. Bored people with nothing much to do are seldom very happy.

Most adults spend a large proportion of their waking lives at work, so it is not surprising that paid work has an important bearing on happiness. Having a satisfying job is strongly connected with happiness. And, as with many other ingredients of happiness, the connection is two-way: job satisfaction contributes to happiness, and happiness in turn fosters job satisfaction. Happy people enjoy their jobs more. Despite media stories about work-related stress and the joys of downshifting, research shows that most people feel at least neutral about their job, and around one in three positively like what they do for a living. Noel Coward once opined that the only way to enjoy life is to work, because work is so much more fun than fun.

Work brings far more than just money. A satisfying job can also bring structure and meaning to one's life, mental and emotional stimulation, personal relationships, regular opportunities to use and develop skills, social status, self-esteem and a sense of identity. Personal relationships are a particularly important benefit of work, and the evidence shows that people who work in small, cohesive groups tend to be the most satisfied with their job and generally happiest.

Pay, on the other hand, has a surprisingly weak influence on job satisfaction – certainly when compared with personal relationships or the nature of the work itself. People doing unpaid voluntary work often enjoy it more than people who are paid to do something similar. In fact, research shows that pay is more often a cause of *dis*satisfaction than satisfaction. Individuals who regard themselves as poorly paid relative to others soon become disgruntled, whereas better pay does surprisingly little to boost satisfaction. People who are highly successful at work typically report enjoying their job for its own sake, not because it is well paid.

The strength of the correlation between job satisfaction and overall happiness varies between different cultures. Among Americans of European origin, job satisfaction is closely linked to overall happiness and to satisfaction with other spheres of life, including satisfaction with marriage, finances, family and health. But the link between job satisfaction and overall happiness is found to be weaker among African-Americans and Asian-Americans. In some cultures and ethnic groups, individuals appear to derive more of their happiness from other areas of life such as their family; jobs are regarded more as a source of income and therefore make a smaller contribution to overall happiness. In highly individualistic societies like the USA, self-worth and happiness derive more from personal achievements and less from being part of a group.

For the same reasons that work provides many ingredients of happiness, unemployment is a powerful cause of unhappiness. Large bodies of evidence confirm that unemployed people are generally much less happy and much less healthy, both mentally and physically, than people with jobs. On average, they experience more depression, more anxiety, lower self-esteem and greater unhappiness than people in employment, even those with low-paid jobs.

The consequences of unemployment extend far beyond the purely financial. In most cases, the psychological, emotional and social effects are much greater. Even in countries where the unemployed receive generous state benefits, they are still very unhappy. Making up for lost wages softens the blow, but only slightly. Unemployment can be particularly damaging for those who have the furthest to fall, notably the middle-aged, the highly educated, and those living in areas of low unemployment where their change in status is more apparent. Unemployment even reduces the happiness of those who remain in work, because it heightens their anxiety that they too might lose their job. Any government that truly wants to promote national happiness should give a high priority to minimising unemployment.

6. *A sense of control*

Another common characteristic of happy people is feeling they have some control over their lives, rather than being passive victims of chance or at the mercy of others. Conversely, a belief that you are helpless and unable to affect what is happening to you, or that your daily life is largely governed by random events beyond your control, is often associated with unhappiness and depression.

Happy people tend to feel more empowered and more in control of their lives than unhappy people. They are also more likely to feel they have the skills, knowledge and motivation to exert that control – a sense that psychologists refer to as self-efficacy. Research shows that young people who report feeling high self-efficacy are happier on average. Education obviously has a major role to play in developing self-efficacy and a sense of control.

7. *A sense of purpose and meaning*
A life that is meaningful and has some purpose to it is more likely to be a happy life. Someone who is swept along by the tide may still be reasonably happy, but someone who knows where they want to go, and why, will probably be happier. Studies have confirmed that people who regard their life as meaningful tend to be happier and more satisfied, other things being equal. Their health benefits too: Japanese researchers have discovered that elderly people who have a strong sense that their lives are meaningful (a concept known in Japanese as *ikigai*) live significantly longer on average than those whose lives lack meaning.

A sense of purpose and meaning can come from many different sources, including family life, career, study, creative activities, politics, religion or voluntary work. Many parents derive a considerable sense of purpose and meaning from parenthood. What these pursuits all have in common is providing long-term goals. According to research, individuals whose daily efforts relate directly to achieving their longer-term goals tend to be happier than those whose strivings are unrelated to their life goals.

Personal goals give a sense of meaning and purpose to the grind of daily life. But they must be realistic and attainable. Having goals or aspirations that exceed what can realistically be achieved is a recipe for unhappiness. When children are young, their parents and teachers usually set their goals for them, and getting the balance right can be tricky. Children need to be stretched so that they can learn and develop, but if the bar is set too high they will experience mostly failure, and their motivation and self-esteem may wilt. If on the other hand the bar is set too low, children may not be sufficiently stimulated and therefore fail to realise their potential. You can only set the bar at the right height if you know the child's individual capabilities and limitations.

8. Resilience

To remain happy, we must be able to cope with a certain amount of upset and stress. Even the most fortunate individuals experience some setbacks, disappointments and problems, no matter how comfortable their circumstances. And of course stress is not something that affects only adults: children and young people also encounter potential sources of stress in their lives, including relationship problems with friends or family, high-stakes exams, and anxieties about their own attractiveness. Like adults, they need to have effective methods for coping.

The capacity to maintain or restore well-being in the face of adversity is referred to by psychologists as resilience, or hardiness. The evidence confirms, unsurprisingly, that resilient individuals are usually happier than those who are more easily cast down by life's inevitable upsets. Individuals who display high levels of resilience are typically found to have supportive personal relationships, persistence, motivation, an ability to plan ahead, and practical knowledge. Resilience is actually a common characteristic of children, prompting one developmental psychologist to call it 'ordinary magic'. Even for children growing up in deprived or difficult circumstances, there is nothing inevitable about future problems. Many of them will cope.

9. Self-esteem

If you are a happy person, the chances are you will feel reasonably good about yourself as well as your life. You will have good self-esteem, to use the jargon. Self-esteem, which has become a somewhat overused term in recent years, is usually defined as how you judge your own worth or value as a person, both rationally and emotionally. The media and self-help books abound with glowing references to its magical powers.

Individuals with high self-esteem are generally found to be happier, healthier and better adjusted than those with low self-esteem. On average, they have better social relationships, cope better with illness and other problems, and are less likely to suffer from anxiety or depression. Studies have found that children who have high self-esteem are statistically less likely to be unemployed when they become adults; they also earn more on average and are less likely to commit crimes. Low self-esteem, on the other hand, can impair social relationships. If you are not happy about yourself, you will probably find it harder to be happy about your relationships with other people as well. Low self-esteem is also associated with a range of other problems including drug and alcohol abuse. Children with low self-esteem are at greater risk of becoming problem drinkers later in life.

Self-esteem is about liking yourself. This makes self-esteem different from satisfaction – which is about how you evaluate your life – and different from overall happiness. In principle, you could have reasonably high self-esteem yet still be dissatisfied with your life and generally unhappy, perhaps because of how you have been treated by other people. Having loads of self-esteem will not prevent you from being a miserable curmudgeon or a vicious swine.[2] That said, self-esteem and satisfaction tend to be quite closely correlated. By and large, people who have high self-esteem are also likely to be satisfied with their lives.

The strength of the association between self-esteem and overall happiness varies according to the kind of society in which people grow up and live. In highly individualistic societies like the USA and UK, self-esteem has a fairly strong influence on overall happiness. However, the association is found to be weaker in more collectivist societies such as Japan, China, India, Bangladesh and Korea, where there is less emphasis on the self and more on harmonising with the group. For example, a study which compared students in the USA and Hong Kong found that maintaining harmony in personal relationship had a bigger influence on the happiness of the Asian students, whereas self-esteem loomed larger in the lives of their American counterparts.

High self-esteem can be a mixed blessing if it is built on self-delusion or vanity, as is sometimes the case. Moreover, trying to boost children's self-esteem by praising them indiscriminately is not a quick way of making them happier or improving their academic performance, as some enthusiasts have claimed. Self-esteem is not all it is cracked up to be. We will return to its complexities and pitfalls in chapter 7.

10. Optimism

A common (though not universal) characteristic of happy people is optimism – that is, a general tendency to expect that life will go well and future events will have favourable outcomes. Like self-esteem, optimism has become a voguish and somewhat overused concept in the self-help literature, where it is presented by some pundits as a form of panacea. Nonetheless, numerous scientific studies have found that optimists tend to be significantly happier, healthier, better able to cope with stress, longer-lived and more successful than pessimists, other things being equal.

You can have too much of a good thing, however. A mindlessly optimistic Pollyanna attitude that flies in the face of reality will create unrealistic expectations. (I have sympathy with the cynic who remarked that a permanently cheerful, optimistic attitude may not solve all your problems, but it will annoy enough people to make it worth the effort.) A certain amount of 'defensive pessimism' can be a good thing if it helps to avoid unnecessary disappointment. We will return to this topic in chapter 7.

11. Outward focus

By and large, happy people do not spend most of their time thinking about themselves and dwelling on their own feelings. Rather, their attention tends to be focused outwards on the world around them. In contrast, a tendency towards brooding introspection and a belief in looking out for number one are common characteristics of unhappy people. The philosopher Bertrand Russell wrote of how he started life as an unhappy child but became happier as he grew older, thanks mainly to a dwindling preoccupation with his own self. Russell argued that a person cannot be happy if they suffer from what he called the disease of self-absorption. 'The man who can centre his thoughts and hopes upon something transcending self', he wrote, 'can find a certain peace in the ordinary troubles of life which is impossible to the pure egoist.'

Self-absorption undermines happiness in many ways. Someone who dwells on their own feelings is unlikely to be brilliant at developing and maintaining close personal relationships. They run the risk of giving little affection and receiving little in return. Self-absorbed people can behave kindly towards others when the need is obvious, but the person to whom kindness comes naturally is more likely to sustain it. The self-absorbed and inwardly-focused can also fall prey to the crippling belief that they alone are responsible for all the bad things that happen to them. Someone who believes, for example, that they are lonely because of fundamental flaws in their personality or appearance may conclude that trying to form new relationships is a waste of time. Their inward focus thereby reinforces their isolation and adds to their unhappiness.

Happiness requires a certain transcendence of the self. Many people unconsciously try to achieve this by distracting themselves with TV, alcohol or recreational drugs, but usually with only limited and temporary success. These tactics might provide some distraction for a few hours, but little more. A better way to achieve outward focus is by regularly engaging with absorbing activities.

The findings from research generally confirm that outward focus is associated with happiness and mental health, including lower rates of depression. Among other things, individuals who are concerned about other people, and not just themselves, are less affected by stress. Outward focus remains important for happiness in old age as well. Studies have found that elderly people whose personal goals and aspirations revolve around an interest in the well-being of others are usually happier than those who are concerned mostly with looking after themselves.

As with many other basic ingredients of happiness, the connection between outward focus and happiness works in both directions. Being outwardly focused contributes to happiness, and being happy makes us more outwardly focused, creating a virtuous circle. The more you avoid thinking about yourself all the time, the happier you become; and the happier you become, the easier it is to avoid thinking about yourself.

The idea that outward focus promotes happiness is, of course, central to many religions and ancient schools of thought, and may contribute to their success. However, outward focus does not fit comfortably with the prevailing attitudes of our current consumerist society. The 'me' culture that predominates in the USA and UK revolves around the self, attaching prime importance to individual choice, personal fulfilment and self-esteem. This mindset does little to encourage the thought that we would all be happier if only we were less self-obsessed. Parts of the self-help industry have added fuel to this fire. Most self-help books are, as their name suggests, all about the self, and the worst examples encourage their disgruntled readers to scrutinise their own navels even more closely.

12. Present- and future-mindedness
We are better equipped to be happy if we can enjoy the present, prepare for the future and avoid dwelling on the past. Happy people are usually able to think ahead, but they do not spend their lives waiting for some imaginary future or endlessly mulling over bad things that happened in the past. They are also capable, at the right times, of losing themselves in the here and now and relishing the present moment.

Our consumerist culture encourages people to strive after things that they believe, often wrongly, will bring them happiness in the future – notably money, material possessions and social recognition. Meanwhile, they find it hard to enjoy the present because their thoughts are focused on a future state they have not yet attained and perhaps never will. Happy people can prepare for the future without having to live there, and they can savour the moment without sticking their head in the sand.

Many philosophers, religious thinkers and self-help gurus have stressed the importance of being able to live in the present. A starting point is to become 'grounded' – that is, gently aware of your current surroundings, rather than fretting about all the things you have to do. Being grounded and focused on the present moment can bring pleasure and calm. It is certainly a useful skill that any busy person would benefit from learning. Various practical techniques have evolved over the centuries for clearing the mind, silencing the cacophony of mental activity and becoming mindful of the present. However, most people notice some improvement if they simply pay attention to their own breathing for a minute or two.

Being rooted in the present can be pleasant, but it does little to produce satisfaction – one of the three fundamental elements of happiness. Often, the course of action that will ultimately bring the greatest satisfaction, and hence the greatest overall happiness, requires a degree of future-mindedness. Happy people generally have a well-developed capacity to control their immediate urges and take the longer view – an important capability that psychologists refer to as delayed gratification.

In a series of experiments conducted in the 1970s and 1980s, American psychologists investigated delayed gratification in children, and its links with other aspects of personality. In a typical experiment, a pre-school child was offered a tempting marshmallow; if the child was able to wait for, say, 15 minutes before eating the marshmallow then he or she was rewarded with a second marshmallow. Some children were able muster the self-control needed to delay their gratification, but others succumbed to temptation and ate the first marshmallow immediately, even though they knew this meant forgoing the second. (You probably know the feeling.)

The important discovery was that children who were better able to delay their gratification at the age of four or five grew up to become more competent adolescents. Follow-up studies conducted a decade later found that individuals who could wait longer to receive a bigger ultimate reward at the age of four or five developed into adolescents who were socially and academically more competent, better able to cope with frustration and stress, and better at communicating than those who lacked self-control. They also achieved more at school. A prominent expert on self-esteem later commented that 'self-control is worth ten times as much as self-esteem'.

13. Humour

Truly happy people usually have a good sense of humour (although there is a certain form of superficial happiness, signified by a cheesy smile and a gleam in the eye, which seems to lack any humour or irony). Conversely, sad or depressed people are generally notable for their lack of hilarity.

Humour helps us roll with the blows. The ability to see the funny or absurd side of life is a useful antidote to misfortune and makes us more resilient. It helps us cope with stress, relieves tension, and can make bad situations seem less threatening. The eighteenth-century poet Matthew Green put it like this: 'Fling but a stone, the giant dies. / Laugh and be well.'

The relatively few scientific studies that have delved into this area have found that humour has a range of psychological and physiological benefits, with no known side effects. Like sleep, humour is safe and pleasant to use. Experiments have shown that making people laugh can temporarily boost certain aspects of their immune system, potentially making them more resistant to infection and disease. Humour can certainly reduce the biological effects of stress, as measured by changes in the levels of the stress-related hormones adrenaline and cortisol. Research has also confirmed that humour in the workplace is correlated with better working relationships, greater job satisfaction and increased productivity. The most creative and productive parts of an organisation are often the noisiest.

Humour is a social lubricant which can help to forge relationships and strengthen existing ones. As such, it promotes connectedness, the most important of all building blocks of happiness. It is probably no coincidence that lonely hearts ads seem to stipulate 'GSOH' more often than 'good looks' or 'own house and car'. Humour is especially handy in difficult social situations, by enabling us to tackle awkward issues in a non-threatening way. Many a true word . . .

14. Playfulness
Children, like young animals of many other species, spend much of their time playing. Indeed, play behaviour is the quintessential characteristic of childhood. Play might seem pointless, but in fact it has important long-term benefits. Through play, children acquire valuable experience and develop their mental and physical capabilities. We will take a closer look at it in chapter 11.

Adults play too, albeit often in more structured ways.

Sports and games are common forms of adult play, and common sources of happiness. So, too, are social leisure activities like making music, voluntary work and going to the pub. What they have in common is their ability to deliver all three basic elements of happiness – pleasure, lack of displeasure and satisfaction.

A less obvious feature of play is its delicate dependence on individual well-being. Play is a highly sensitive barometer of mental and physical health. A child who is feeling anxious, sad, hungry or ill will probably not be playful. Play behaviour is one of the first things to go when we are feeling less than well. As such, it can provide a valuable insight into the current state of individuals and organisations. The least creative and productive sections of an organisation are often the least playful.

A personal characteristic that is closely related to playfulness is openness to new experiences. By and large, happy people have a more welcoming attitude towards new experiences and cope better with change. Openness to new experiences and a willingness to change have become increasingly important in a complex world where the demands are evolving at an accelerating pace.

15. Wisdom

As we saw earlier, happiness depends to a considerable extent on how we *think* about the world, as well as our emotional responses. Someone who can think straight and solve real-life problems is better equipped to be happy.

One of the most valuable gifts that parents and teachers can bestow on children is wisdom – which is not as grand and rarefied as it might sound. There is nothing particularly mysterious or exclusive about wisdom. What it boils down to is an armoury of pragmatic knowledge about the world, together with some effective ways of thinking about problems. It is *not* the same as 'common sense', which often amounts to little more than prejudice or being wise after the event. Wisdom means being able to understand and deal with the challenges, both great and small, that we all encounter in everyday life. Wise people can identify the problem and then work out how to resolve it in a practical way. They remain objective and avoid being blinded by their own emotions. Wise people also recognise the inherent uncertainties of life, appreciate the limits of their own knowledge, and cope well with ambiguity.

The great philosophers of ancient Greece taught that people are happier if they acquire the thinking skills that enable them to make the right choices, develop the right attitudes, and cope with adversity. The evidence from modern science bears this out. Various studies have shown that individuals who possess wisdom tend to have happier lives. Wisdom makes a particularly big contribution to happiness in old age.

None of this implies that children must attend philosophy classes in order to be happy (although there is much to recommend this idea). It simply means that parents and teachers can help children greatly by equipping them with practical strategies for coping with everyday problems. These can include very simple rules of thumb, such as always trying to learn from bad experiences ('what does not destroy me makes me stronger'), not setting wildly unrealistic goals, not seeing everything in black and white, and accepting that bad things sometimes just happen.

One of the main ways in which children acquire wisdom is by observing how their parents behave. Children are more inclined to do what their parents *do* than what they *say*, which means that parents need to think about their own behaviour and set a good example. Education obviously plays a key role as well. Well-educated people live healthier and happier lives, partly because they have the knowledge and wisdom to make the right choices and avoid harm. We will return to education and its contribution to happiness in later chapters.

16. Freedom from excessive materialism

Too many people in wealthy nations live their lives as though acquiring money and material possessions will bring them enduring happiness. In fact, as we shall see later, wealth has surprisingly little lasting impact on happiness. Acquiring more money or possessions can make us feel better for a while, but the rise in mood tends to be modest and short-lived. We soon get used to what we have and our expectations rise, leading us to want ever more.

More importantly, the process of trying to acquire wealth can actually make us *less* happy if it gets in the way of things that really do matter, such as personal relationships or a sense of purpose and meaning. As we will see in chapter 8, there is good evidence that highly materialistic people are less happy on average than those who have other priorities in life.

17. Regular experience of flow

A fairly regular occurrence for most happy people is a particular state of optimal experience which is sometimes referred to as *flow*.[3]

Flow occurs when you are utterly absorbed in an activity. That activity might be something mundane like reading a book or socialising, or it might be more demanding, like playing a musical instrument or climbing a mountain. Whatever the activity is, you have chosen to perform it for its own sake and have a clear sense of what you are trying to do; you are also completely focused on the task in hand and nothing else seems to matter. (In this way, flow is an excellent antidote to self-absorption.) Your attention is firmly rooted in the present, rather than flitting anxiously between the past and future as often happens in normal experience. In addition, you might notice a change in your perception of time, which can feel either as though it has speeded up or slowed down. The sensation of flow can be intensely rewarding, but it may not feel especially pleasurable. Someone in flow will probably not be whooping with joy: the gratification usually comes later, when looking back on the experience.

Flow requires you to be fully engaged in a task that is sufficiently challenging to stretch your skills, but not so difficult that it becomes stressful. Someone in flow can feel intensely alive, as though they were *meant* to be doing what they are doing. Think of James Bond performing some feat of derring-do and saving the world (again). Bond feels more than mere physical pleasure – indeed, he might feel quite the reverse if the villains temporarily have the upper hand. Rather, he feels at one with himself and fulfilled. In contrast, an essentially passive pastime like watching TV is unlikely to produce flow because it makes so little demand on the viewer.

Because flow requires active engagement with a challenging task, it helps to develop skills. There are some obvious parallels here with play. A child who is absorbed in playing may well be experiencing flow; and play, like flow, helps children to develop their skills. Sadly, few children experience flow whilst sitting in the classroom, and even fewer experience it whilst sitting in front of the TV. Moreover, their parents do not always present ideal role models for creating flow if they routinely come home from work exhausted and slump in front of the TV.

To discover the delights of flow, you must make some initial investment of effort. That said, flow does seem to be a common human experience, even if for some people it is an infrequent one. Research has found that 80–90 per cent of people report experiencing flow at least occasionally in their lives, regardless of their nationality, cultural background or affluence. Extremely poor, disabled people report experiencing flow, as do street children living rough in developing nations. Indeed, surviving on the streets provides rich opportunities for flow, because it is a highly demanding lifestyle that regularly stretches the child's social, mental and physical skills to the limit. This might help to explain why street children often respond badly to welfare programmes that seek to bring them back into formal education. Many drop out after a few weeks or months, despite expressing a desire to study and improve their prospects. For children used to surviving on their wits, sitting in a classroom for hours can be immensely boring. The streets present many stresses and dangers, but they also provide flow.

Those of us living much more cosseted lives in wealthy nations have plenty of opportunities to experience flow. Activities that reliably produce it include playing sports, making music, painting, dancing, reading, studying, socialising, taking part in religious rituals and pursuing hobbies. Sports people, athletes and musicians regularly experience flow, and they often report that it helps their performance. One of the main reasons why art, sports and games have for so long been a central feature of all human cultures is probably because they are such rich and reliable sources of flow. Social interactions, if they are sufficiently complex and absorbing, can also generate flow.

Paid work can be a regular source of opportunities to experience flow. Researchers find that people with relatively complex and demanding jobs, including teachers, surgeons, musicians, social workers, artisans, soldiers and academics, are more likely to describe their jobs as providing flow than junior office workers and those with routine blue-collar jobs. Nonetheless, almost any job or activity is capable of providing opportunities for flow, as long as it is approached with the right attitude – which means becoming fully engaged with the task and building in personal challenges to make it more stimulating. It's not what you do but the way that you do it.

Two pictures of happiness

We have just run through a list of 17 characteristics commonly displayed by happy people, as distilled from scientific research. But what does happiness look like in practice? What are the hallmarks of a happy child who has the makings of a happy adult? The most vivid pictures of happiness can be found in the pages of fiction, where the shades of grey that characterise most real people can be conveniently lost. One of my personal favourite role models is William Brown, the eleven-year-old hero of Richmal Crompton's 1920s-era *William* books.

The irrepressible William is an admirably happy person on almost every count. For a start, he scores highly on connectedness, social skills and emotional competence. He has a coterie of bosom chums (Ginger, Douglas and Henry, aka 'The Outlaws') of whom he is the undisputed leader. He effortlessly dominates all those around him through his strength of character, imagination, drive, courage and physical prowess. He is an effective (if ungrammatical) communicator. He is free from anxiety to the point of being reckless. Nothing worries or fazes him; there is no rule he is unwilling to break, and no red-faced adult he is afraid to defy. In any situation, no matter how dire, he somehow manages to remain in control.

William's resilience, optimism and self-esteem are boundless, making him virtually bulletproof in the face of adversity. In one typical incident, Douglas queries William's suggestion that they should all dig for gold. William challenges Douglas to give him one good reason why they shouldn't dig for gold. Because they won't find any, is Douglas's simple answer. But that is not good enough for William. How does Douglas know they won't find gold? Has Douglas ever tried? Has he ever dug for gold? Does he know anyone who's ever dug for gold? No. Well then, concludes William triumphantly, how can Douglas possibly *know* they won't find any?

When it comes to playfulness and exploration, William is matchless. To him, the main attraction of any game is the extent to which it presents a danger to life and limb. If there is a tall tree, he will climb it; if there is an abandoned house, he will break in and explore it. Falls, cuts, bruises and adult wrath are no deterrent. One of the few aspects of schooling that William finds tolerable is science, and that is because he likes to experiment. In fact, he likes to experiment with his experiments. He feels compelled to heat things he has been told not to heat, just to see what happens. And if in the process he loses his eyebrows – well, that only adds to his pride and pleasure. He would find little pleasure in many of today's safety-conscious science classes.

Nothing can dampen William's spirits for long. He is a truly happy boy who has all the essential qualities to become a truly happy and highly successful adult (although in present-day England, his long-suffering parents would probably take him to their doctor, and emerge with a diagnosis of ADHD and a prescription for Ritalin).

Another fictional exemplar of happiness is the vain, impulsive and childish Mr Toad in *The Wind in the Willows*. Mr Toad may not seem the most obvious archetype of happiness, and he certainly has his weak spots. But he also has notable strengths. Like William, Mr Toad has a rich network of close and supportive friends. Thanks to his loyal pals Badger, Water Rat and Mole, Toad gets his house back after it has been occupied by the nasty Wild Wooders.

Toad is highly sociable. As Ratty remarks, it is never the wrong time to call on Toad. 'Early or late, he's always the same fellow. Always good tempered, always glad to see you, always sorry when you go!' Toad's communication skills are not bad either, though perhaps not as superb as he might believe. ('I have the gift of conversation,' boasts Toad. 'I've been told that I ought to have a *salon*, whatever that may be.')

Toad scores especially highly when it comes to engagement. Indeed, he personifies engagement in a rather extreme form, with his succession of all-consuming crazes. First he is mad about travelling by horse and cart; then he falls passionately in love with fast cars. When Toad is behind the wheel of a motor he is in flow, and nothing else matters. Rat describes him as 'like an animal walking in a happy dream'. Toad is possessed. His new craze lands him in terrible trouble because he simply cannot leave cars alone, but Toad is unrepentant. He will not admit that his car-stealing antics were folly. To him, the experience was 'simply glorious'.

Toad's affectionate nature helps to compensate for his other failings, notably his boastfulness and conceit. Intelligence is not one of his strengths, either. Nonetheless, Toad is good-hearted, loved by his friends and manages to live an eventful and happy life. One could do worse.

The characteristics of very happy people

What about *very* happy people? What are the characteristics of those fortunate few individuals who would, metaphorically speaking, win medals in the Happiness Olympics?

To find out, the American psychologists Ed Diener and Martin Seligman investigated individuals who ranked in the top 10 per cent of consistently very happy people. Their most striking finding was that very happy people were highly connected. Compared to averagely happy or unhappy people, they had stronger and richer personal relationships of all sorts. They were also more sociable, more extroverted, and more agreeable. However, Diener and Seligman uncovered nothing absolutely unique about the personalities or circumstances of very happy people. They did not appear to experience a larger number of objectively good or pleasurable events than the rest of us, and their great happiness could not be accounted for by great wealth or conventional success.

The finding that very happy people are characterised above all else by their connectedness and sociability underlines one of the central themes of this book – that personal relationships are the single most important building block of happiness. Good relationships may not be sufficient by themselves to make a happy person, because other things matter as well, but they are almost always necessary. It is difficult to be lonely and happy at the same time.

FIVE

Being connected

Only connect!
E. M. FORSTER, *Howard's End* (1910)

Relationships rule, OK?

We have seen that connectedness is an almost universal feature of happy people. Personal relationships, especially the close ones, are enormously important for happiness; they contribute more than money, fame, conventional success, material possessions, intelligence or even health. Loneliness, on the other hand, breeds unhappiness and poor health.

Throughout history, wise people have understood that relationships are essential for happiness, health and success. Among them was the Greek philosopher Epicurus, who lived between 341 and 270 BC. He wrote that: 'Of all the means that wisdom provides to help one live one's entire life in happiness, the greatest by far is the possession of friendship.' The nineteenth-century writer William Morris was even more effusive: 'Fellowship is heaven, and lack of fellowship is hell: fellowship is life, and lack of fellowship is death.' Regrettably, our current consumerist society, with its overriding focus on the self, does little to foster connectedness. Some parts of the self-help industry also give insufficient weight to this fundamental aspect of human nature.

In recent decades, the centrality of personal relationships to happiness has been amply borne out by scientific research. Relationships exert a major influence on happiness throughout the lifespan, from childhood to old age. For instance, adolescents who have good relationships with their peers are found to be happier, on average, than those whose peer relationships are less satisfactory. Similarly, adults who are part of one or more social groups are happier than those who feel less connected.

People with good relationships also tend to be more successful at school, at work and in other ways, including financially. Researchers have found that individuals with extensive social networks make faster progress in their careers, earn more money and are less likely to be unemployed. As one eminent academic put it, your address book is probably worth more to you in the long run than your school or university qualifications. However, the quality of those relationships matters more than their sheer quantity; having a few close, supportive relationships is more beneficial than being casually acquainted with hundreds of semi-strangers.

In addition to being happier, people with good personal relationships also tend to be healthier. Individuals with close friends and confidants, friendly neighbours and supportive workmates are generally found to have better mental and physical health than those who are isolated. Personal relationships contribute more to mental and physical health than do money or fame. By the same token, social isolation and loneliness are strongly associated with unhappiness, depression and poor physical health. On average, lonely people have shorter, unhealthier and unhappier lives.

Individuals whose poor social skills damage their personal relationships may face the prospect of persistent unhappiness. Thomas Hardy paints a depressing picture of just such a person in the form of Michael Henchard in *The Mayor of Casterbridge*. The dogged Henchard rises from rags to riches, eventually becoming a successful businessman and mayor, but his murky past catches up with him and he dies a broken man, alone and in poverty. Throughout his rise and fall, Henchard remains a lonely and isolated figure, thanks to fundamental flaws in his character. His harshness, cynicism, bad temper and indifference to other people's feelings alienate his friends and associates. When his business fails and he is declared bankrupt, he refuses help from his business partner and is finally rejected even by his own daughter. Henchard's downfall and lonely death are at least partly the result of his social and emotional incompetence.

Maintaining close relationships requires a certain amount of motivation and effort, as well as basic social skills. If two friends or partners spend very little time together then their relationship may suffer, no matter how socially and emotionally competent they are. Friends sometimes drift apart as they get older and circumstances change, creating gaps that must be filled with new relationships. As the great eighteenth-century scholar Samuel Johnson remarked: 'If a man does not make new acquaintances as he advances through life, he will soon find himself alone. A man, Sir, should keep his friendship in constant repair.'

The fact that personal relationships are central to happiness should come as no surprise: after all, we humans are fundamentally social beings. The ability to develop relationships is a universal characteristic of our species, as Charles Darwin observed in *The Descent of Man:*

> Man is a social animal. We see this in his dislike of solitude, and in his wish for society beyond that of his own family. Solitary confinement is one of the severest punishments which can be inflicted. Some authors suppose that man primevally lived in single families; but at the present day, though single families, or only two or three together, roam the solitudes of some savage lands, they always, as far as I can discover, hold friendly relations with other families inhabiting the same district.

Humans are not the only social animals, of course. Many other species are intensely social as well. Observations of social animals in their natural habitats have repeatedly revealed that survival and well-being can depend critically on the individual's social relationships. For instance, long-term studies of baboons in the wild have found that adult females who have good social networks also have lower levels of the stress hormone cortisol in their bloodstream and produce healthier, longer-lived offspring.

The evolutionary history of our own species means that we are 'designed' (by natural selection) to live in relatively small social groups, surrounded by individuals who are familiar to us and with whom we conduct complex and subtle relationships. That is ultimately why personal relationships are so central to our happiness and mental health.

The evolutionary biologist Robin Dunbar has drawn

some intriguing inferences about the likely social behaviour of our ancient ancestors, by comparing the brains and behavioural characteristics of modern humans with those of our closest biological relatives, the apes and monkeys.[1] His analysis suggests that the maximum sustainable group size for humans is roughly 150 individuals. This is the biggest social group that can maintain its integrity on the basis of individuals having direct personal knowledge of each other and of all the two-way relationships in the group. Once a group gets much bigger than about 150, so the theory goes, everyone finds it hard to keep track of all the many different relationships. Our brains are not big enough to juggle the enormous complexities of thousands of relationships, each with its own history and undertones. In groups that are much larger than about 150, individuals tend to be lumped together into categories or subgroups, and notions of 'us and them' creep in.

In line with this prediction, anthropologists find that the surviving hunter-gatherer peoples, including the Kung San of southern Africa, the Yanomamo of Venezuela and hunter-gatherer societies in New Guinea, Indonesia, Africa and South America, typically do live in groups of up to about 150 individuals. Indeed, social groupings of around 150 seem to crop up throughout human history. For example, archaeologists estimate that Neolithic villages in Mesopotamia, inhabited 8,000 years ago, probably housed between 150 and 200 people. And in professional armies the typical size of a company, which is the basic unit for independent action, has been between 100 and 200 throughout history.

Trust

Another important and heartening lesson from biology is that social relationships are not simply about extracting the maximum immediate benefit from other people. According to a pernicious idea that has leached out from economics, human relationships can be reduced to economic transactions in which each individual seeks to maximise his or her own selfish benefit. Classical economic theory assumes that we all act in our own selfish interest; it predicts, for example, that we should generally be unwilling to trust strangers with our money unless we have proof of their bona fides.

This calculating view of life is epitomised by Charles Dickens's character Thomas Gradgrind, in *Hard Times*. Gradgrind, a former businessman turned politician, is a firm believer in the value of facts and the pointlessness of feelings. He will have no truck with trust:

> It was a fundamental principle of the Gradgrind philosophy that everything was to be paid for. Nobody was ever on any account to give anybody anything, or render anybody help without purchase. Gratitude was to be abolished, and the virtues springing from it were not to be. Every inch of the existence of mankind, from birth to death, was to be a bargain across a counter. And if we didn't get to Heaven that way, it was not a politico-economical place, and we had no business there.

Gratifyingly, science lends no support to this deeply unattractive philosophy. Psychological research has found that individuals who are generally inclined to assume the best of other people, and therefore to trust them, tend to be happier than those whose inclination is to be suspicious and distrustful. And there is a good reason for this.

Biological theory, backed by empirical evidence, strongly implies that we are predisposed to trust each other. Evolution favours personality traits and behaviour patterns that tend to maximise the survival and reproductive success of the genes that give rise to them. But that certainly does not mean we are 'designed' to behave selfishly in all circumstances. On the contrary, trusting others and behaving altruistically is often the best thing to do.

Natural selection has equipped us with brains that suit us for living in social groups. One way in which we are adapted for group living is to be predisposed to trust others, up to a point, so that we can cooperate with them and reap the considerable benefits that cooperation brings. If I scratch your back then you will probably scratch mine one day, and both of us will be better off than if we had not helped each other. Evolutionary biologists refer to this phenomenon as reciprocal altruism, and it is observed in many other social species including apes, monkeys and birds.

Nakedly selfish behaviour is simply not an optimal strategy in a social group where individuals know each other and remember the history of their previous interactions. If you accept help from someone you know, but later refuse to help that individual, you risk being regarded by other group members as a cheat who is not to be trusted. And in a group-living species, being distrusted and ostracised can have serious implications for an individual's well-being. As the philosopher Bertrand Russell presciently argued in 1930: 'Man depends upon co-operation, and has been provided by nature with the instructive apparatus out of which the friendliness required for co-operation can spring.'

The impulse to trust others and cooperate with them is deep-rooted and ancient. This is not just biological theorising or wishful thinking: it is borne out by hard data. Carefully controlled psychological experiments have established that, contrary to what simple economic theory predicts, real people actually do trust others and want to cooperate with them – even in situations that are explicitly concerned with money. Reciprocity is absolutely central to human social behaviour. The feeling of obligation that comes from being given something is a powerful psychological force, which is daily exploited the world over by salespeople and other persuaders.

Scientists have been investigating the biology and psychology of trust using so-called trust-and-reciprocity games, in which volunteers take part in financial transactions with another person under experimental conditions. When people play these games they often display a considerable degree of trust in the strangers with whom they are playing, and their trust is usually reciprocated. The results show that the more you trust someone, the more likely they are to trust you.

In one series of experiments conducted at the University of Zurich, volunteers were given real money to invest with an anonymous other person (the 'trustee'). Three different scenarios were used. In one scenario, the investor was instructed to threaten their trustee with a financial penalty if the trustee failed to deliver a specified return on the investment. In a second scenario the trustee knew about the possibility of a penalty, but the investor was told not to mention it. And in the third scenario, neither investor nor trustee knew anything about the possibility of a penalty. The scenario that in practice produced the biggest returns for investors was the second one, in which sanctions were known to be an option but were not mentioned. The least successful scenario was the one in which the trustee was explicitly threatened with punishment. Investors who trusted strangers ended up making bigger profits than those who treated their co-player with suspicion.

Experiments such as these have repeatedly found that most people respond better when they are trusted than when they are treated with suspicion. Trust breeds trust, whereas sanctions that are intended to prevent cheating can actually make people *more* inclined to cheat, if they think they can get away with it. Trusting others really does pay dividends.

Scientists have started to explore the neurobiological basis of trust, using brain-scanning techniques to monitor brain activity patterns in situations where people are called upon to trust or distrust others. In a typical experiment, volunteers' brains are monitored while they play a 'trust' game such as the Prisoner's Dilemma, in which each player must independently choose whether or not to trust the other player.[2] Brain scanning has revealed that when someone trusts and cooperates with another person, certain areas of their brain become more active; and the brain areas that light up are those known to be involved with the emotional experience of feeling good (the so-called reward centres). This groundbreaking research implies that we are indeed predisposed to trust other people, because doing so is emotionally rewarding. The decision whether to trust someone and cooperate with them is not purely a matter of rational calculation or moral judgment: our brains are built in such a way that it actually *feels good* to trust and be trusted.

Extensive research has also established that – contrary to popular mythology – we are surprisingly poor at judging when other people are lying to us. We have a marked 'truth bias' which makes us inclined to assume that others are telling the truth, especially when the other person appears to be generally friendly or if we have a close personal relationship with them.

Evolutionary thinking also casts light on some other, apparently very modern, problems. The environment in which our species evolved was radically different in many respects from the environment in which most of us now live. Culture and technology have evolved at a vastly greater pace than human biology. The wheel was probably invented around 3500 BC, which is less than 300 generations ago, and within the space of a few thousand years we have catapulted ourselves from a hunter-gatherer existence to life as it is now led in places like London, Los Angeles and Tokyo. But a few thousand years is a mere fraction of an instant when compared against the huge timescales of biological evolution. In terms of human genetics, nothing much has happened since the dawn of civilisation: our bodies and brains are essentially the same as those of our hunter-gatherer ancestors who lived during the most recent stages of human evolution. A human born 50,000 years ago would have been biologically capable of becoming an IT consultant or an interior designer.

Discrepancies between our current environment and the ancestral environment for which we are biologically adapted can give rise to problems. Consider diet, for example. Fatty or sugary foodstuffs rich in calories were hard to obtain throughout most of human evolutionary history, but people in affluent societies are now surrounded by limitless, cheap supplies. We have inherited from our ancestors a liking for sweet or fatty foods and a propensity to stuff ourselves with them whenever we have the opportunity. Fifty thousand years ago that was an adaptive trait; it would have helped our ancestors to survive in a harsher world where food supplies were often unpredictable and intermittent. In our current environment, however, a predisposition to gorge on junk food and sugary drinks leads to obesity, diabetes and heart disease on a massive scale.

Similar reasoning can be applied to our social environment. We humans have spent nearly all of our long evolutionary history living in social groups where everyone knows everyone else. But the current reality for many people in industrialised nations is dramatically different. The mobile and fragmented nature of urban society means that many individuals are no longer part of a tightly-knit network of family, relatives and close friends. Someone living in a big city might take part in hundreds of casual social interactions every day, yet still have no real connection or meaningful relationship with anyone. They can feel lonely despite being immersed in an ocean of humanity. When our social environment drifts too far out of kilter with our biological legacy we can expect unhappiness to ensue.

In certain respects, industrialised societies mitigate against personal happiness. One of their potential pitfalls is that we have fewer opportunities than our hunter-gatherer ancestors to *test* our relationships. When life was a real struggle, and survival depended on cooperation, people soon found out who they could trust. But modern humans living in safe, predictable environments can end up feeling doubtful about their relationships because these are so seldom put to the test. As Epicurus said, 'It is not so much our friends' help that helps us as the confident knowledge that they will help us.' We may not know who our true friends are until we experience a crisis that tests the relationship. Some may turn out to be fair-weather friends who slither away at the first sign of real trouble, while others stand fast and help. Paradoxically, the very safety and stability of urban life can leave us feeling less confident about the strength of our relationships and therefore less connected.

Our current environment also clashes with our biology by continually offering us an array of tempting sources of quick and easy pleasures which compete with our personal relationships. When someone feels in need of cheering up, their response may well be to flop in front of the TV and consume comfort food or alcohol rather than make the effort to socialise. But such responses probably do more harm than good if they become a way of life. Staying in alone and eating ice cream in front of the TV is unlikely to provide a long-term remedy for unhappiness.

Personal relationships can be eroded by current life-styles in other ways as well. Take commuting, for example. Research confirms, unsurprisingly, that people who regularly commute long distances to and from work are measurably unhappier on average than those who work closer to home. Commuting can be a deeply unpleasant and frustrating experience, which partly explains why those who do a lot of it tend to feel less happy. But that is not the whole story. Commuting can also diminish happiness by hampering social relationships. If your home and workplace are far apart, it may be difficult to socialise freely with people from both environments. Moreover, spending a lot of time travelling each day will leave less time for family and friends. Such constraints may get in the way of relationships and hence erode happiness.

Social capitalism

In recent years, social scientists, economists and politicians have become increasingly interested in a concept known as social capital, which refers to the many great benefits that social relationships bring to society as a whole, as well as to individuals.[3] According to one formal definition, social capital consists of the social networks within a community or society, together with the shared norms, values and understandings that facilitate cooperation within or among groups. Social capital arises from the networks of personal relationships between friends, neighbours and colleagues, and it encompasses such things as neighbourliness, community spirit, social cohesion, citizenship and trust. In that sense, it is a new way of thinking about some old concepts.

The reason why social capital has been attracting attention is because it brings enormous tangible benefits to society. Researchers have been uncovering more and more evidence of links between social capital and desirable outcomes in terms of economic growth, crime, health and education. Among other things, citizens with good networks of relationships have fewer mental health problems, recover faster from illness, smoke less and live longer. They are also less likely to commit crime or to be the victim of crime. A society rich in social capital should therefore be better off in many ways, not least because it should need to spend less money on hospitals, prisons and antidepressant drugs.

Regrettably, the evidence also suggests that in recent decades social capital has been declining rather than expanding in wealthy nations like the USA and UK. The American political scientist Robert Putnam, who is one of the leading thinkers in this field, blames various social trends in Western society for undermining personal relationships and thereby reducing social capital. Three of the main culprits are the 'me' culture of individualism, the workaholic long-hours culture, and TV. All three have the unintended effect of disconnecting us from other people and from social structures. Putnam's seminal book on the decline of social capital in the USA is called *Bowling Alone*, its title signifying the fact that Americans no longer go bowling together in league teams as they once did in their millions.

Over the past few decades the UK has grown to resemble the USA in many respects, becoming a more individualistic society at the expense of social capital. Some statistics reveal the current state of play. On the positive side, there are still more than half a million voluntary and community groups in the UK, ranging from national and international organisations to small local groups. However, a government survey in 2001 found that less than a third (32 per cent) of adults in Britain had taken part in some form of voluntary work within the previous year. Another large survey found that 34 per cent of people saw or spoke to friends less than once a week, and 42 per cent knew fewer than five other people to whom they could turn in a crisis. Research also shows that people under the age of 30 are the least neighbourly and the least likely to be civically engaged with their communities.

The UK has certainly become a country of ever smaller households, in which a growing proportion of the population is living alone. More than a quarter (29 per cent) of all households in Britain in 2003 consisted of one person living alone (up from 18 per cent in 1971) and more than half the population now live either alone or with only one other person. In fact, there are now more single-person households in Britain than there are traditional nuclear families: in 2003, only 22 per cent of households consisted of a couple with dependent children, down from 35 per cent in 1971. The average number of people living together in a typical British household has fallen progressively over the past 30 years.[4] As a consequence, the total number of households has risen by more than 30 per cent, despite an actual population growth of only 5 per cent. No wonder house prices have risen so much.

The long-hours working culture is another feature of life in the UK that eats into social capital. As the media frequently remind us, we work the longest hours in Europe. Even according to official government statistics, a quarter of all employed men in the UK are working more than 50 hours a week.[5] And when we are not at work, many of us are slumped in front of the TV rather than socialising. Adults in the UK spend an average of three hours a day watching TV. Add that to the commuting and the 50-hour working week and you can see why there are fewer hours left for keeping personal relationships alive. And without those relationships we are unlikely to be happy, no matter how much money we earn.

Marriage

Let us turn now to a particular sort of relationship that has a big influence on happiness – marriage. According to a large body of empirical data, married people are significantly happier on average than unmarried people, including those who have never married and those who are divorced, separated or widowed. Moreover, marriage has a stronger positive influence on happiness than cohabitation, which in turn does more for happiness than living alone (at least, in societies where cohabitation is widely tolerated).

An association between marriage and happiness is found

in most societies; one international comparison found that marriage was positively correlated with happiness in 16 out of 17 nations.[6] The correlation tends to be stronger in countries such as the USA and UK where divorce is relatively easy to obtain, presumably because fewer people in these countries are trapped in unhappy marriages. Incidentally, recent research has overturned the commonly held belief that men benefit more than women from being married. In fact, men and women appear to benefit about equally.

Happiness is not the only potential advantage of marriage. Married people also enjoy better mental and physical health. On average, they live longer than unmarried people, are less likely to commit suicide and have better-paid jobs. For example, a British study involving 20,000 men found that married men lived three years longer and earned £3,000 a year more on average than single men. Another study found that middle-aged married people were better off than single people in terms of physical health, mobility and freedom from depression. Marriage also contributes to social capital: research shows that married people are more likely than single people to trust their neighbours and be trusted by their neighbours.

Marriage can boost happiness in various ways, including practical ones like providing financial security, burden-sharing and sex. One reason why married people live longer is that they tend to live healthier lifestyles than single people. Psychological and emotional factors undoubtedly contribute as well.

Marriage appears to be unlike several other potential sources of happiness, in that its effects tend to be long-lasting. As we shall see in chapter 8, pleasurable experiences such as receiving a large sum of money usually provide only a short-term boost to happiness; we adjust to most good or bad events and their effects soon wear off. Marriage is different, however. A successful marriage can make one or both partners measurably happier for decades. In one American study, researchers tracked 24,000 people whose marital status had changed, either because they got married or divorced. The results revealed marked changes in happiness that often persisted for years, with married people generally becoming happier over time and divorced people heading in the opposite direction. Indeed, in some cases the impact of marriage or divorce actually increased over time rather than diminishing.

Of course, not all marriages lead to happiness. A substantial proportion of them end in separation or divorce, often with dismal consequences for the happiness of both partners. On current statistics, around one in three marriages in the UK will end in divorce. Around 160,000 couples get divorced each year in the UK, which has one of the highest divorce rates in Europe. You are statistically more likely to divorce if you married when you were young, if you gave birth before you were married, or if you have been divorced previously.

Many children are affected by divorce. Approximately half of all divorces involve couples with children, the majority of whom are under the age of ten. More than a quarter (28 per cent) of all British children living in families headed by a married couple will experience divorce within their family before they reach the age of 16.

Divorce can have undesirable consequences for children, although many adjust remarkably well and lasting damage is not inevitable. A review of more than 200 research studies found that the immediate distress of parental separation usually fades with time, and most children eventually settle into a pattern of normal development. Nonetheless, most children experience acute unhappiness during the early stages of the divorce process, and some suffer enduring effects. A large, long-term study in the UK found that individuals whose parents had divorced tended to be less happy in adult life than those whose parents had stayed together. One of the reasons why the children of divorce may be less happy in adult life is because they are significantly more likely to become divorced themselves. The evidence also indicates that they face a greater risk of behaviour problems, difficulties in school, low educational achievement, low income, and becoming a parent at an early age.

Research suggests that a marriage is more likely to be successful and long-lasting if the partners share similar values and interests and if they are broadly similar in attractiveness. Jealousy and trouble may arise if one partner is much more attractive than the other. One of the implications for parents is that they should try to help their children develop realistic attitudes towards choosing a partner. In particular, young people need to grasp the distinction between lust and the extra ingredients that are usually needed to sustain a long-lasting and happy relationship. As the poet John Donne so aptly put it: 'Love built on beauty, soon as beauty, dies.'

According to the evidence, then, anyone who wants to improve their long-term prospects for happiness should probably get married at some stage. In reality, the trend in the UK and other wealthy nations has been moving in the opposite direction. Since the early 1970s there has been a long-term decline in the number of people getting married each year in the UK, and the number of marriages in 2001 was the lowest since 1897.[7] Currently, just over half of all men and women are married, compared with two-thirds in 1971.[8] Much the same has been going on in other countries: one international comparison of developed nations found that between 1950 and 1985 marriage rates had declined in 22 out of the 27 countries studied. There is also a strong trend to marry later in life. The average age at which English men now marry for the first time is 31, while for women it is 29; in 1961, by comparison, it was 26 and 23. Even so, the majority of people do still get married at some point in their life; current statistics suggest that only about 16 per cent of men and just over 10 per cent of women who were born in the 1960s will never marry.

Although marriage and other forms of close personal relationship are vital for most people's happiness, a few individuals do find happiness in a solitary life, whether by choice or circumstance. Some notable geniuses, including Beethoven, Goya, Newton, Descartes and Wittgenstein, seem to have derived their happiness more from their work than from their relationships. But they are the exceptions. For most of us, personal relationships form the bedrock of happiness. And we are far more likely to form and maintain those relationships if, as children, we have acquired the necessary social and emotional skills and attitudes. Parents and schools have pivotal roles to play in helping children to become connected, and hence happy.

SIX

Authentic ingredients

You should pray to have a sound mind in a sound body.
JUVENAL (*c.* AD 60–130), *Satires*

We saw in the previous chapter that personal relationships are crucial for happiness. But many other ingredients also contribute to making a happy person. In this chapter we will look at the more important ones, ranging from genes and culture to education and health. Each one can have a substantial influence on an individual's capacity for pleasure, displeasure or satisfaction, and thus on their overall happiness.

Geography

How happy you are will depend to some extent on where in the world you were brought up and live. This is not surprising. Happiness reflects our attitudes, which are partly shaped by the values and norms of our culture. And of course nations differ in more tangible ways like wealth, health, education and equality.

There is abundant evidence that nations differ considerably in their average levels of satisfaction and happiness. Take the countries of Europe, for example. Since the early 1970s, annual surveys of European citizens have been uncovering large and consistent national differences in satisfaction and happiness. Year after year, the Danes, Dutch, Irish and British have revealed themselves to be more satisfied with their lives, on average, than the French, Italians and Portuguese. The Danes have consistently come at or near the top of the league table, with more than half of all Danes rating themselves as very satisfied with their lives – a far higher proportion than in Portugal. (But averages are only averages, of course: even in 'unhappy' countries there are still a fair number of happy individuals, just as there are unhappy people in 'happy' countries.)

Even bigger differences emerge when other regions of the globe are compared. In one international study, for example, researchers analysed data from 55 nations which between them represented three-quarters of the world's population. Such comparisons generally find that the populations of wealthy nations are happier on average than those of very poor nations. Even the Portuguese, a relatively gloomy lot by European standards, are happy in comparison with people in several developing nations, where more than half the population rate themselves as unhappy or very unhappy. Why do nations differ in this way?

National wealth has some bearing on national happiness, but it accounts for only a fraction of the observed differences. Other factors, including culture and politics, also play substantial roles. Several of the countries that usually appear near the bottom of global league tables for happiness were once part of the former Soviet Union. For example, Russia, Ukraine, Belarus and Azerbaijan have some of the least satisfied and unhappiest populations in the world, who rate themselves as less happy even than people in very poor countries such as Bangladesh. According to a 1990s survey covering six continents, the unhappiest people on the planet live in Moldova.

The countries whose populations are happiest tend to have an individualistic culture, relatively high levels of social equality and good human rights. They include Denmark, Sweden, the USA, UK, Netherlands, Canada and Iceland. Average levels of satisfaction and happiness are also found to be somewhat higher in societies that have mature democratic institutions. In one study, researchers compared different cantons of Switzerland that had different degrees of devolution. The results indicated that people tended to be happier in regions with more local autonomy and more direct democracy. More devolved forms of democratic government might help to make people happier by giving them more control over what happens to them.

A nation's economic policies can have a big impact on happiness. One reason is unemployment which, as we saw in chapter 4, is a major cause of unhappiness. Financial and social equality also play a role. A 25-year comparison of eight nations found that those with the biggest inequalities in income were also the least happy. A range of other evidence indicates that levels of happiness are generally lower in countries where extreme wealth co-exists with extreme poverty. One implication is that rising economic prosperity may not produce greater happiness if it is accompanied by greater inequality.

One of the more powerful societal influences on happiness is the degree of individualism. Highly individualistic societies like the USA place great emphasis on the needs, choices and fulfilment of the individual. By comparison, more collectivist societies like Japan and China put greater weight on harmonious social relationships and the interdependence of individuals. People in collectivist societies appear to measure their own self-worth and well-being more in terms of how well their group is doing. Displays of personal happiness can be seen as inappropriate if they relate solely to the individual's private experience.

The emotional dimensions of happiness, namely pleasure and displeasure, are found to play a bigger role in shaping personal happiness in individualistic cultures than in more collectivist societies. Thus feeling good is a bigger part of being happy for an American than it is, say, in Japan, China or India. Some psychologists have suggested that the rise in loneliness, social isolation and marital breakdown in many developed nations over the past 50 years may stem partly from the increasingly individualistic tendency to view pleasure, rather than satisfaction, as the key 'performance indicator' of personal relationships. The quest for immediate pleasure may not be a problem in the early stages of a relationship, but pleasure alone is unlikely to provide sufficiently solid foundations for a close friendship, partnership or marriage lasting several decades. One of the pitfalls of the 'me' society is the triumph of the heart over the head.

International surveys of satisfaction and happiness have thrown up another, somewhat surprising, finding. You might have formed the impression that we humans are a pretty miserable and mixed-up lot these days, regardless of where we live. The media remind us that depression, suicide, drug abuse, crime, divorce and family breakdown are growing problems in developed nations. And yet research consistently finds that most people, when asked, say they are happy. In most nations that have so far been studied, the majority of people describe themselves as happy or very happy. Most people also report being satisfied with key areas of their lives such as their marriage, health and job. This holds true more or less regardless of gender, wealth, ethnic origin or age; for example, most adolescents rate themselves as happy. Even people whose objective circumstances are bad, including those suffering from severe disabilities, usually rate themselves as moderately happy.

In more than 80 per cent of the many nations for which data are available, the average level of happiness is above the midway or neutral mark on whatever measurement scale is used. When happiness or satisfaction with life is rated on a scale of 0 to 10, the average score in most nations is about 7.5.[1] Indeed, most people in developed countries rate themselves as happier than average, which is obviously a statistical impossibility. Believing oneself to be above average appears to be the normal state for most people, whether it refers to happiness or driving ability.

In most countries, self-professed happy people outnumber unhappy people by about three to one, and in some wealthier nations the ratio is even higher. A typical study, which assessed 29,000 Finnish adults, found that 79 per cent rated themselves as fairly or very happy, whereas only 8 per cent said they were fairly or very unhappy. Thus, happy Finns outnumbered unhappy Finns almost ten to one. Most people also report experiencing more pleasure than displeasure in their daily lives; for example, a large British study found that seven out of ten people had experienced feelings of pleasure for at least half of the previous day, whereas fewer than one in six had experienced mostly unpleasant feelings.

The finding that most people are happy should be treated

with some caution, however. In many Western nations, being happy is regarded as socially desirable, while unhappiness has a certain stigma attached to it. In the USA, in particular, happiness is more than just an inalienable right: it is virtually a legal obligation. Individuals are regarded as somehow accountable for their own happiness, implying that anyone who is unhappy has failed in some way and must therefore be flawed. It may be no coincidence that the word 'sad' has come to mean pathetically inadequate or unfashionable. The social desirability of being happy – or at least *appearing* to be happy – may dispose some people to present themselves as happier than they really are. They may try, consciously or unconsciously, to modify how others see them – a process that psychologists refer to as 'impression management'. Scientists must take account of the potential distortions caused by impression management when analysing data on happiness.

The social desirability of happiness is not equally evident in all cultures, however. In China, for example, excessive displays of happiness are often frowned upon. A study of Chinese students found that they valued personal happiness less than Americans and spent less of their time thinking about whether or not they were happy. More generally, the evidence suggests that Asians typically feel less obliged to appear happy than Americans.

The observation that most people are fairly happy seems less surprising from a biological perspective. As we saw in chapter 3, we function better, both mentally and physically, when we are happy; we are more energetic, more successful, more sociable, more creative, healthier and longer-lived. So it makes sense that happiness should be a common state for humanity.

Genes

Whenever the causes of happiness are debated, there is a good chance someone will assert that happiness is 'all in the genes', with the implication that individuals can do little or nothing to change their own happiness. According to a more sophisticated version of this idea, everyone has their own genetically determined 'set point' for happiness, somewhat like the thermostat on a central heating system. The implication here is that our personal 'set point' has been determined by our genes, and therefore any attempt to make ourselves or our children happier is futile.

The notion that happiness is somehow 'all in the genes' can have damaging consequences if it creates a sense of being powerless to alter a fixed destiny. Unsurprisingly, research shows that parents who believe there is little they can do to influence their children's development tend to be less successful in helping their children to flourish.

Fortunately (or this would have been a short and rather dispiriting book) the notion that personal happiness is genetically hard-wired is scientifically misconceived and demonstrably wrong. Genes do of course affect happiness in countless different ways – for example, through their manifold influences on personality, health and even physical appearance. But they certainly do not explain the whole picture. Indeed, they do not even explain many of the most interesting parts of the picture.

Simple-minded genetic explanations cannot account for some prominent features of happiness, such as the fact that individuals can and do become happier or unhappier as a consequence of what happens to them. Certain sorts of life event, such as getting married, getting divorced, suffering bereavement, becoming a parent, having a major career success or losing your job, can have a big impact on happiness that in some cases may last for years. If there were such a thing as a personal 'set point' for happiness, then its setting would obviously have to change in response to experience.

Happiness is heavily dependent upon our attitudes and beliefs. This is especially true for satisfaction, the thinking element of happiness. And our attitudes and beliefs are not directly inherited through our genes: they are acquired through experience. Even someone born with an inherited disposition towards gloomy moods can nonetheless modify their state of happiness by learning to think and behave differently.

Another problem with the notion that happiness is 'all in the genes' is the fact that it varies according to where people live. As we have just seen, average levels of satisfaction and happiness differ considerably between countries. Genetic differences cannot possibly account for these national characteristics. Genetically speaking, there is precious little difference between Danes and Portuguese, or between Americans and Bangladeshis, yet these nations differ markedly in their average levels of satisfaction and happiness.

More telling still is the fact that immigrants generally acquire the happiness characteristics of the nation to which they move, not the nation in which they were born (implying that one way of acquiring happiness might be to move to Denmark). Furthermore, national levels of happiness can change rapidly in response to social, economic or political events. According to survey data, the Russian population became markedly less happy during the 1980s and 1990s as the Soviet Union fell apart. However, the genetic makeup of a population simply does not change within the space of a few years.

If the idea of happiness being genetically determined is so dubious, then why does it have such currency among the public, the media and even some scientists? Hardly a week goes by without the media announcing a new and supposedly direct causal link between a newly discovered gene and some complex human characteristic such as intelligence, criminality, promiscuity or language – so why not a gene for happiness? The problem here lies with a basic misconception about the nature of genes and what they do. Genes do not make behaviour patterns or emotions – let alone a highly complex mental state such as happiness, which involves (among other things) memory, emotion and rational thought. Genes make proteins.

According to recent research, the human genome consists of surprisingly few genes. Whereas only a few years ago scientists thought it took at least 100,000 different genes to build a human, the current conclusion is that each of us has only about 25,000 genes (most of which are also found in other species). Between them, your 25,000 genes must contribute to building your entire body and nervous system. They do this by switching on and off in immensely complex patterns that change over time. Your brain alone consists of more than one hundred thousand million (10^{11}) separate nerve cells, all interconnected in fantastically elaborate networks. So the idea that one of those 25,000 genes might code specifically for a multidimensional characteristic like happiness looks rather implausible.

Each of us is the unique product of a process known as development, which starts at the moment of conception and continues until we die. Development involves the assembly of the mind and personality as well as the physical body and brain. Your capacity for happiness is a product of your development and, as such, depends both on the genes you inherited from your parents and the experiences you have had since you were conceived.

Development is not a matter of *either* nature (genes) *or* nurture (environment). Rather, it is a continuous process in which our genes and our experiences interact with each other to shape our minds and bodies. Development can be thought of as somewhat like baking a cake, with genes and experiences as the ingredients. When you inspect the eventual cake, you cannot tell which ingredients gave rise to any one characteristic. The particular texture or flavour of the cake cannot be ascribed uniquely to, say, the eggs or the temperature at which it was baked. In development, as in baking, many different ingredients interact with each other. Whether one particular gene will dispose you to be more or less happy will depend on which other genes you have inherited and the environment in which those genes are being expressed.

The specific combination of genes you inherited from your parents will influence your happiness, but it does this in all sorts of indirect ways that also depend on your past experiences and environment. For example, one way in which genetic factors affect happiness is by influencing personality and temperament. A certain combination of genes might dispose someone to be more sociable, say. But that person's sociability would only make them happier if they were living in the right sort of environment, spoke the right language and possessed the necessary social skills. A highly sociable person stuck on a desert island would probably be lonely and depressed. To add to the complexity, an individual's behaviour will in turn affect their environment and hence the course of their future development. For instance, a smiley baby will elicit more positive responses from its parents, thereby changing its early social environment. Each of us is an active agent in our own development.

Another common error in the 'nature versus nurture' arena is the belief that any inherited or genetic character-istic must necessarily be fixed and unalterable. This is not true. Certain genes or combinations of genes may equip us with certain predispositions, but they do not rigidly determine how we behave, think or feel from moment to moment. It would be equally wrong to assume that all environmental influences are impermanent and malleable: in fact, some can exert long-lasting effects on feelings and behaviour which are hard to erase. Traumatic experiences such as physical abuse, sexual abuse or combat can leave deep emotional scars.

Long-term studies often find that an individual's general level of happiness tends to remain fairly stable when measured over intervals of a year or more. But the fact that a person's overall happiness might not change greatly over time does not mean it is fixed and unalterable, nor does it demonstrate that happiness is 'genetic'. Many of the environmental influences that affect happiness also remain stable over long periods. A person's social situ-ation, beliefs, attitudes, health, educational background and work environment might not vary much over the course of a year or more, so it should come as no surprise if their overall happiness does not change dramatically either.

Debates about the influence of genes on human develop-ment and happiness might seem faintly abstruse, but they have important practical implications. Perhaps the most important of these is that we can do a lot to change our happiness, for better or for worse. Inheriting a predis-position to be more or less happy in a particular set of

circumstances does not render us powerless to make ourselves or our children happier by modifying our behaviour,
attitudes and environment. Science emphatically does not
support the assertion, made by two American psychologists in the 1990s, that trying to be happier is as futile as
trying to be taller. At the very least, you can make the most
of the genes you inherited.

Health

You might assume that physical health would have a major
bearing on happiness. Surely someone could not be happy
if they were ill? In fact, the relationship between happiness
and physical health turns out to be less than clear cut.

Various studies have found that happiness relates more
strongly to people's mental health than it does to their
objective physical health – that is, their health as assessed
independently by a doctor. However, reasonably strong
associations are found between happiness and people's
perception of their own health: their so-called subjective
health. Objective health and subjective health are two distinct things. You could feel healthy yet have a serious disease such as early-stage cancer or coronary heart disease.
Conversely, you could feel unwell yet have no detectable
signs of any disease. Our subjective perception of our own
physical health has a stronger bearing on our happiness
than does our objective physical health. Moreover, as
we saw earlier, people with serious illnesses or disabilities
often regain near-normal levels of happiness once they
have had time to adjust to their condition.

Even the observed association between subjective physical health and happiness may be partly a by-product of
something else. An individual's perception of their own
health is influenced by their personality, past experience

and current emotional state. Someone who is highly anxious, for example, will tend to pay more attention to physical symptoms and feel more concerned about their health than someone whose mind is on other things. The heightened state of physiological arousal that accompanies anxiety makes us more sensitive to subtle physical symptoms. Moreover, it can create real physical symptoms of its own, including headaches, breathlessness, palpitations and digestive problems. An anxious mind may then interpret those symptoms as evidence of something more serious. As we saw in chapter 4, anxiety is a major contributor to unhappiness.

In line with this, research with twins has found that the links between happiness, subjective health and objective health are influenced to some extent by genetic factors, and that the same genes appear to affect both happiness and subjective health. It may be that certain combinations of genes predispose some individuals to be generally more anxious. Their greater anxiety makes them more likely to feel unwell, which makes them even more anxious and hence unhappy. In this way, their subjective health has a big influence on their happiness. Someone who is generally less anxious may notice fewer apparent symptoms and be less bothered by them.

Up to half of all patients who seek professional medical help are suffering from psychological and emotional problems, but they turn out to have no detectable physical disease despite experiencing pain, fatigue, breathlessness or other symptoms. Some of these patients keep returning to their doctor over and over again, distressed and dissatisfied. These are the 'worried well', whose problems prove difficult to diagnose or treat.

Long-term studies indicate that the influence of subjective health on happiness becomes even stronger in old age. Objective health obviously tends to deteriorate as we get older, and it may be that an ability to feel reasonably well despite physical decline is an important part of remaining happy.

Sleep and exercise

One of the quickest and easiest ways of making yourself thoroughly unhappy and unhealthy is to get inadequate sleep. Sleep deprivation remains a basic method of torture and coercion around the world, beloved of secret police forces and oppressive regimes.

When someone is very tired, their mood drops and they become emotionally fragile; they feel low, irritable, and less able to cope with sudden demands. Lack of sleep causes a marked deterioration in social and communication skills, making it harder to deal successfully with other people or maintain relationships. Even our vocabulary shrinks noticeably. Memory, judgment and decision-making all decline, with potentially severe consequences for performance in the classroom or at work. Tiredness also makes it much harder to experience flow, the optimal state that arises when we are fully immersed in a challenging task. In fact, it severely curtails our scope for living life to the full.

Sleep deprivation can impair physical health as well, producing measurable changes in hormone levels and immune functioning, and greatly increasing the risk of having an accident. Tired drivers are much more likely to crash their cars, and often do. The hallmark of a sleep-related vehicle accident is the lack of skid marks. Young people who sleep badly are found to be at greater risk of smoking, drinking excessively and taking illicit drugs. All in all, getting insufficient sleep is bad news. If you want to be happy and healthy then you must have a sufficient quantity and quality of sleep, and at the right times.

Unfortunately, inadequate sleep and chronic tiredness are alarmingly widespread. The incessant demands and temptations of the 24/7 society squeeze sleep at both ends of the day: we get up early in the morning to go to school or work, and we stay up late at night to be entertained. According to one prevailing attitude, sleep is merely unproductive downtime which would be better spent working or playing. Insomnia and other sleep problems are rife, adding to the toll of sleeplessness. In consequence, a substantial proportion of children, teenagers and adults in the UK, USA and other developed nations get less sleep than they require to function on peak form. A large majority of us try to counteract our daytime sleepiness by regularly dosing ourselves with caffeine, but even the world's most widely consumed psychoactive drug cannot replace sleep.

Daytime tiredness resulting from inadequate sleep is a common but widely neglected cause of low mood, academic underperformance and behaviour problems among young children and adolescents. The evidence suggests that inadequate sleep affects at least one in six young people, but some scientists maintain that more than a third are affected. Studies of children in their normal home environments show that poor-quality sleep is often associated with easily avoidable lifestyle choices such as going to bed at varying times, staying up late to watch TV and consuming large amounts of caffeinated soft drinks.

Childhood and adolescence are periods when social, emotional and intellectual capabilities develop most rapidly and are most malleable. But these are precisely the capabilities that are most acutely impaired by lack of sleep.

Numerous scientific studies have shown that children who get insufficient or low-quality sleep end up feeling tired during the day, are much less able to perform effectively in the classroom, and are more likely to display behaviour problems. In fact, the effects of sleep deprivation on mental abilities and physical coordination are strikingly similar in several respects to those of alcohol, which means that sleep-deprived children can end up behaving as though they have drunk a glass or three of wine. More worrying still is the emerging evidence that undiagnosed sleep problems may be contributing to some common childhood behavioural disorders, notably Attention Deficit/ Hyperactivity Disorder (ADHD).

Whether or not you get sufficient sleep, your mood and energy will naturally fluctuate during the course of the day, in line with your biological circadian rhythms. Your sense of well-being and vitality will therefore depend partly on the time of day. Most people feel somewhat livelier and happier in the morning than they do in the afternoon, although there are distinct differences between early-rising 'larks' and late-to-bed 'owls'. Mood can be affected by relatively small disturbances to circadian rhythms, so the time at which you wake up or go to bed can make a difference to how you feel during the day.

Physical activity is another important contributor to health and happiness. People who regularly take physical exercise are usually happier as well as physically healthier than those who spend their days sitting at a desk. (Oops.) Couch potatoes tend to be unhappy people.

Measurements have confirmed that even a brisk ten-minute walk can help to lift mood and dispel gloom for a few hours. More vigorous and regular exercise produces bigger and longer-lasting improvements in mood and vitality. For those who do it regularly, exercise can be a rich source of pleasure and satisfaction. There is good evidence that exercise reduces anxiety and helps to cope with stress. It even provides relief in some cases of mild depression. The psychological and emotional benefits of exercise are particularly apparent in older people, especially if the exercise is allied with social contact arising from involvement in organised sports or classes.

The immediate mood-enhancing effects of exercise help to explain the association between sport and happiness. Regular participation in sport contributes to happiness in other ways as well, notably by providing social contact, developing skills and improving self-esteem. Sport can make people feel better about themselves in various ways: for example, developing new physical skills brings a sense of control, while a leaner body boosts self-esteem. Research has uncovered firm connections between physical activity and self-esteem in children as well as adults.

Unfortunately, many children and teenagers live alarmingly sedentary lives. According to recent research, American children and adolescents spend an average of only 13 minutes a day in any form of vigorous activity, and remain completely inactive for more than 75 per cent of their waking hours. Much the same is true for British children: government research in the late 1990s found that only half of all 15-year-old girls in England were achieving the recommended minimum of at least two bouts of vigorous exercise a week. As with inadequate sleep, parents must shoulder some of the responsibility.

The sloths among us can perhaps take solace from evidence that you do not need a lot of exercise to feel happier. An American study of very happy people – those in the top 10 per cent of consistently very happy individuals – found that they did not exercise more than averagely happy people.

Education
Education has for decades been regarded more as a route to employment and material success than a source of happiness. The evidence shows that intelligence, as measured by IQ tests, has little bearing on happiness, and that academic attainment, as measured by conventional exams, has only a modest influence. But it would be quite wrong to conclude that education has little to do with happiness. In fact, education in the broad sense plays a major role in fostering happiness and health.

Research has revealed a consistent, if modest, association between educational level and happiness. People who have received more years of education tend to be somewhat happier than those who have been educated only to a lower level. So, for example, university graduates are happier on average than people who left school at the minimum age. This correlation between education and happiness is stronger in poor countries, but it still holds true in rich nations like the UK and Switzerland. A major long-term study in the UK found that those who had continued their education beyond the age of 16 were happier when assessed again as adults, and that individuals who had displayed negative attitudes towards schooling when young were less happy as adults.

It is not hard to see how education would promote long-term happiness and well-being. A good, rounded education should foster many of the basic ingredients of happiness which we saw in chapter 4, including social and emotional competence, communication skills, engagement in meaningful activity, a sense of control, resilience, self-esteem, outward focus, future-mindedness and wisdom.

Consider, for example, engagement in meaningful activity. Education helps individuals obtain satisfying work, with all the benefits that brings including personal relationships, money, self-esteem and a sense of purpose. The statistics confirm that better-educated people have better-paid and more satisfying jobs on average (albeit that some also have higher aspirations and expose themselves to more work-related stress). They are also found to have a stronger sense of purpose and meaning. Conversely, poorly educated people are at greater risk of being unemployed, which is a powerful cause of unhappiness and poor physical health. The children of poorly educated parents are also more likely to suffer from mental health problems such as depression, anxiety, behaviour problems and hyperactivity.

Education makes us more resilient by helping us to cope with adversity. Better-educated people have better problem-solving skills. The wisdom they acquire through education equips them to deal more effectively with the inevitable problems of everyday life. The emotional elements of happiness, especially the absence of displeasure, also benefit from education. Research shows that better-educated people tend to experience lower levels of unpleasant emotions like anxiety, anger and depression, and fewer physical symptoms such as aches and pains. The knowledge and problem-solving skills provided by education can liberate us from irrational worries that would otherwise leave us prey to anxiety.

Education can promote physical health as well. Better-educated people are generally more aware of the connections between lifestyle and health, and are therefore better placed to live healthier lives (even if some fail to do so in practice). Research confirms that, on average, better-educated people do have healthier lifestyles and enjoy better physical health, especially in middle and old age. Studies of elderly people have uncovered strong positive correlations between educational level, vitality and health. Overall, better-educated people live longer, although the evidence suggests that this is at least partly a result of their larger average incomes. (Rich people live longer.) If anything, the happiness and health benefits of education become even more evident in old age. A major American investigation of aging found that men who had received more education in their youth were typically happier and healthier in old age than those who had received less education. Another study of elderly Americans discovered that low levels of education were associated in old age with physical inactivity, obesity, smoking, a sense of lacking control, and unhappiness.

The benefits of education are not restricted to individuals: they extend to society as a whole, in the form of social capital. There is clear evidence of strong links between education and various aspects of social capital, including trust, neighbourliness, civic engagement and social support.

Education can be a two-edged sword, however. If it encourages someone to develop unrealistic ambitions, it may set them up for frustration and disappointment. Some highly educated people end up feeling dissatisfied with their lives, and therefore unhappier, because of unreasonable aspirations. However, a rounded education should help each individual to understand their own strengths and limitations. We will return to education later.

Religion

Religion, which the *Oxford Dictionary* defines as the belief in and worship of a superhuman controlling power, undeniably contributes to the happiness of many millions of people around the world. Research, mostly conducted in the USA, has found that religious people tend to be somewhat happier than non-religious people, other things being equal. They also have a lower suicide rate and live longer: Americans who go to church at least once a week live about four years longer on average than those who never go. However, the USA is a much more religious nation than the UK and most other European countries.

According to a major international poll conducted for the BBC in 2004, the highest levels of religious belief are generally found in the poorest countries, with Nigeria, India and Indonesia coming top.[2] But the USA is an anomaly – despite being the world's richest nation, it is also one of the most religious. In the USA, 91 per cent of people say they believe in God or a higher power, compared with 67 per cent in the UK. More disconcertingly, 71 per cent of Americans (the same proportion as in Lebanon) say they are willing to die for their God or their religious beliefs, compared with only 19 per cent of Britons. The BBC poll found the UK to be one of the least religious nations in the world. A quarter of Britons never pray, compared with only 9 per cent of Americans, while 29 per cent of Britons think the world would be a more peaceful place if people didn't believe in God or a higher power – a view shared by only 6 per cent of Americans.

A separate poll conducted in the USA in 2004 found that more than 60 per cent of Americans believe in the literal, word-for-word truth of the Genesis account of the world being created in six days, the Old Testament story of Noah's Ark and the story of Moses parting the Red Sea. Another major survey in 2003 found that 82 per cent of Americans believe in miracles and 78 per cent believe in angels. Even in the USA, however, religion is not a prerequisite for happiness. A study of very happy Americans (those in the top 10 per cent for happiness) found that they did not participate in any more religious activity than Americans who were only averagely happy or unhappy.

What is it about religion that can make people happier and longer-lived? When thinking about this issue it is useful to distinguish between religious *activity*, such as going to church, and religious *belief*. The evidence suggests that both can contribute to happiness, but in different ways.

One of the reasons why religious people are happier is because they tend to be more connected. Active membership of a church is accompanied by social interactions and supportive personal relationships. This might help to explain why the psychological and emotional benefits of religious activity are found to be greatest among individuals who might otherwise be socially isolated, including single, retired, elderly and sick people. In other sections of the population, such as college students, religious activity is less strongly linked to happiness. However, simply going to church may do little to boost happiness unless it is accompanied by religious belief. Researchers have found that people who attend church for non-religious reasons, such as wanting to make friends or gain other benefits, tend to have poorer mental health than those who go primarily because of their faith.

Religion can be a powerful buffer against stress arising from social or economic deprivation. The social support from fellow churchgoers, together with religious faith itself, can alleviate the psychological and emotional impact of adverse events. In line with this, researchers have found that religious activity worldwide is most prevalent among high-risk groups including the poor, the elderly, the ill, the uneducated, the unmarried, ethnic minorities and those threatened by political oppression or famine.

Religion boosts happiness in other ways as well, such as giving individuals a strong sense of purpose and meaning in life. It also encourages people to think beyond their own selfish interests; as we saw in chapter 4, having an outward focus is one of the key ingredients of happiness, whereas the inward-looking mindset of the consumerist 'me' culture is a recipe for unhappiness. Another possible reason why humanity has always been drawn to religion in one form or another is that it provides the comfort of certainty about the world. This might account for the growing popularity in the USA and other parts of the world of the more fundamentalist religions and churches.

Physical health can also benefit. Most religions discourage certain forms of behaviour that may damage health, such as taking psychoactive drugs, and religious people generally tend to have healthier lifestyles. Their close personal relationships may also be more stable. Religious couples are statistically less likely to divorce, unless they are of mixed faith. However, there is no evidence that going to church by itself makes marriages happier, and couples who stay together primarily for religious reasons are found to experience more, not less, marital strife.

Religion, then, can be a rich source of comfort, support and happiness. But it can also have its downsides. For instance, researchers at the Royal Free and University College Medical School in London uncovered evidence that religious belief is statistically associated with poorer clinical outcomes among hospital patients. A study of patients admitted to a London hospital found that individuals who had strong religious beliefs were more than twice as likely to have deteriorated or failed to improve when clinically assessed nine months later. Indeed, strong religious belief was a stronger predictor of poor clinical outcome than the patient's actual medical condition as assessed by doctors at the time of admission.

Furthermore, while most studies have found positive links between religiosity and mental health, some have uncovered negative effects. For example, an investigation involving several thousand people found that religiosity was correlated with displeasure: highly religious individuals were less likely to judge their current mood as pleasant. Similarly, a review of 80 published studies found that although religion was generally associated with a reduced risk of depression, individuals with some types of religious affiliation actually had an elevated risk of depression.

Overall, the evidence suggests that at least some of the happiness-promoting aspects of religion, including personal relationships and outward focus, could be attained in other ways that do not require religious faith. However, one of the reasons why religion has been such a central feature of human life for so long is presumably because it does provide a firm structure for encouraging people to behave and think in ways that make them feel happier.

Looking good

Are beautiful people happier? In a just world the answer would be no. Regrettably, the facts are otherwise: there is abundant evidence that physically attractive individuals tend to have happier and more successful lives than those of us who are less alluring. The reasons are not hard to fathom. Attractive people usually feel good about themselves, and their higher self-esteem in turn boosts their happiness. However, the consequences of attractiveness extend far beyond mere self-esteem.

Psychological experiments have revealed that we all have a tendency to attribute more positive characteristics to physically attractive people. Attractive children are far more likely to be judged as above average in their general competence, academic ability, social skills, social appeal and emotional adjustment, compared to unattractive children. Similarly, attractive adults are consistently judged to be more competent at their jobs. Even the state of your teeth affects how others assess you. One study found that men with good teeth were judged, on the basis of their photo alone, to be more socially competent, better psychologically adjusted and more intellectually capable than men with visible evidence of dental problems. So make sure you floss.

This shameful bias towards good-looking people holds true for males and females, children and adults. For similar reasons, we are all inclined to believe that unattractive individuals have more negative characteristics – an aspect of human nature that has not escaped Hollywood casting directors. You will have noticed that gorgeous screen villains and ugly screen heroes are in a minority. TV and films have a strong bias towards keeping ugly people off our screens. And in many cultures, ugly is currently equated with fat. A recent analysis of more than a thousand TV characters from prime-time fictional programmes on American TV found that the proportion who were overweight or obese was less than half that of the real population of the USA.[3] Moreover, the relatively few tubby characters who were permitted to appear on American TV were consistently less likely to be portrayed in romantic situations.

Our tendency to judge physically attractive people more favourably applies even when the individuals in question are known to us in person. Studies have shown that attractive children and adults are appraised more positively than unattractive children and adults, even when those making the appraisal know them personally and therefore have other information on which to base their assessment.

It gets worse. As well as judging attractive people more positively, we also follow through on our judgment by actually behaving more positively towards them, whether or not we know them. Researchers have found that physically attractive children receive more care and attention, more positive social interactions and fewer negative interactions than unattractive children.

Humanity's bias in favour of beautiful people seems to affect them in turn, because attractive individuals actually display more positive behavioural traits. In addition to receiving more positive responses from other people, attractive children tend to respond in kind by behaving in a more positive and attractive way. This virtuous circle stacks the cards even more in favour of good-lookers.

The upshot of all this is that attractive people reap substantial benefits from their pleasing appearance. Various studies have found that attractive children are on average more popular, more competent and psychologically better adjusted than unattractive children. Similarly, attractive adults are generally more popular and more successful in their jobs than unattractive adults; they also have more sex, better physical health, better social skills and somewhat higher self-esteem, on average. (There are, of course, plenty of exceptions, and you have probably met a few.)

By the same token, children and adults who are physically unattractive may be at some disadvantage. There is clear evidence, for example, that children who are overweight or obese are at significantly greater risk of depression. Girls are especially vulnerable. Similarly, children who are unusually short in stature are more likely to experience anxiety, low self-esteem, depression and social problems. Their intellectual and social development may also suffer. One reason, according to research, is that the parents of unusually short children tend to regard them as more vulnerable, and therefore insulate them from everyday experience that would contribute to their development.

Just to complete this depressing picture, scientists have established experimentally that we all tend to agree about who is physically attractive. When large samples of people are shown photos of strangers' faces and asked to rate their attractiveness, they display a remarkably high level of agreement, including when rating faces of individuals from other ethnic groups. There seems to be something universal about physical beauty which transcends national and cultural boundaries. Experiments have even shown that babies will spend longer gazing at faces that are judged by adults to be attractive. One of the key features that guides our assessment of facial attractiveness is symmetry: given the choice, we generally prefer highly symmetrical faces to lopsided ones.

All in all, the evidence shows that being physically attractive gives an individual various advantages that contribute to their happiness. Other people will tend to appraise them more favourably, respond more positively towards them, and receive more positive responses from them. The sixteenth-century writer Michel de Montaigne was on the right track (if slightly overstating the case) when he wrote: 'I cannot say often enough how much I consider beauty a powerful and advantageous quality. We have no quality that surpasses it in credit. It holds the first place in human relations; it presents itself before the rest, seduces and prepossesses our judgment with great authority and a wondrous impression.'

Before you despair about the unfairness of a world in which beautiful people receive the added bonus of happiness, bear this in mind. Narcissism is bad for you. Research has shown that individuals who place an unusually high value on their own appearance, and who have a strong desire to be regarded as attractive, tend to have poorer mental and physical health than those whose desires are less nakedly cosmetic. Similarly, researchers have found that people whose life goals centre round their own physical appearance tend to feel less energetic, are more prone to depression and experience more physical symptoms of illness.

A final comforting thought (especially for people who look like me) is that there is more to attractiveness than physical appearance alone. Better still, as we saw in chapter 3, being happy makes us more attractive. As Charles Dickens put it, 'cheerfulness and contentment are great beautifiers'. So, even if we fall far short of the unfeasible standards set by the media, we can at least improve on what nature gave us by being happier.

SEVEN

Snares and delusions

Pleasure in the flesh admits no increase when once the pain of want has been removed; after that it only admits of variation.

EPICURUS (341–270 BC)

Most of us spend our lives trying to acquire, do, or hang onto, things we think will make us or our children happy. The snag is that some supposed sources of happiness actually make little difference, and one or two can even have the reverse effect. A prime example is the popular belief that acquiring material wealth is a reliable way of acquiring happiness. In this chapter we will look at some of the more common blind alleys down which people disappear while pursuing happiness.

Mindless pleasure
Self-help guides often recommend that we boost our mood by indulging in occasional treats like shopping, eating chocolate, having a massage or taking a weekend break. The simple proposition is that pleasure will make us happy.

The same thought lies behind so much advertising; buy this product, whispers the voice, and you will be happy. Sprinkling our lives with small pleasures clearly can give a lift, and research has confirmed that people who deliberately build more pleasurable activities into their daily lives do indeed feel better as a result. There is nothing inherently wrong with pleasure. The problem is that the quick fix of pleasure alone is not a reliable route to lasting happiness. We have our brains to thank for this inconvenient fact.

The human brain is built to be most sensitive to new information; it responds more to change than to constancy. We adapt, or habituate, to new circumstances, with important consequences for happiness. Habituation means that pleasurable experiences usually produce only a temporary lift. Eating chocolate can be delightful, but not if you have already wolfed down several slabs of the stuff. A sunny day can be cheering if you are used to the British climate, but blue skies create less jollity in California. Sinking into a hot bath can feel terrific when you are cold and tired, but the animal pleasure soon fades once you have warmed up. And so on.

Habituation makes good biological sense. Pleasure, anxiety, fear and other emotions have evolved because they guide us (and other animals) to respond appropriately in different situations. Feeling fearful if you see a dangerous predator is obviously beneficial because it impels you to run away or defend yourself. Pleasure guides us to do things that satisfy some need or desire. Once that desire has been satisfied, however, the pleasure evaporates. Even the plainest food will taste delicious if you are starving, whereas the most exquisite titbits may be nauseating if you are already stuffed full. Pleasure must die away so that we can move on to the next activity. If it did not, we could become locked into whatever pleasurable activity we were currently engaged in. Our hunter-gatherer ancestors would not have survived long if they had sat back in a permanent glow of contentment every time they did something pleasurable.

Pleasure, then, is by its very nature transient and self-limiting: it will start to wane after a while. Thus, only relatively recent experiences tend to have a major impact on happiness. The evidence shows that the effects on happiness of most experiences, both good and bad, have generally faded away within a few months. Even spectacularly pleasurable events, like suddenly acquiring a large sum of money, may not produce lasting changes in happiness. Researchers have found, for example, that most lottery winners do not become permanently much happier than the rest of us; a few months after receiving their windfall most of them are only averagely happy.

Thanks to habituation, anyone who tried to derive their happiness solely from pleasure (as distinct from satisfaction) must continually expose themselves to new or stronger pleasures in order to maintain a constant level of happiness. The same old pleasures simply fail to work after a while, and the only recourse is to increase the dose or switch to a new one. Psychologists refer to this phenomenon as the 'hedonic treadmill'. Someone who becomes trapped on the hedonic treadmill is drawn into a continuous process of escalating, but ultimately self-defeating, pleasure-seeking. Most of the world's successful religions and philosophies have long been familiar with this basic aspect of human nature.[1]

Anyone who nonetheless does attempt to derive their happiness mostly from pleasure is recommended to adopt a strategy of little but often. Research indicates that happiness is shaped more by the frequency of pleasurable experiences than by the intensity of those experiences. As Benjamin Franklin rightly said, 'Happiness is produced not so much by great pieces of good fortune that seldom happen as by little advantages that occur every day.'

Intensely pleasurable experiences have a surprisingly muted effect on happiness. This is partly because they can make everyday life seem bland by comparison; mundane pleasures have less impact if they are overshadowed by an outstandingly wonderful experience. One of the reasons why lottery winners usually revert to being only averagely happy is that the initial joy of winning makes the ordinary business of life seem less pleasurable by contrast. An American study of major lottery winners found that their new wealth actually reduced their ability to derive pleasure from everyday activities they had previously enjoyed. All in all, it seems that the commonplace pleasures of daily life contribute more to happiness than intense but unusual delights.

Attempting to build happiness from pleasure alone is problematic for another reason as well: intense pleasure is often accompanied by intense displeasure. In practice, good and bad experiences often go hand in hand, because the more active and engaged we are with life, the more experiences we have – both pleasant and unpleasant. Consider, for example, the low-life characters in Irvine Welsh's novel *Trainspotting*. They live for intense, chemically induced pleasure – if not heroin then massive doses of alcohol, with emotionless sex and random violence as chasers. Along the way they try, often unsuccessfully, to dodge the accompanying displeasures inherent in their lifestyle, which include HIV, unemployment, physical injury, poverty and imprisonment. The pursuit of extreme pleasure can be a distinctly two-edged sword. Epicurus put it like this: 'No pleasure is in itself evil, but the things which produce certain pleasures entail annoyances many times greater than the pleasures themselves.'

To make matters worse, our minds do not react equally to pleasant and unpleasant experiences. Research has revealed that unpleasant experiences have a proportionally greater psychological impact, and for good reason: they are potentially threatening to our well-being. There are relatively few things in life that can make you feel much better, but many that can make you feel worse.

Our generally greater sensitivity towards negative events helps to explain why the behaviour of real people often fails to match the rational predictions of market economics. The fear of losing a sum of money has a bigger influence on our behaviour than does the prospect of gaining the same amount. Classical economic theory predicts that loss and gain are symmetrical and equally balanced. In reality, however, our psychological responses to loss are stronger than our responses to gain. We are naturally averse to losing.[2] This greater sensitivity to negative stimuli also holds true when it comes to judging other people. Researchers have found that critical or negative information about other people has more influence on our judgment than positive information.

The general lesson, then, is that we adjust to changes in our circumstances, and therefore pleasurable events provide only a transient boost to overall happiness. However, there are some important exceptions to this principle. Events that involve close personal relationships – notably marriage, separation and divorce – can give rise to long-lasting changes in happiness, as we saw in chapter 5. Losing your job can also have enduring effects. Long-term research has shown that although individuals adjust to some extent after becoming unemployed, many fail to regain their former level of happiness even after finding a new job.

An easy life
Something else that will not guarantee eternal bliss is living an undemanding life devoid of stress. Downshifting, though much in vogue, is no sure-fire recipe for happiness. Neither is early retirement if it involves exchanging stimulating work for empty inactivity. As Tom Lehrer put it, life is like a sewer: what you get out of it depends on what you put into it. A happy life is typically a rich and eventful life which involves extensive engagement with activities and other people. Being a parent, for example, can be challenging and at times stressful, but most parents regard parenthood as ultimately satisfying and fulfilling.

Nonetheless, we do all need to relax from time to time, and the most common leisure 'activity' in the UK and other wealthy nations is watching TV. But despite its popularity, watching TV is actually correlated with *un*happiness. Researchers have found that the more time people spend in front of the box, the less happy they are likely to be.

One possible explanation for this negative correlation between happiness and TV viewing is that people who watch a lot of TV have less satisfactory personal relationships. (Interestingly, those who regularly watch TV soaps are found to be slightly happier than those who watch other types of programmes. They might conceivably derive some happiness from vicarious 'relationships' with the fictional characters. Or perhaps they realise that their own life seems rather good in comparison to the torrid, trauma-packed lives of most soap characters.) An essentially passive pastime like watching TV can deliver a certain amount of easy pleasure, but it has little potential to provide satisfaction or flow in the way that more engaging activities can.

Now, I admit that TV is a soft target. It is easy to preach that we would all be happier if only we spent more time playing sports or reading mind-expanding books instead of vegetating in front of the box. But the reality is that most of us do not. Why? One reason may be that engaging in almost any activity that generates satisfaction or flow requires some initial effort. To play most sports, for example, you must get changed, run around and probably experience physical discomfort before the benefits start to accrue. Flopping in front of the TV has no initial hurdle and the payback is immediate. Paradoxically, the inhabitants of wealthy nations may also be spoilt by choice. The sheer range of options for passing free time can be stifling – especially for children or adolescents, who may consequently stick on their default setting, which often means watching TV. Furthermore, parents do not always present good role models. After a long day at work, tired parents may not feel like immersing themselves in challenging, flow-producing activities, but prefer instead to languish in front of the TV (and in front of their children).

Unlike TV, holidays really do have the potential to engender happiness. The evidence suggests that they do this as much by reducing displeasure as by providing pleasure or satisfaction. A successful holiday can relieve anxiety – or, at least, temporarily exchange one set of anxieties for another. When we are on holiday we are licensed to stop fretting for a week or two about all the usual problems in our lives. That said, holidays can equally be a rich source of relationship-killing strife and disaster.

Another significant and widely overlooked benefit of taking a holiday is simply getting more sleep. As we saw in the previous chapter, large numbers of people, including many children and adolescents, simply do not get sleep of sufficient quantity and quality during their frenetic lives, and rely on weekends and holidays to catch up. Getting rid of accumulated fatigue by sleeping longer and better should make anyone feel happier and more alive. So don't feel guilty about lie-ins and siestas, especially when you are on holiday. That is what holidays should be for.

Youth and sex

According to popular wisdom, gilded youth is the happiest time of our lives, whereas old age brings inevitable decline and wrinkly woe. In line with this belief, surveys have found that most young people expect to become happier over the next few years, whereas older adults typically expect their happiness to decline as they become elderly.

But, like so much of what passes for common sense, this turns out to be untrue. In reality, young people are not generally happier than the elderly. Old age may spell a decline in physical health and often wealth, but the empirical evidence shows that it does not spell a systematic decline in happiness.

Numerous studies have found that measures of happiness and satisfaction show little, if any, consistent change across the lifespan. The proportion of people who feel reasonably happy or satisfied with their life is roughly the same among teenagers as it is among elderly people. Moreover, this appears to be true regardless of where people live. For instance, researchers have found that very elderly people living in rural Africa are just as likely to be happy as young people, despite old age and hardship.

If anything, we tend to become slightly happier with advancing years. Older people often feel more satisfied with their life, perhaps because their aspirations become more realistic as a result of experience. Research has also found that elderly people do slightly better in terms of pleasure. Many older people have learned, partly through trial and error, how to behave in ways that maximise their pleasure and satisfaction while minimising displeasure. They may also care less what other people think of them, which is generally a good idea.

The ingredients that contribute most to happiness in old age are not always the same ones that build happiness in childhood or early adulthood. In particular, wisdom becomes a more significant factor in old age. (As we saw in chapter 4, wisdom means pragmatic knowledge about life, together with effective tactics for solving problems.) The wisdom that comes from experience can help us to avoid pitfalls and extract more pleasure from life. Emotional stability is another important ingredient of happiness in old age; older people tend to experience less intense emotions, with shallower troughs of displeasure and smaller peaks of pleasure. That said, elderly people do derive much of their happiness from the same things as anyone else, and especially from personal relationships.

Let us now turn briefly to gender – another basic personal characteristic that has only a minor bearing on happiness. Broadly speaking, men and women do not differ much when it comes to happiness (although women are at greater risk from depression). The evidence indicates that young women tend to be slightly happier than young men, whereas older women tend to be unhappier than older men. But these differences are relatively modest. By and large, knowing simply whether someone is male or female will tell you very little about how happy they are likely to be.

There are, however, some subtle statistical differences between the sexes when it comes to happiness. Women report experiencing more intense emotions than men, both positive and negative, and a slightly higher frequency of unpleasant emotions like sadness, anxiety, fear and guilt. For instance, women are slightly more likely than men to report that they have been experiencing unpleasant emotional strain within the previous 24 hours. They are also more likely than men to say they wish for happiness in their life, as opposed to other goals such as money or success. But again, these differences are relatively slight. Overall, there is no clear evidence that women are generally more or less happy than men. Other factors, such as personal relationships, employment and educational background, make far more difference.

Intelligence

Now here is some bad news for members of Mensa, the club for people who achieve very high scores on IQ tests. There is no systematic connection between IQ and happiness. Numerous scientific studies have failed to find any correlation between intelligence, as measured by IQ tests, and happiness. People with high IQs are no happier, on average, than the rest of us. You do not require a great intellect to be happy. Indeed, you do not even require an average level of mental functioning: plenty of people with varying degrees of mental disability are happy. Equally, the evidence contradicts Ernest Hemingway's observation that 'Happiness in intelligent people is the rarest thing I know.'

The absence of any clear link between IQ and happiness

should not come as a great surprise, since some would argue that IQ scores do not reveal a great deal else of profound interest either. People with high IQs do tend to perform better in their jobs, other things being equal. However, they do not invariably achieve greatness, because other attributes including motivation, social and emotional competence, communication skills, resilience and wisdom make a big difference in the real world. One eminent psychologist commented that the biggest achievement in the lives of many Mensa members was having joined Mensa.

Intelligence in the narrow IQ sense makes little difference to happiness, but education is an entirely different matter. As we saw in the previous chapter, the more education you or your children have received, the happier you are likely to be.

Empty self-esteem

Self-esteem, otherwise known as valuing yourself, is one of the more common characteristics of happy people, as we saw in chapter 4.[3] Children and adults with high self-esteem are generally happier, healthier and more successful than those with low self-esteem, other things being equal. However, the concept of self-esteem is frequently stretched beyond its sensible limits, resulting in some widespread misconceptions among parents and educators.

Low self-esteem has come to be regarded as a source of many of society's ills, including educational failure, drug abuse and criminality. One influential media pundit even described low self-esteem as the root of all evil in the world. In similar vein, various experts recommend raising self-esteem as a fast track to happiness and achievement.

A whole industry has grown in response to this faith in the power of self-esteem, with the USA as its homeland.

The self-esteem industry strikes a chord in our consumerist 'me' culture, with its emphasis on individualism, self-improvement and feeling good. Thousands of books, websites and organisations have been created in order to explain, discuss and boost self-esteem. You can get some sense of the sheer scale of this business by searching the web for 'self-esteem'. When I tried this, Google returned more than two million hits, starting with the National Association for Self-Esteem, while the American Amazon website listed 42,082 books on the subject, starting with *The Self-Esteem Workbook*. (British Amazon listed a mere 3,719 titles.)

Swept along by this tide of enthusiasm, some parents and teachers have come to believe that raising children's self-esteem is a sort of panacea – a 'social vaccine' that will boost their academic performance and protect them from depression, drug abuse, antisocial behaviour and a host of other undesirable outcomes. In pursuit of this seductive vision, some adults have taken to showering children with praise, almost regardless of their actual achievement or behaviour.

The reality, however, turns out to be much less clear cut than the rhetoric implies. Low self-esteem is not the root of all evil, and raising self-esteem is not an easy way to make everything well. The evidence from research suggests that low self-esteem in children is more often a *consequence*, not a *cause*, of problems like educational underachievement, drug abuse or depression.

The evidence also casts doubt on the belief that raising self-esteem is a simple and effective way of boosting children's academic performance. Although some studies have found that high self-esteem is associated with better performance, others have found that the linkage works the other way round – in other words, that good performance is more a cause of high self-esteem than a consequence. If children acquire self-esteem as a consequence of doing well in school, it does not necessarily follow that raising their self-esteem will improve their academic achievement. (To muddy the waters even more, a number of published studies have failed to find any clear association between self-esteem and performance.)

To unravel this conundrum, we need to distinguish between two different types of self-esteem – namely, global self-esteem, which is how you judge yourself in general, and specific self-esteem, which is how you judge a specific aspect of yourself, such as your performance in the classroom or at work, your physical appearance, your sporting ability or your intelligence. You can feel good about certain aspects of yourself but not others. For instance, a child might have high specific self-esteem about their sporting ability but low specific self-esteem about their academic achievement.

Research indicates that global self-esteem has a stronger influence on children's overall happiness, whereas academic self-esteem (that is, how they feel specifically about their performance in school) has a stronger influence on how they behave in the classroom. This implies that raising children's global self-esteem should help to make them happier, but it may not do much to improve their exam grades or their classroom behaviour.

Academic self-esteem can contribute to global self-esteem, and hence to overall happiness. However, the extent to which academic self-esteem will boost a particular child's happiness depends on how much importance that child attaches to academic achievement, as opposed to other aspects of their life. If an individual places little value on academic achievement, their success or failure in school will have less impact on their global self-esteem or happiness. Furthermore, the importance an individual attaches to academic self-esteem varies according to their experience of success or failure in that arena. We all tend unconsciously to assign a higher priority to those areas of our life in which we experience success, and lower priority to those in which we do less well. The upshot is that academic achievement will make less difference to a child's global self-esteem (and hence happiness) if that child has previously done badly at school.

In sum, there is little solid evidence that boosting children's self-esteem is an easy or particularly effective way of improving their performance or behaviour in school. The most that can be said is that self-esteem and academic performance tend to be mutually reinforcing, although the influence may not be very strong. In practical terms, this means that simply showering children with praise, regardless of what they have actually done, is unlikely to transform them into immaculately behaved high achievers.

The image of self-esteem as a universal panacea has been further undermined by research suggesting that too much of it can be a bad thing. A major British report concluded that low self-esteem is not the root cause of antisocial behaviour in children: on the contrary, the individuals who are most likely to become bullies, criminals or racists are those with *high* levels of confidence and self-esteem. Children with excessively high self-esteem are inclined to respond aggressively when someone challenges their inflated view of themselves. As Samuel Johnson observed more than two hundred years ago, 'He that overvalues himself will undervalue others, and he that undervalues others will oppress them.' Very low self-esteem can indeed be harmful, but only to the individual concerned, whereas excessively high self-esteem can harm others as well. The report's author, Professor Nicholas Emler, concluded that 'The widespread belief in raising self-esteem as an all-purpose cure for social problems has created a huge market for self-help manuals and educational programmes that is threatening to become the psychotherapeutic equivalent of snake oil.'

Healthy self-esteem – the sort that does contribute to happiness – is based on a realistic assessment of one's own worth. Healthy self-esteem means being content with who you really are, warts and all. However, some individuals form an inflated view of their own worth and become overly concerned with preserving their sense of being deeply wonderful. Empty self-esteem can turn into self-delusion, vanity or narcissism. A fictional example of relatively benign excessive self-esteem is provided by Mr Toad in *The Wind in the Willows*. Although in many respects Toad is an excellent and happy fellow – sociable, loved by his close friends, good-natured and brimming with enthusiasm – his overblown self-esteem is one of his less endearing qualities. At times he becomes so puffed-up with conceit that he sings a song to himself about how clever, handsome and popular he is.

Vanity is often a psychological defence mechanism for individuals who lack confidence in their own worth. To protect their fragile self-esteem they unconsciously pump themselves up by continually reminding themselves (and everyone else) how terrific they are. Such self-deception may make them feel better for a while, but it is easily punctured and does little to bolster real happiness.

Some individuals become unhealthily dependent for their self-esteem on what others think of them. Their sense of their own worth relies on receiving approval or praise from others, rather than feeling genuinely good about themselves. As a consequence they may become excessively concerned to create a favourable impression or avoid offending anyone. A strong need for social approval is generally bad for psychological health and happiness, not least because that approval can easily evaporate. The ancient Taoist scripture the *Tao Te Ching* issued this warning against such folly: 'Chase after money and security and your heart will never unclench. Care about people's approval and you will be their prisoner.'

To be a truly happy person, a child must develop the inner resources to cope with the inevitable disappointments, failures and frustrations of life. A steady diet of indiscriminate praise from parents and teachers will do little to develop those inner resources. The overpraised child comes to interpret anything short of glowing praise as criticism, and anything less than instant success as failure. Ironically, the end result may be a child with low self-esteem. Parents who shower their children with praise in pursuit of high self-esteem can end up devaluing the currency. Worse, they may be inadvertently encouraging their children to regard effusive praise as the minimum price to do anything. The sociologist Frank Furedi has argued that indiscriminate praise turns children into self-centred and unmotivated brats who are unable to handle disappointment or respect other people's feelings.

In conclusion, self-esteem is a complex concept that should be regarded with a degree of caution. Too much self-esteem of the wrong sort can do more harm than good. For self-esteem to be healthy, it must be tempered by reality. The practical implication for parents is that they should be reasonably honest with their children – loving them unconditionally, and praising their achievements, but not trying to convince them that everything they do and say is perfect.

Mindless optimism

A similar note of caution applies to optimism which, like self-esteem, has come to be widely regarded as a cure for many ills. Positive thinking and optimism are highly valued in the individualistic cultures of the USA and UK. There is little doubt that healthy optimism, like healthy self-esteem, can be highly beneficial: as we saw in chapter 4, optimistic people tend to be happier, healthier and longer-lived than pessimists, other things being equal. But, just as with self-esteem, optimism can be toxic if it is built on self-delusion or taken to excess.

The simplistic assumption that optimism is always good and pessimism is always bad does not stand up to scrutiny. For instance, one major long-term study found that individuals who were cheerful optimists as children died significantly *younger* on average than their gloomier classmates, possibly because they were more willing to expose themselves to risks (although it must be said that many other studies have found positive associations between optimism and lifespan). Research has also uncovered some intriguing associations between an optimistic, individualistic outlook on life and the rising tide of suicide among young men in many wealthy nations. An analysis of data from a large sample of wealthy nations found that the suicide rate among young males was strongly correlated with measures of individualism and optimism.

Optimism can be a mixed blessing even in the business environment, where it has traditionally been viewed with undiluted approval. An analysis in the *Harvard Business*

Review by two distinguished academics concluded that biased thinking and organisational pressures often lead managers to become excessively optimistic about big projects. This may partly account for the embarrassing fact that most major business initiatives never pay off.

Pessimism is not a uniformly bad characteristic either. The American psychologist Julie Norem has compiled a compelling body of evidence that what she calls 'defensive pessimism' is an effective strategy for some individuals, particularly those who naturally tend to be anxious. Pessimism forces them to confront their anxieties and take pre-emptive action to prevent their fears from coming true. By responding in this way, defensive pessimists take control of their lives and keep their anxieties in check. Optimism can work well for individuals who are generally less anxious, but for those of us who tend to fret, a healthy dose of defensive pessimism may be positively beneficial.[4] There is no universal, one-size-fits-all solution to making happy people.

Intemperate optimism has its sceptics in the world of fiction as well. Voltaire's eighteenth-century fable *Candide*, for example, chronicles the exotic adventures of a naïve young man in a dangerous world. Candide is under the sway of his absurdly optimistic tutor, the philosopher Doctor Pangloss, who repeatedly assures Candide that 'all is for the best in this best of all possible worlds'. Candide's stolidly upbeat view of the world helps him cope with numerous problems, but it also leads him and Doctor Pangloss into many avoidable disasters.

Candide eventually begins to doubt the wisdom of his tutor's optimism. He asks Pangloss: 'When you were hanged, dissected, severely beaten, and tugging at the oar in the galley, did you always think that things in this world were for the best?' Pangloss remains resolute that things are indeed all for the best, and dies horribly as a consequence. After yet more mayhem, the truth finally dawns on Candide that optimism can be taken too far. Having endured a prodigious number of whippings, kicks on the backside and beatings with a bull's pizzle on the soles of his feet; having been in an earthquake, having seen Doctor Pangloss hanged and burned alive, and having been 'ignominiously used by a vile Persian, plundered by order of the divan and drubbed by a company of philosophers', a wiser and less optimistic Candide concludes that although he once believed all was for the best, he is now 'entirely undeceived'.

The eponymous heroine of Eleanor Porter's *Pollyanna* is, if anything, even more relentlessly upbeat than Doctor Pangloss. However, whereas Voltaire was writing for satirical effect, Eleanor Porter seems to have intended her sickly-sweet creation to be taken seriously.

Eleven-year-old orphan Pollyanna rights the wrongs of the world, and eases the sorrows that beset her and everyone around her. She does this by playing her Special Game, which consists of finding something to be glad about in everything, no matter how bad it may appear (or be). Pollyanna's secret is 'an overwhelming, unquenchable gladness for everything that has happened or is going to happen'. When Pollyanna is run over by a car and paralysed from the waist down, an eminent doctor tells her she will never walk again. Needless to say, Pollyanna applies her awesome powers of optimism to defy medical science, and is soon on her feet again, spraying joy and indiscriminate gladness in all directions.

The practical lesson for parents is to encourage children to look on the bright side, but also to remain realistic.

There is little point in trying to persuade children that everything in life will always be wonderful, because it won't. We all experience disappointments and setbacks, and harbouring unrealistically optimistic expectations just makes them harder to cope with.

Drugs

Unhappy or anxious people often seek chemical assistance to make themselves happier or less anxious. Alcohol, cannabis, cocaine and other mood-altering drugs rapidly produce pleasure or reduce displeasure by tapping directly into ancient brain mechanisms that evolved to control our emotions and behaviour. That is why around 3.5 million people a year consume illicit drugs in the UK, more than half of whom use heroin, cocaine or crack cocaine. Most of the rest of the population uses alcohol. Even caffeine, which is by far the most widely consumed mood-altering drug on the planet, produces a measurable lift in mood, fending off the daytime tiredness that affects so many of us in our chronically sleep-deprived society.

Drugs do not bring fully rounded happiness, however, because they cannot create satisfaction. A mood-enhancing or anxiety-reducing drug might make someone feel better for a few hours, but it will not make them feel more satisfied with their life – usually the reverse. Bertrand Russell described drunkenness as a state in which unhappiness could be briefly halted through a process of 'temporary suicide'. Taking drugs, like watching TV, is at best a temporary fix. Drugs do not provide a lasting solution because a crucial part of happiness is being satisfied with your life, and knowing you were responsible for achieving that satisfaction.

That said, there is clearly more to alcohol than just the

chemistry of mood. In places like the UK, alcohol is an essentially social drug, and much of the pleasure (if not happiness) derived from drinking it stems from these social aspects. When we drink in the company of friends we experience far more than just the pharmacological effects of C_2H_5OH. As Samuel Johnson put it, 'There is nothing which has yet been contrived by man, by which so much happiness is produced as by a good tavern or inn.'

Alcohol, the grandmother of all mood-enhancing drugs, has been a prominent part of human existence for several thousand years. Opinions differ as to when humans first discovered the joys of booze (which, incidentally, is said to be one of the oldest words in the English language). Wine production was well established in the Middle East by 4000 BC, and there is some evidence that wine was being drunk in Transcaucasia eight thousand years ago, before even the wheel was invented. More recently, scientific experiments have confirmed what billions of people have happily discovered for themselves: that moderate doses of alcohol reduce anxiety and self-consciousness, make us more sociable, and induce a pleasant glow of well-being.

Quick fixes

Many people in wealthy nations feel vaguely unsatisfied with their lot, despite their money, cars, interesting jobs, good health, schools, foreign holidays, widescreen TVs, mobile phones, football and centrally heated homes. In search of the missing ingredient, growing numbers have sought solace in one of the numerous brands of New Age beliefs. For centuries, gurus and charlatans have offered a dazzling array of practices, faiths and philosophies that purport to bring lasting happiness. Whether they actually work is another matter. Few have ever been put to any form of objective or verifiable test. There are certainly good reasons for being sceptical about much of what is on offer.

Keeping an open mind and being willing to experiment in the quest for happiness has much to recommend it as a strategy. But suspending rational thought and critical judgment is less sensible. American research has found that individuals who believe in magic, space aliens, after-death experiences or the miraculous powers of meditation, prayer and faith are no happier, no more relaxed and no less stressed on average than people who hold more evidence-based beliefs about the nature of reality.

Some popular techniques for improving well-being and happiness really do work, however. In particular, there is reasonably good scientific evidence that practising certain forms of meditation can boost happiness and reduce anxiety, as well as producing measurable physical changes including reductions in heart rate and blood pressure.[5]

Those philosophies that have proved to be genuinely effective in enhancing the happiness of their practitioners have certain basic features in common with modern science, even if the concepts are expressed in a very different sort of language. In particular, they recognise the fundamental truths that there is no single, universal key to happiness, and that happiness is as much a product of what goes on in the mind as the physical environment. They also recognise that enhancing happiness takes time and patience. There are no quick fixes.

EIGHT

Wealth and celebrity

The moral flabbiness born of the exclusive worship of
the bitch-goddess *success*. That – with the squalid cash
interpretation put on the word success – is our national
disease.

WILLIAM JAMES, letter (1906)

Jane Austen famously wrote that a large income was the
best recipe for happiness she had heard of. Well, she was
wrong. Happiness is much more a product of psychological
wealth than material wealth.

The assets that contribute most to human happiness are
attitudes, experiences and personal relationships, but you
would not guess that from the way we behave. Many of
us act as though money, material possessions and social
recognition were the real passports to happiness, and we
cling onto this belief despite blatant evidence to the contrary. Thanks to the media, we know that celebrities, prin-
cesses, footballers, pop stars and captains of industry are
just as capable as anyone else of living unhappy and taw-
dry lives. Money and fame are clearly no guarantees of

144

happiness. What, then, is the true relationship between happiness and those two dominant gods of our era – wealth and celebrity?

Money, money, money

Life for some people is dominated by a quest for money and material possessions. The global advertising industry spends billions each year persuading us that buying certain brands will make us happier, and we elect governments that act as though economic growth and rising incomes were the keys to happiness. Most of us, it seems, implicitly believe that happiness can be bought.

According to research, the majority of people in developed nations regard money as a primary goal in life and think it will make their lives better. Three out of four American students entering university in the 1990s rated wealth as a very important or essential goal – more than double the proportion who gave that response in the 1970s. One study even found that Americans assess people who are successful, happy and rich to be morally superior to the poor and unhappy, and more likely to go to heaven. The philosophy seems to be that if you 'have it all' in this life then you will also be blessed in the afterlife. And American culture is not the only one to equate wealth with virtue.

Our faith in the power of money to make us happier does not stand up to much scrutiny, however. By the standards of our grandparents most of us are fabulously rich, but we do not appear to be fabulously happy. Thanks to economic growth, the populations of developed nations have become much wealthier since the mid-twentieth century. In the UK, for example, the average disposable income per person (adjusted for inflation) more than doubled between 1971 and 2000, and a level of wealth that was average in 1950s Britain would now fall below the poverty line. However, this huge growth in real wealth has not been accompanied by a huge growth in personal happiness. Indeed, according to some analyses people are slightly less happy now than they were in the past. Dramatic increases in wealth over the past 50 years have added remarkably little to the stock of human happiness.

Money does of course have some bearing on happiness. Whilst it may not add much to the happiness of people who are already well off, it does make a difference to people who have very little. A basic minimum amount of wealth provides a crucial bulwark against many sources of stress and unhappiness. Possessing sufficient money means not having to worry about food or shelter. Poverty makes happiness much harder to attain. Even in wealthy nations, children whose parents have financial problems are found to be at greater risk of unhappiness and low self-esteem, partly as a consequence of receiving less parental support. And individuals who experienced poverty in childhood are more likely to become unhappy adults, especially if childhood poverty is combined with other risk factors such as being born to a young mother.

The connection between poverty and unhappiness becomes even more apparent when viewed on a global scale. International comparisons consistently find that the inhabitants of wealthy nations such as the UK, USA, Sweden and Switzerland are happier on average than the inhabitants of very poor nations. Even so, there is more to national happiness than national wealth: as we saw in chapter 6, several of the unhappiest populations on the planet live in former Soviet countries such as Moldova, Ukraine, Russia and Belarus, which are not the very poorest.

The existence of a broad, worldwide association between national wealth and national happiness is easy to understand. We all require a certain minimum quality of life to be happy. If you are hungry, ill and have no roof over your head, you will find it harder to be happy, no matter how strong your personal relationships or philosophical outlook. And by almost every objective measure, the average quality of life in the world's poorest nations is substantially lower than in rich nations. The majority of people in very poor countries like Chad, Ethiopia and Bangladesh have poorer housing, education, healthcare, literacy, civil rights and economic equality, so it is no wonder that they also tend to be less satisfied with their lives and less happy.[1]

For someone living in abject poverty, even a small increment in wealth can bring big improvements in quality of life and their ability to satisfy basic needs. However, increases in personal wealth produce comparable increases in personal happiness only up to a point where basic human needs such as food, shelter, clean water and healthcare have been catered for. Beyond this basic level, further rises in wealth make proportionally smaller differences to happiness. Economists have estimated that this cut-off point comes at a level of material wealth roughly equivalent to that of the UK in the 1950s.

Within a wealthy nation like present-day Britain, richer individuals are still happier on average than poorer individuals – but only slightly happier. Knowing only how wealthy someone is will tell you relatively little about how happy they are likely to be, because individual differences in income account for less than 4 per cent of the individual differences in happiness. Thus, for most people in wealthy nations, additional wealth has surprisingly little bearing on happiness.

One way of illustrating the relative impotence of money is to compare its ability to 'buy' happiness against other assets that really *do* make a difference, such as personal relationships and employment. The economists Andrew Clark and Andrew Oswald have applied clever statistical techniques to estimate the equivalent monetary value of various life events which are known to make people happier or unhappier. Using data from UK studies, they calculated how much money the average person would have to receive in order to compensate (in terms of happiness) for a bad life event like losing their job, and how much money they would have to lose in order to negate the immediate effects of a good life event like getting married.

Their calculations revealed that marriage, divorce, becoming unemployed and other major life events make far bigger differences to happiness than even very large changes in income. For instance, Clark and Oswald estimated that the average Briton would have to receive a sum of money equivalent to more than seven times the national average annual income to leave them feeling no less happy after losing their job. The break-up of a marriage would also require a six-figure sum to offset its immediate detrimental effects on happiness. Conversely, getting married boosts happiness by roughly the same extent as receiving four times the national average annual income. Broadly speaking, you would have to receive a windfall of more than a million pounds to transform you from an unhappy person into a happy person – and even then, the effect would only be temporary.

Why does money fail to produce great happiness, in defiance of popular wisdom? A simple answer is that material wealth is not a basic human psychological need whereas, say, being connected with other people *is*. Such an answer might well have been given by many of the philosophers of ancient Greece. Take Diogenes, for example, who died around 320 BC. He chose to live in abject poverty, sleeping rough and relying for his food on begging. Diogenes did this to demonstrate that a man can be happy no matter how poor he is in material terms. His whole lifestyle was intended as a graphic reproof to his compatriots, who had made the fundamental error of equating happiness with wealth and luxury. A disregard for material wealth is a common theme in most major religions as well.[2]

A more searching explanation as to why money buys relatively little happiness in wealthy nations rests on three psychological processes, each of which dilutes the psychological benefits of rising wealth. These processes are habituation ('the shine wears off'), rising aspirations ('the more you have, the more you want') and social comparison ('keeping up with the Joneses').

Habituation, which we encountered in the previous chapter, means that our emotional response to a new source of pleasure tends to dwindle over time. Extra money or a prized new possession may make us feel better for a while, but the shine will wear off. Thus, lottery winners are little or no happier than anyone else a few months after their win; they habituate to the new pleasures that money can buy, and before long their happiness is more or less back to where it started.

The additional happiness generated by extra wealth is also eroded by rising aspirations. The reality of human psychology is that the more we have, the more we want; and the more we want, the less satisfied we are with what we already have. Our material aspirations are inclined to expand in line with increasing wealth, offsetting its psychological benefits. As Ralph Waldo Emerson said, 'Want is a growing giant whom the coat of Have was never large enough to cover.' Experiments have confirmed that our financial aspirations generally do grow bigger as we grow richer. Thus, someone earning, say, £30,000 a year might feel that an income of £60,000 would enable them to fulfil their desires, whereas someone on £100,000 might feel they needed £250,000 a year to be satisfied. The bigger the gap between your current earnings and your aspirations, the less satisfied you are likely to be with your lot. Fat cats can be just as dissatisfied with their pay packets as the rest of us.

Once again, though, popular assumptions about the nature and causes of happiness are at odds with reality. Research has found that most people believe their material aspirations remain roughly constant over the years. Younger people therefore assume they will be happier in the future, as they become wealthier. Most people also believe they were less happy in the past, when they earned less money. In reality, however, we do not generally become much happier as we get older and wealthier, nor do we become much less happy if our income drops on retirement. As we saw in the previous chapter, happiness actually tends to remain fairly stable over the lifespan.

A third reason why greater wealth does not make us feel much happier for long is because of a phenomenon that psychologists refer to as the social comparison effect (otherwise known as 'keeping up with the Joneses'). In an affluent nation like the UK, personal wealth is more of a relative quantity than an absolute one. What matters is not so much feeling better off than you were before as feeling better off *than other people*. The American writer H. L. Mencken summed this up when he defined a wealthy man as one whose income is $100 a year higher than his wife's sister's husband.

The social comparison effect means that someone who earns, say, £30,000 a year would feel better off surrounded by friends, neighbours and colleagues earning £25,000 than if peers were earning £35,000 a year. Research has shown that a majority of people would opt for a situation in which they were paid £50,000 a year while others received £25,000, in preference to one in which they were paid £100,000 while others received £250,000. In other words, most of us would prefer to be *relatively* wealthy even if that meant being absolutely poorer. Experiments have also confirmed that our happiness tends to decline when we are in the presence of others who receive an increase in their wealth.

The social comparison effect is most conspicuous in the case of money and material possessions, but the general principle applies in other spheres, including health and employment. For example, one experiment found that people felt happier after they had been exposed to someone who appeared to be receiving treatment for a serious kidney disease. Ambrose Bierce was not being entirely cynical when he defined happiness as an agreeable sensation arising from contemplating the misery of others. Similarly, research has found that workers who lose their jobs suffer a smaller decline in their happiness if they are living in a community where there is already high unemployment.

Our inherent tendency to judge what we have by comparison with what others have means we can remain dissatisfied despite being wealthier than our parents' generation. I might feel happier for a while if I acquire a shiny new car, but if my friends and neighbours also acquire shiny new cars then I might not feel much happier. Similarly, if most people in a community or a nation become wealthier then they might not feel much happier because their *relative* wealth will not have changed. This may help to explain why the UK, USA and other prosperous nations have not become dramatically happier in recent decades.

A less obvious consequence of the social comparison effect is that if only a minority of individuals within a community or nation become much wealthier then the average level of happiness in the population may actually *drop*, because the majority of people feel less wealthy in comparison. Evidence from several countries bears this out. The average happiness of a population does indeed tend to decline if the disparity in wealth between the richest and the poorest grows bigger.

Thanks to the social comparison effect the connection between your wealth and your happiness is not entirely under your control, because it depends to some extent on other people. What you can, do, however, is choose who you compare yourself with. Most of us, by definition, are neither at the top of the economic pile nor the bottom. In principle, therefore, we have some degree of choice about who to judge ourselves against. Psychology tells us that looking down upon the less fortunate should make us feel happier, while looking enviously upwards towards the better off will make us feel worse. With this aspect of human nature presumably in mind, Samuel Johnson's fictional character Rasselas proclaims that he longs to see the miseries of the world because the sight of them is necessary for happiness.

In practice, however, we are inclined to put ourselves at a psychological disadvantage when making social comparisons, by looking upwards rather than downwards. To make matters worse, the social comparison effect is greatly amplified by the media (a point we shall return to later). All those obscenely rich football stars, celebrities and business moguls we keep reading about and seeing on our TV screens may actually be making the rest of us *less* happy.

Research has revealed that the social comparison effect operates somewhat differently in happy and unhappy people. Individuals who are already unhappy are more inclined than happy people to make upward comparisons, and therefore to feel even worse off. In one experiment, volunteers performed a puzzle-solving task in the presence of a stooge who either performed better or worse than they did. Happy subjects typically compared themselves with stooges who performed worse than them, which made them feel better about their own performance. However, *un*happy subjects tended to compare themselves with stooges who outperformed them, which made them feel worse. This link between unhappiness and an inclination to make upward comparisons is mutually reinforcing: the glummer you feel, the more you compare yourself to people who are better off, and the glummer you become. Happy people have another advantage, in that they are generally less sensitive to social comparisons, whether upward or downward. They just seem to be more comfortable in their own skin and less dependent for their happiness on what other people do or think.

So, thanks to habituation, rising aspirations and the social comparison effect, new money or material possessions will probably not make you feel much happier for long. What is more, the process of pursuing that wealth can make you *un*happy. There is good evidence that highly materialistic people are less happy on average than those whose priorities lie elsewhere. Individuals who attach a high priority to financial success tend to be less happy, less satisfied with their lives and more anxious than individuals for whom other life goals are more important. The same is true for children. Studies have found, for example, that children whose main aim in life is to be rich and famous are at greater risk of becoming depressed. None of this would have come as any surprise to Plato and Aristotle, who regarded the pursuit of money for its own sake as dehumanising.

For some individuals, excessive materialism is a reflection of low self-esteem, an exaggerated need for social approval or some other psychological problem. But a more commonplace reason why materialism breeds unhappiness is because the pursuit of wealth often conflicts with other, more fundamental, priorities.

We all have only a limited amount of time, and tensions easily arise between acquiring wealth and looking after our personal relationships and other truly important aspects of our lives. The potential conflict between the pursuit of wealth and the pursuit of happiness might account for anecdotal evidence that many individuals who reach the heights of material success are unhappy. Conceivably, their wealth and ascendancy might have been acquired at the expense of their family life, close friendships and other crucial ingredients of happiness. It is not the money per se that makes them unhappy, but the single-minded pursuit of that money. Tellingly, the Biblical maxim is commonly misquoted as 'money is the root of all evil', whereas what it actually says is 'the *love* of money is the root of all evil'.

If wealth does not buy much happiness, and chasing after it can actually make us unhappy, then why are most of us so fixated on it? One reason may be simply that money is very easy to quantify. You can measure exactly how much money an item will cost, or a job will pay, but it is hard to judge in advance how much pleasure or satisfaction you will derive from them. The media also play a role, as we shall see later.

The bitch-goddess celebrity

We turn now to another god of our current era – celebrity. We live in a culture where it is commonplace to desire social recognition, to regard it as a source of happiness, and to admire (or even worship) those who have it. For many, fame has replaced money as the ultimate goal in life, although the two are assumed to go hand in hand anyway.

Once upon a time, individuals achieved fame through their actions and achievements. To be celebrated, you generally had to be wise, virtuous, brave, beautiful, rich, powerful, or some combination of these. Now, however, celebrity has become an end in its own right, and almost anyone can aspire to it. Some celebrities are famous mainly for being famous.

Craving celebrity or social recognition has certain similarities with craving wealth. In both cases the goal is external rather than intrinsic, and any happiness derived from it will be eroded by habituation, rising aspirations and the social comparison effect. Someone who does achieve a degree of fame may not remain happier for long, and they will probably want more. As Bertrand Russell pointed out, someone who desires glory might envy Napoleon; but Napoleon envied Caesar, Caesar envied Alexander, and Alexander probably envied Hercules, who never existed. The truth is that there will always be someone out there who is richer, more successful and more famous than you.

The pursuit of fame, like the pursuit of wealth, is more often a recipe for unhappiness. Researchers have found that children and adults whose main aspirations in life centre round money, fame or their own physical appearance tend to have poorer mental health than those who are more concerned with intrinsic goals like developing close relationships or helping others. Individuals who hanker after looking good and being recognised have higher levels of depression and anxiety, and experience more physical symptoms such as headaches and lack of vitality.

One large study of pre-teen children found that those who believed fame and money to be the roots of happiness were more vulnerable to depression. The children's role models, who included pop singers and the writer J. K. Rowling, were admired more for their wealth or their physical appearance than for their skills. In contrast, the happier children were more interested in their own personal relationships, and in the processes whereby they could pursue their life goals (i.e., in the means as well as the ends). More generally, research shows that children and adults who regard happiness as an end point are more likely to be depressed than those who regard it as a process. (To use the self-help terminology, happiness should be regarded as a journey rather than a destination.)

The pursuit of celebrity can be observed at its most naked on reality TV shows, where 'ordinary' people undergo varying degrees of public humiliation in their quest for social recognition. The psychologist Oliver James has argued that the worst of these programmes damage the mental health of the contestants, very few of whom ever achieve their fantasy of lasting success or fame. Reality TV can even harm those who watch it, according to James, because it reinforces the pernicious belief that fame is a quick way of becoming attractive, successful and happy.

Those at greatest risk are individuals with low self-esteem.

If we cannot be famous ourselves, the next best thing may be to worship those who are. According to recent surveys, around a third of us indulge in some form of 'celebrity worship', varying along a spectrum from the innocuous to the downright pathological. In its milder forms, celebrity worship amounts to little more than harmless entertainment. At the other end of the scale, however, lurk individuals who have become obsessed with every detail of their idol's life and deluded into believing they have a personal relationship. In its more pathological forms, celebrity worship can manifest itself in stalking and other potentially dangerous behaviour.

Psychologists who have investigated celebrity worshippers have found that those who display the most extreme form are more likely to exhibit measurable difficulties with their thinking, learning and language skills. These psychological deficits may have contributed to their worship problem. Intense celebrity worshippers also tend to have moody, emotional, neurotic personalities, making them more prone to anxiety, unhappiness and depression. However, celebrity worshippers do not appear to be generally lonelier than average, casting doubt on the 'common sense' assumption that celebrity worship is simply a substitute for real personal relationships.

Evolutionary theory can throw some interesting, if speculative, light on this seemingly contemporary phenomenon. Celebrity worship may in fact have ancient biological roots. Some evolutionary psychologists have suggested that celebrity worship reflects a more fundamental human desire to emulate successful individuals.

According to this theory, we are predisposed to pay particular attention to highly successful individuals in our social group, to learn from their behaviour, and to copy them. It makes sense that our hunter-gatherer ancestors would have benefited from aping their most successful peers. However, this predisposition to notice and emulate successful individuals did not evolve to cope with a modern world equipped with global electronic communication. The mass media can inadvertently trick our brains into forming imaginary relationships with celebrities we have never met, and whose admirable qualities may be more synthetic than real – which brings us back to TV and advertising.

Why TV and advertising are bad for you

Wealth and celebrity usually fail to provide lasting happiness, and the dogged quest for them can distort lives and generate unhappiness. Now add to this cocktail the baleful influence of the media and advertising, and the outlook grows even worse.

The mass media and the advertising industry have the potential to undermine happiness in several ways. They eat up large chunks of our time that could be spent doing things which really do make us happier. They reinforce the myth that wealth and celebrity are passports to happiness. They undermine our satisfaction by amplifying the social comparison effect. And just for good measure, they persuade us and our children to consume junk food and soft drinks that make us fat and unhealthy.

Consider the simple matter of time: watching TV consumes large amounts of it and therefore has opportunity costs. Adults and children in the UK spend an average of about three hours a day watching TV. And while we are watching TV, we and our children are not doing things that could contribute to our happiness and well-being, such as building and maintaining personal relationships, engaging in meaningful activities, playing with friends, exercising or getting enough sleep. One of the more banal reasons why many children and adolescents suffer from daytime tiredness is because they routinely stay up late to watch TV.

A second way in which the media and advertising undermine happiness is by continually reinforcing the implicit message that happiness can be bought in the form of material possessions and brands. One of the basic ingredients of happiness, as we saw in chapter 4, is freedom from excessive materialism. But the aim of most advertising is to make us *more* materialistic. Advertising exists to create or reinforce desires, which is why businesses spend billions on it every year. Its insidious influence was well understood even in ancient Greece, where the philosopher Epicurus launched a fierce attack on consumerism and marketing. Writing around 300 BC, Epicurus argued that the world of commerce stimulates unnecessary and artificial cravings in people who do not understand their true needs, and thereby makes them unhappy.

Advertising works hard and intelligently to persuade us that products and brands have the power to make us and our children happier. One of the simple ways it does this, quite successfully, is by repeatedly linking images of the product or brand with images of love, close friendship, freedom, physical attractiveness or other genuine sources of happiness. Like Pavlov's dogs salivating at the sound of a bell, we unconsciously learn to associate these two stimuli which have been repeatedly paired on our screens. We see the brand and unconsciously associate it with happiness. We learn to yearn for the trainers, the car or the perfume possessed in the advert by the beautiful young person surrounded by beautiful young friends. We see the beefy 4×4 racing across the unspoilt wilderness and imagine that owning one of these aggressive vehicles will somehow liberate us, even if we do live in traffic-choked urban Britain.

The Pavlovian conditioning does occasionally backfire, however. One of the great advertising disasters of all times was a 1960s campaign for a now-defunct brand of cigarette known as Strand. Over an image of a rugged-looking man in a trench coat standing under a street lamp, the slogan ran 'You're never alone with a Strand.' The advert itself was highly regarded among critics. But associating any product with loneliness – one of the prime causes of unhappiness – was not such a terrific idea. Smokers in their droves stopped buying Strand cigarettes and the campaign was rapidly shelved.

As well as fomenting desires for new possessions, the media and advertising can leave us feeling less satisfied with what we already have. They do this by presenting the world through a lens that massively amplifies the social comparison effect. As we saw earlier, we tend to feel less happy when comparing ourselves with people who are better off than us. In the distant pre-media past, people judged their own lives and possessions largely by comparison with their friends and neighbours. Now, however, the media routinely invite us to measure ourselves against the stratospherically high standards of the wealthiest, most famous and most impossibly gorgeous individuals on the planet.

TV programmes, adverts, films and magazines portray a world of rich, beautiful, successful and happy people with perfect bodies, ravishing partners and fabulous houses (even though the truth is often different behind the glossy façade, as some celebrities have been known to become depressed, divorced or addicted to drugs). We learn that a well-known footballer is paid as much as several hundred nurses, and perhaps wonder if he is really worth it. But we also imagine what it would be like to have all that money and adulation, and how much happier it would make us. This continual parading of extreme wealth, glamour and celebrity can leave us feeling less satisfied with our own relatively paltry lot, like small children with our noses pressed against the sweetshop window.

The malignant shadow of the social comparison effect spreads beyond money and material possessions, to encompass even our bodies and our partners' bodies. Psychological experiments have demonstrated that when men and women view images of highly attractive members of their own sex, they judge themselves to be less physically attractive. Not surprisingly, their self-esteem drops. In one study, women who watched music videos featuring idealised images of highly attractive young women felt measurably more dissatisfied with their own body. In other experiments, men who were shown images of highly attractive women reported feeling less committed towards their partner, compared to when they were shown images of averagely attractive women. Similarly, women reported feeling less committed towards their partner after seeing images of high-status men. These sorts of insidious social comparison effects are generally short-lived and relatively modest in size, but the images that stimulate them are ever-present. We are daily bombarded with words and pictures that almost seem designed to make us feel dissatisfied.

Another way in which advertising and marketing inadvertently reduce happiness is, paradoxically, by exposing us to an excessive range of consumer choices. A conventional belief among marketeers and economists is that the more choices consumers are given, the better. But psychological research suggests otherwise. In fact, too much choice can be unpleasant, to the extent that it puts people off buying. Faced with too many options, we may freeze and buy nothing at all, or feel dissatisfied with what we have bought. Researchers have found that when consumers are asked to choose from half a dozen different types of jam they will happily pick one they like, but confronted with two dozen types of jam they may buy none at all, because they do not want to feel they might have chosen the 'wrong' one. Sometimes, less really is more.

The American psychologist Barry Schwartz has discovered that some individuals, whom he calls 'maximizers', consistently feel a need to ensure that they make optimal decisions and always choose the very best. When maximisers are faced with a large range of competing options they feel pressurised and are inclined to regret their decision later. Maximisers are found to be generally less happy, less satisfied with their lives and more prone to depression than individuals who are normally content to settle for a choice that is good enough ('satisficers').

Children are especially vulnerable to the corrosive influences of TV and advertising, in terms of both their mental and physical well-being. For decades, scientists, policymakers and pundits have been debating whether violent TV programmes make children more inclined to behave aggressively. The controversy remains unresolved. Untangling the specific influence of TV violence from the many other factors that affect children's behaviour is extremely difficult, and several big studies have failed to find any clear causal links between violent programming and violent behaviour among viewers. Many other factors will also be in play, some less obvious than others. For instance, research has discovered that pre-school children who watch a lot of TV are statistically more likely to have a mother who is clinically depressed.

Nonetheless, credible evidence has emerged over the years to suggest that there is at least cause for concern. For example, a major American study, conducted over a 17-year period, found that individuals who had watched a lot of TV during their adolescence were significantly more likely to behave aggressively years later. Those who had watched three or more hours of TV a day in their mid-teens were five times more likely to commit aggressive acts than those who had watched TV for less than one hour a day. This connection held true even after the investigators had allowed for the effects of other factors including childhood neglect, low family income, living in a violent neighbourhood, poor parental education and psychiatric disorders.

Roald Dahl parodies the insidious influence of TV in his book *Charlie and the Chocolate Factory*, through the ghastly Mike Teavee. This nine-year-old monster does almost nothing other than watch TV; he is usually to be found in front of an enormous television set, his eyes glued to a programme in which criminals are shooting each other. Mike Teavee has no fewer than 18 toy guns attached to his body, and every so often blasts off several rounds from one of these weapons. In one of his rare and irritable lapses into conversation, the small addict boasts that he watches *all* of the shows *every* day, 'even the rotten ones, where there's no shooting'.

Although the links between TV viewing and violent behaviour remain scientifically controversial, not even its staunchest defenders would argue that spending several hours a day watching junk TV *improves* children's social and emotional development. The best that can be said is that it may do no lasting harm.

Some critics argue that TV exposes children to poor role models which convey unhealthy stereotypes. In many TV soaps the conventional way in which characters deal with everyday conflict is to shout and posture, if not resort to outright violence. In real life, however, individuals who can only respond by becoming angry and aggressive are unlikely to flourish. Soap opera tactics are a recipe for unhappiness.

Poor social skills are not the only potential risk. Recently published research in the USA has uncovered troubling evidence that TV viewing in early life is linked to reduced attention spans in school-aged children, and perhaps even ADHD (Attention Deficit/Hyperactivity Disorder). A long-term study, which tracked more than a thousand children, discovered that those who watched the most hours per day of TV at the ages of one and three years were significantly more likely to display attention problems when assessed again at the age of seven. Again, the implication is that pre-school children should not be allowed to spend too many hours a day parked in front of the TV.

Whether or not TV damages children's minds, it certainly does little to improve their physical health. Clear evidence from numerous published studies shows that children who spend a lot of time watching TV are on average fatter and less healthy than children who spend less time in front of the box. One investigation, for example, found that adolescents who watched more than two hours of TV a day were much more likely to be overweight a few years later than those who had watched less than two hours a day. Similarly, a large American study, based on a sample of more than 15,000 teenagers, found that 14–18-year-olds who watched four hours or more of TV a day (as a quarter of American teenagers do) were much more likely to be overweight than those who watched an hour or less.

One simple and obvious reason why young people who watch more TV are fatter is because they get less exercise. Research has repeatedly found that the more time people spend watching TV each week, the less physically active they are on average. A negative correlation between TV viewing and physical exercise is hardly surprising, since you cannot easily do both at the same time. However, time is not the only reason why TV and inactivity go hand in hand. Indeed, researchers have found that adolescents who spend a lot of time on certain other sedentary activities like reading and homework tend to take *more* exercise. There appears to be something specific to TV that discourages physical activity.

Avid TV viewers are fatter and unhealthier for another reason as well: they consume more high-calorie convenience foods, snacks and soft drinks. A mass of research evidence, accumulated over several decades, shows that the more time children spend watching TV, the higher their average intake of calories, snack foods, fat and carbonated soft drinks. Children who watch a lot of TV are also found to eat less fruit and vegetables. Experiments have even shown that exposing children to food adverts elicits an immediate increase in their consumption of snack foods. Moreover, obese children are more susceptible than slim children to being influenced in this way, and are better at remembering food-related adverts.

The connection between TV viewing and unhealthy diets is not hard to unravel. The main reason why children who watch a lot of TV consume more junk food and soft drinks is because they are exposed to a lot of advertising, the purpose of which is to persuade them to do precisely that. Vast sums of money are spent on advertising food and drink, and much of that marketing muscle is targeted specifically at children. According to the independent Food Commission, the food industry's global advertising budget is a remarkable 40 billion dollars a year – more than the gross domestic product of an average-sized country. In wealthy nations like the UK, food and drink adverts account for about half of all the advertising broadcast during children's TV programmes, and most of these adverts are for products of dubious nutritional value. Advertising on this monumental scale completely dwarfs all the worthy efforts to educate children about nutrition and healthy eating.

Food and drink manufacturers do not spend billions without good reason, and there is no doubt that advertising really does work. Numerous studies have shown that even very young children display strong preferences for the branded food and drink products they have seen in adverts. Research has also found that the more time children spend viewing TV, the more requests they make to their parents for the advertised products, and the more of those products are actually found in their house. In other words, children ask for, and get, what they see in adverts. Moreover, the effects of advertising are not limited to persuading children to prefer one brand over another, as its defenders often claim. Instead, the evidence indicates that advertising shapes children's preferences for whole categories or types of food. Rather than merely persuading children to choose, say, McDonald's instead of Burger King, or Pepsi instead of Coke, advertising also boosts their desire for fast food and soft drinks in general.

Although TV is the main medium through which the

manufacturers of junk food and sugary drinks market their wares to children, it is by no means the only one. Advertisers exploit a range of other outlets to target children, including radio, magazines, vending machines, voucher schemes, text messaging, educational sponsorship and celebrity endorsements. The British Football Association and several leading football clubs have justifiably been criticised for promoting fast food, confectionery and soft drinks to children as part of lucrative marketing deals.

In sum, then, TV and advertising have the potential to make you and your children dissatisfied, fat, unhealthy and unhappy.

What governments could do

Faulty beliefs about the connections between wealth, fame and happiness distort people's priorities and decisions every day of their lives. They seek money, material possessions and social recognition on the mistaken assumption that these will make them enduringly happier.

Similar faulty beliefs distort the economic and social policies of national governments around the world, many of which behave as though economic growth were the key to happiness. However, a growing minority of economists, including Richard Layard and Andrew Oswald in the UK, are arguing that Western governments should give more explicit priority to improving personal happiness, even if that means turning away from the conventional preoccupation with economic growth.

The small Himalayan kingdom of Bhutan appears to be the sole exception to the rule that national governments pay little more than lip service to happiness. The government of Bhutan has officially declared that 'gross national happiness' is more important than gross national product.

Precisely how 'gross national happiness' is defined remains unclear, although it reportedly takes account of a sustainable balance among the economic, social, emotional and cultural needs of the people. An optimist would attribute Bhutan's enlightened attitude to its Buddhist heritage, though a cynic might also point to its extremely small gross national product.

Most other governments continue to give a much higher priority to economic growth, as though greater personal incomes will inevitably generate greater personal happiness. A basic minimum level of wealth is certainly needed for happiness – although, as we saw earlier, this level is probably about that of the UK in the 1950s. Once people have the basic requirements, such as somewhere to live, enough to eat and drink, education and access to healthcare, then further large increases in wealth do not generate comparably large increases in happiness. Unemployment, on the other hand, is a powerful cause of unhappiness: as we saw in chapter 4, unemployed people are much less happy, less healthy and shorter-lived than people with jobs. Any government that is intent on raising national happiness will give a high priority to minimising unemployment.

Governments that truly wanted to make people happier would behave differently in other ways as well. In addition to bearing down hard on unemployment, they would seek to reduce inequalities in wealth. There is good evidence that reducing the disparity between the richest and poorest in a society tends to raise the average level of happiness. Pro-happiness governments would spend more on improving mental health. They would also use economic, social and educational policies to promote close personal relationships. Education could promote personal relationships by paying more attention to the development of children's social skills and emotional literacy (a theme to which we shall be returning later).

A radical pro-happiness government would acknowledge that rampant consumerism and advertising undermine unhappiness, and it might even consider using taxation or regulation to discourage them. The American psychologist Tim Kasser has argued that advertising is a form of environmental pollution which damages mental health and reduces human happiness. He has proposed that governments should tax advertising or force advertisers to issue a health warning. Imagine that.

NINE

The story so far

Be not solitary, be not idle.
ROBERT BURTON, *The Anatomy of Melancholy*
(1621–51)

In the next two chapters we will consider how parenting and education influence children's long-term potential for happiness. Among other things, we will see that certain styles of parenting behaviour are associated with better outcomes than others, and that an excessive emphasis on measurable academic attainment can hinder children's social and emotional development. Before launching into this, however, it might be an idea briefly to remind ourselves of the key points about the nature and origins of happiness.

Happiness is arguably the most important thing in life. It can be measured, and scientists have discovered a fair amount about its make-up, causes and consequences. Happiness is a blend of three distinct elements – namely, pleasure, the absence of displeasure, and satisfaction. Different combinations of these three can combine to produce the same overall level of happiness. Pleasure and displeasure are concerned with how we feel (emotion), whereas satisfaction depends on how we think (cognition). A common error is to equate happiness with pleasure alone. In fact, pleasurable experiences generally provide only a temporary boost to happiness.

Besides being inherently desirable in its own right, happiness breeds success and is good for physical health. On average, happy people are more energetic, more sociable, more attractive, more creative and better at thinking. They are also healthier and live longer than unhappy people. Furthermore, happiness does not appear to have any significant drawbacks; for example, being happy does not make us less objective or less creative. Unpleasant emotions like sadness and anxiety are not wholly bad, however, because they have important protective functions, analogous to physical pain. The capacity to feel sad, anxious, angry or fearful in the right circumstances is highly beneficial, even if it does not feel good at the time.

Happiness is influenced by external events (i.e., what happens to us) but it also depends critically on how we perceive, think about and respond to those events. Personality plays an important role.

The most common characteristics of happy people are:

- *Connectedness* (having close relationships with other people)
- *Social and emotional competence* (understanding and responding appropriately to your own emotions and other people's emotions)
- *Freedom from excessive anxiety* (fretting only when there are good reasons to fret)
- *Communication skills* (being able to transmit and

receive information and feelings through all the available channels)

- *Engagement in meaningful activity* (and especially not being unemployed)
- *A sense of control* (feeling that you have some influence over what happens to you)
- *A sense of purpose and meaning* (feeling that your current activity, or your life as a whole, has some broader significance)
- *Resilience* (the ability to cope with adversity)
- *Self-esteem* (valuing yourself, but without being vain or narcissistic)
- *Optimism* (expecting the best, but without being a Pollyanna)
- *Outward focus* (thinking mostly about other people and the world around you, rather than continually brooding about yourself)
- *Present- and future-mindedness* (the ability both to enjoy the moment and to take the longer view)
- *Humour* (being able to laugh at yourself and the absurdities of life)
- *Playfulness* (having fun, experimenting with new ways of doing things, and relishing novel experiences)
- *Wisdom* (pragmatic knowledge about the world and how to tackle real-life problems)
- *Freedom from excessive materialism* (not distorting your life by pursuing money, material possessions or social recognition at the expense of things that contribute far more to happiness, notably personal relationships)
- *Regular experience of flow* (plentiful opportunities, at work or elsewhere, to become absorbed in challenging tasks that create the optimal experience known as flow)

Of all the many different characteristics of happy people, connectedness is the most important and universal. Our relationships with other people are absolutely central to happiness. We humans are fundamentally social animals, and personal relationships are crucial for our mental and physical well-being. Close relationships are associated with greater happiness, whereas lonely people are at much greater risk of unhappiness, depression, poor health and a shorter lifespan.

Self-esteem and optimism are associated with happiness, but they are not the universal panaceas they are sometimes cracked up to be. Healthy self-esteem, based on a realistic assessment of your qualities and achievements, is a good thing. However, empty or excessive self-esteem can be corrosive if it is built on self-delusion, vanity or meaningless praise from parents and teachers. Contrary to popular belief, boosting children's self-esteem is not a quick way of boosting their performance in school or keeping them out of trouble. Optimism must also be grounded in reality.

Many different factors shape the development of happiness during each individual's lifetime. The main ones include social and cultural influences, genes, health, sleep, physical activity, education, religion and physical attractiveness.

Genes affect our capacity for happiness in many ways, including through their influences on personality and health. But this does not imply that happiness is somehow 'all in the genes' and therefore unalterable. You can do a great deal to change your own happiness and your children's happiness, for better or for worse. Engagement in meaningful activity or work is a significant source of happiness, with benefits extending far beyond the purely financial. Conversely, unemployment is a major cause of unhappiness and ill health.

Individuals who have received extensive education tend to be happier and healthier than those who have had less education, especially in old age. However, intelligence (in the narrow sense, as measured by conventional IQ tests) makes little difference to happiness. Physical activity and exercise can lift mood and improve happiness in various ways. Getting sleep of sufficient quantity and quality is essential for happiness and for mental and physical well-being more generally, although many adults and children do not get enough.

Several things that are widely assumed to affect happiness actually have little bearing on it. Age and gender make little difference: old people are no less happy on average than young people, and men are just as happy (or unhappy) as women. Leisure activities can be a source of happiness if they are intrinsically rewarding, but watching a lot of TV is associated with unhappiness.

Money and material possessions make remarkably little lasting difference to happiness. For most people in affluent nations, even large increases in personal wealth produce only small and temporary increases in happiness. The psychological benefits of wealth and fame are eroded by habituation (getting used to what you have), rising aspirations (wanting more) and social comparison (wanting more than other people). Nonetheless, most individuals and most governments behave as though wealth were the key to happiness. The media and advertising add fuel to the flames by stimulating our desires and amplifying the social comparison effect. The pursuit of wealth or celebrity can create unhappiness if it interferes with things that really do matter, notably close personal relationships.

The happy implication of all this is that parents, teachers and other adults can do a great deal to help children flourish and become happier, both in childhood and later in life. In the next two chapters we will consider how.

TEN

The authoritative parent

All happy families resemble one another, but each unhappy family is unhappy in its own way.

LEO TOLSTOY, *Anna Karenina* (1875–7)

You will be unsurprised to learn that parents really do have a profound influence on their children's capacity for happiness. Parental attitudes and behaviour affect children's happiness both directly and indirectly – for example, through their influences on children's social and emotional competence, communication skills, wisdom, education and health. Some styles of parenting promote happiness, while others do the reverse. The consequences can be extensive and long-lasting.

An impressive body of data, accumulated from decades of research, confirms that children who grow up with loving, supportive parents are generally happier and more successful, both in childhood and later in life, than children who lack this advantage. Having loving and supportive parents is one of the strongest predictors of academic success: indeed, the evidence suggests that it makes a bigger difference to children's educational attainment than which school they attend. The longer-term ramifications are, if anything, even more compelling. Numerous studies have found that individuals who have a warm, loving relationship with their parents when young tend to be happier as adults, including in middle and old age. They also earn more money and are less likely to be unemployed. In fact, good family relationships in childhood have a bigger influence on individuals' later career success than how well they did in school.

By the same token, children and young people whose parents are unloving and unsupportive are, on average, less successful in school, more vulnerable to depression, more likely to use drugs, less successful in their other personal relationships and generally less happy, both as children and in adult life. And of course parents who subject their children to physical or emotional abuse can inflict severe and lasting damage on their mental health.

Parenting undoubtedly plays a crucial role in the development of happiness. That said, almost any adult has the capacity to be a good parent, even if some lack confidence in their own ability. Parenting can be hard work, but that does not mean you have to be a highly trained expert to do it well. As we shall see, good parenting is more a matter of having the right basic attitudes than always doing precisely the right things every minute of the day. We will start by looking at the most basic attitude of all – love.

All you need (to begin with) is love

More than half a century ago the British psychiatrist John Bowlby made a far-reaching advance in the understanding of parenthood, when he brought a new biological perspective to bear on his clinical experience. As a practising psychiatrist, Bowlby had encountered many teenagers and adults with severe behavioural and emotional problems. He was struck by the fact that a large proportion of these troubled individuals came from disrupted family backgrounds, often involving marked disturbances in their relationship with one or both parents.

Bowlby realised that the nature of the early relationship between the child and its primary caregiver (who is usually, but not necessarily, its mother) has a profound effect on the child's future development. He also saw that this made sense in biological terms. In the uncertain and dangerous world inhabited by our ancient ancestors, infants who immediately sought the safety of their parent or other caregiver in times of danger would have had a better chance of surviving. Infants who stayed close to their parent in situations of heightened threat would have been less likely to succumb to accidents, predators and other dangers. The formation of a strong emotional bond, or attachment, between the infant and its parent is a normal biological process which helps to protect the infant during the vulnerable early years of life. Bowlby also observed that the quality of this attachment varies considerably, depending largely on the parent's behaviour. By about the age of three, virtually every child will have formed an attachment to at least one primary caregiver, usually its mother. (The rare exceptions would be children living in extremely deprived conditions such as the Romanian orphanages of the 1980s.) But not all infants are *securely* attached.

To become securely attached, an infant must be wholly confident, on the basis of consistent experience, that its caregiver is responsive to its needs and unconditionally available to provide help whenever help is needed. A child will form an attachment even to an abusive or neglectful parent, but that attachment will probably not be secure. Similarly, a mother who is unloving, unresponsive, inconsistent and unpredictable is unlikely to have a securely attached child.

Decades of observational and experimental research have reinforced and extended John Bowlby's original insights. The findings have confirmed, among other things, that securely attached children are usually happier than insecurely attached children.

Secure attachment promotes happiness in several ways. For example, it encourages exploration and play. The securely attached infant uses its mother or caregiver as a safe, dependable base from which to explore the world and acquire the experience that will help it develop. An infant who feels unconditionally loved and secure is better able to cope with uncertainty, and can therefore afford to explore, play and take risks. Experiments have revealed that securely attached infants are generally less fearful or angry than insecurely attached infants, even in situations that are intended to provoke fear or anger. For the same reasons, insecurely attached infants are less exploratory and less playful. They have learned that they do not have a dependable safe haven and cannot rely on their caregiver if they need comfort or help. They consequently become cautious and inclined to cling to the familiar. Insecure early attachment is a risk factor for a whole range of psychological and emotional problems later in life.

A child's early relationship with its parents can have an enduring impact on playfulness that is apparent even in old age. A long-term American investigation of aging (known as the Harvard Study) discovered that men whose parents had been affectionless and lacking in warmth towards them in childhood were less playful in middle and old age. When assessed at the ages of 45 and 65, these offspring of cold parents were much less likely to play games with friends, engage in sports or take proper holidays. They were also less happy. The same study also found that secure attachment in early childhood had a significant bearing on individuals' earnings decades later. The best long-term predictor of high income in middle and old age was whether the man's mother had made him feel loved when he was a child.

The importance of secure attachment extends far beyond promoting exploration and play. Secure attachment also provides the right conditions for the development of other building blocks of happiness – notably social and emotional competence and freedom from excessive anxiety. Research has shown that securely attached children are generally better at understanding and dealing with emotions, including negative emotions like sadness and anger.

Securely attached infants display higher levels of social and emotional competence when interacting with their peers and are less likely to display uncontrolled anger. Compared to insecurely attached children, they are found to have more successful social relationships and fewer behaviour problems. Overall, securely attached children are more competent at dealing with life. Insecure attachment, on the other hand, can impair children's social and emotional development. Experience teaches them that their mother will sometimes ignore or rebuff them. They must work harder at monitoring their mother's behaviour and soliciting responses from her. Insecurely attached infants therefore tend to become anxious and attention-seeking.

Style with substance
Secure attachment built on unconditional love is the bedrock from which children develop and flourish. But there is a bit more to producing happy, flourishing children than secure attachment alone.

The overall style of behaviour that parents adopt with their children has far-reaching implications. In this context, some psychologists find it helpful to distinguish between four broadly different styles of parenting, which I will refer to here as *authoritative* parenting, *authoritarian* parenting, *indulgent* parenting and *uninvolved* parenting.[1] For reasons we are about to explore, authoritative parenting is generally regarded as a Good Thing, the others less so.

Authoritative parenting is distinguished from the other parenting styles by three main features, which psychologists sometimes refer to as 'acceptance-involvement', 'strictness-supervision' and 'psychological autonomy-granting'. In everyday English, this means that authoritative parents love their children unconditionally and accept them for who they are, keep a close eye on them, provide plenty of support, set firm boundaries, and grant considerable freedom within those boundaries. Authoritative parents monitor their children and intervene when necessary, but let them get on with things when there is no need to interfere. They mean what they say, and do not shy away from conflict when enforcing the boundaries they have set. In sum, authoritative parents are:

- Warm, supportive and unconditionally loving, but not overindulgent
- Aware and involved, but not interfering or overly controlling

- Clear and firm about boundaries, but not excessively risk-averse
- Permissive within those boundaries, but not neglectful

Authoritarian parents, in contrast, have a colder parenting style which is more demanding but less responsive to their children's real needs. Authoritarian parents are highly controlling, but not very warm or loving. They intervene frequently, issuing commands, criticisms and occasional praise, but do this in an inconsistent and unpredictable way. They expect their children to obey their instructions without explanation, and may use emotional tactics to get their way, such as making their children feel guilty, ashamed or unloved. Authoritarian parents often interfere when there is no real need to interfere, and issue threats without always carrying them through. At the extreme, some highly authoritarian parents resort to physical or emotional abuse in their attempts to control their children, which obviously can cause lasting psychological damage. Children who are beaten or denied any affection are at significantly greater risk of becoming abusive parents themselves, thereby perpetuating the cycle.

Some research has indicated that the authoritarian parenting style is more prevalent among parents of lower educational level. It has also been suggested that middle-class parents in the UK have become more authoritarian in recent years because of their higher (and sometimes unrealistically high) expectations about their children's behaviour, academic attainment and career prospects.

Indulgent parents are undemanding, permissive and set few clear boundaries. They are warm and loving, but lax. They often respond to their children's wishes, even when these are unreasonable or inappropriate. Punishments are seldom threatened, let alone carried through, and the children often appear to have the upper hand in the relationship. Indulgent parents try to be kind, but they shy away from conflict or difficulty.

A parody of indulgent parenting can be found in Roald Dahl's *Charlie and the Chocolate Factory*, in the form of Mr and Mrs Salt. Their daughter Veruca is an obnoxious little girl who has been spoiled rotten by her rich parents. She gains entry to Willy Wonka's fabulous chocolate factory by winning one of the coveted Golden Tickets – but only thanks to her doting father, who has bought half a million Wonka chocolate bars and made his employees unwrap them until a Golden Ticket is found. Veruca arrives at the chocolate factory in a silver mink coat and keeps demanding to have everything she sees. Predictably, Veruca Salt receives a fitting punishment. Despite already owning two dogs, four cats, six rabbits, two parakeets, three canaries, a green parrot, a turtle, a bowl of goldfish, a cage of white mice and a hamster, she demands one of Willy Wonka's trained squirrels. They are not for sale, even though Mr Salt invites Wonka to name his price, but Veruca decides to take one anyway. She is mobbed by the squirrels, who rightly judge her to be a bad nut and throw her down the rubbish chute. Just for good measure, they throw her indulgent parents down there too.

Uninvolved parents, who make up our fourth category, are undemanding, permissive and set few clear boundaries, largely because they don't really care very much. Unlike authoritative parents, they are neither warm nor firm and they do not monitor their children. Instead, they are laid back and unresponsive to an extent that can sometimes seem reckless. In extreme cases, uninvolved parenting may stray into outright neglect. Roald Dahl also helpfully supplies us with a parody of uninvolved parenting – this time in the shape of Mr and Mrs Wormwood in *Matilda*. The gormless Wormwoods are so wrapped up in their own empty suburban lives that they fail to notice their daughter Matilda is an extraordinarily brilliant little girl who has taught herself to read by the age of three. To them, she is little more than an annoying scab.

My brief pen portraits of authoritative, authoritarian, indulgent and uninvolved parenting are inevitably oversimplifications of a complex reality. Most real parents do not fit neatly into just one of the four categories, and many display a mix of two or more different styles, albeit often with a dominant theme. Moreover, the same parents may display different parenting styles on different occasions or towards different children. Think, for example, of Harry Potter's adoptive parents, the ghastly Mr and Mrs Dursley of No. 4 Privet Drive.

In their behaviour towards the orphaned Harry, the Dursleys are predominantly *authoritarian* caregivers, with a streak of *uninvolved*. They are fussy, demanding and overcontrolling, but also cold, unloving and ultimately indifferent. They do not accept Harry for who he is, and there is no warmth in the relationship. The Dursleys often talk about Harry in front of him, as though he was not there, and Mr Dursley's idea of a morning greeting is to bark an order at him. Harry is given precious little autonomy or support, and is even made to sleep in the cupboard under the stairs. 'Don't ask questions' is the first rule for a quiet life in the Dursley household.

In sharp contrast, the Dursleys' fawning attitude towards their biological son, the egregious Dudley, falls firmly into the *indulgent* camp. While Harry can do no right in their eyes, 'ickle Dudleykins' can do no wrong.

Their fat, greedy offspring's every whim is indulged, often in response to the threat of a massive tantrum. Dudley knows that if he screws up his face and bawls, his mother will give him pretty well anything he wants. On Dudley's birthday, Harry watches him unwrap a racing bike, a cine camera, a remote-control aeroplane, sixteen new computer games, a video recorder and a gold wristwatch. And still Dudley is not happy.

The authoritative difference

My earlier assertion that authoritative parenting is generally a Good Thing is backed up by reassuringly large amounts of data from psychological research.

Numerous studies have found that authoritative parenting is associated with more secure attachment, less anxiety, higher self-esteem, better achievement in school and at work, greater satisfaction with life, and greater overall happiness, both in childhood and later in life. On average, children of authoritative parents are happier, academically more successful, emotionally better adjusted and have better personal relationships than children of authoritarian, indulgent or uninvolved parents. They adapt better to school or university and perform better in both. As if that were not enough, studies have also found that children of authoritative parents are less likely to smoke, take illicit drugs or abuse alcohol. They even eat more fruit. So how does authoritative parenting actually affect children's development and thereby contribute to their greater happiness and success?

Probably the most powerful component of authoritative parenting is unconditional love and acceptance. The children of authoritative parents do not have to keep on earning their parents' affection by behaving in particular ways:

they are loved and accepted for who they are, not what they do. The unconditional love and acceptance that lies at the heart of authoritative parenting helps to create secure attachment, with all the manifold benefits that brings. Authoritarian, indulgent or uninvolved parents are more likely to have insecurely attached children.

As well as encouraging secure attachment, authoritative parenting promotes many of the other features that characterise happy people. Among other things, it fosters connectedness, freedom from excessive anxiety, a sense of control, resilience, self-esteem, optimism, outward focus, playfulness and freedom from excessive materialism. Let us look at each of these characteristics in turn, and consider how authoritative parenting helps to build them.

Connectedness

Personal relationships, as I have repeatedly stressed, are fundamental to happiness throughout life. Having a rich network of close, supportive relationships with partner, friends, family and colleagues is probably the single most important ingredient of happiness. But in order to develop and maintain those relationships, any individual must possess at least a minimum level of social skills and emotional literacy. Helping children to become socially and emotionally competent is therefore one of the most effective ways of helping them become happy. And according to research, that is precisely what authoritative parenting does.

The children of authoritative parents are found to have better social skills and more successful relationships with their peers during childhood, adolescence and early adulthood. They also display a better understanding of other people's thoughts and emotions, which helps them to behave more appropriately. In contrast, authoritarian parenting appears to be bad news for the development of emotional literacy, especially where aggression is concerned. The children of highly authoritarian parents are more inclined to interpret other people's intentions as hostile, even when they are not. This unfortunate propensity makes them more likely to behave aggressively.

One of the biggest obstacles any child can face when it comes to personal relationships is shyness. Again, the children of authoritative parents are at an advantage. Research has found that overcontrolling authoritarian parents and overprotective indulgent parents are more likely than authoritative parents to have shy children. It is not hard to see why. Shyness has been defined as a tendency to respond in social contexts with heightened anxiety, self-consciousness and reticence, reflecting the fact that it affects both feelings and visible behaviour.[2] A parent who consistently overprotects or overcontrols their child is sending a message that the world is a hostile place. At the same time, they are restricting the child's opportunities to develop social and emotional competence through playing freely with other children. It is therefore unsurprising if the child comes to respond in a shy, cautious way in social encounters.[3]

Freedom from excessive anxiety

A second aspect of happiness that authoritative parenting helps to create is freedom from excessive anxiety. Authoritative parents are involved and supportive; they monitor their children, take notice of what they are doing, and respond to their needs. They may not always do precisely what their children want, but they do at least respond. Their children therefore learn from an early age that someone is looking after them and they have a reliable safe haven in case of trouble.

The securely attached child has less need to monitor its parents, because it implicitly knows they will be there if help is required. The child also has less need to be clingy or use attention-seeking tactics like temper tantrums. By creating this inherent sense of security, authoritative parenting insulates the developing child against the nagging anxiety that can so easily undermine happiness.

A sense of control

A sense of control is another ingredient of happiness that flourishes under authoritative parenting. Research shows that children of authoritative parents have a stronger sense of being in control of their lives than do children of authoritarian, indulgent or uninvolved parents.[4] This makes them more self-confident and independent.

The pathway from authoritative parenting to a sense of control is not hard to discern. One of the defining features of authoritative parents is their willingness to grant their children considerable autonomy. Having set clear boundaries for what is and is not permissible, they step back and let their children get on with it. They keep a close eye on what their children are up to, but do not interfere unnecessarily. Children who are given plenty of autonomy within a safe environment feel more in control of their lives – as indeed they are.

In contrast, children of authoritarian parents are subjected to a lot of parental control and have little autonomy. They feel less sense of control because they actually have less control. This, in turn, can foster anxiety – which, as we have seen, is an ingredient of unhappiness. A poor sense of control can also have unwelcome ramifications in other areas of children's lives, including even their future sex lives. Researchers have found that adults who had highly controlling authoritarian mothers tend to be less self-confident in sexual matters. Uninvolved parenting can also store up problems; for example, young adolescents with uninvolved mothers drink more alcohol, are more likely to smoke, and have more behaviour problems on average than adolescents with authoritative mothers.

The self-confidence born from a strong sense of control goes hand in hand with competence. A self-confident, independent child is better placed to acquire and develop new skills than one who lacks confidence, and the evidence bears this out. The children of authoritative parents are generally found to behave more competently in the classroom. Their competence is enhanced by receiving better quality criticism: authoritative parents give their children good support, which includes telling them when they have got something wrong and advising them how to do it better. Authoritative parents offer constructive criticism, with the emphasis on the constructive.

Studies have found that young children whose parents simply tell them off whenever they make mistakes tend to become less confident over time and more inclined to avoid tackling difficult tasks, whereas children whose parents provide constructive criticism become more confident and more competent. In one experiment, mothers were asked to teach their two-year-old infants a difficult task; the same mothers and infants were then assessed again a year later. The children of authoritative mothers, who had been encouraged with praise, guidance and constructive criticism, were more persistent and less inclined to avoid challenges than those whose mothers had simply criticised their mistakes a year earlier. Undiluted criticism had made the children feel ashamed of their mistakes and therefore more reluctant to expose themselves to further ridicule. Other research has found that young children with authoritative mothers are more persistent, waste less time on irrelevant tasks, and are less likely to appear helpless in classroom situations.

One practical take-home message here is that parental criticism should be directed specifically at the child's actions, and not generally at the child as a person. 'Criticise the behaviour, not the child' is one of the golden rules of good parenting. Moreover, the aim of any criticism should be constructive rather than purely negative. Repeatedly telling a child that he or she is bad or stupid will do nothing to help them improve, and may become a self-fulfilling prophecy.

Authoritative parents are responsive to their children's needs, but this does not mean they are overly permissive: they set clear boundaries and enforce them. However, some of the more traditional guidebooks for parents of babies and young children seem to confuse responsiveness with indulgence. In the past, some childcare experts encouraged – nay, ordered – parents to ignore their babies or infants when they cried, and to respond only according to a rigid schedule. But the research evidence shows that ignoring children, or training them to be quiet, is rarely a good idea. More often than not, the child simply learns that it must work even harder to gain parental attention. Meanwhile, the foundations of a secure attachment are being undermined. Similar principles apply to dealing with older children. Authoritative parents set firm boundaries, but they do not turn their backs on their children or let arguments over petty disciplinary rules damage their relationship. There is much to recommend the old adage that you should never let the sun go down on a quarrel.

Resilience
Another reason why children of authoritative parents are happier is because they tend to be more resilient, making them better able to cope with the problems and setbacks that life will inevitably throw at them.

One of the most notable scientific studies of resilience was conducted by the psychologist Emmy Werner, who tracked the development of children born on the Hawaiian island of Kauai over a 40-year period. Around a third of these children proved to be remarkably resilient. They grew up to be well-balanced, happy and successful adults despite experiencing severe problems in childhood, including poverty and abuse. If anything, the outcome was somewhat better for resilient individuals than those who had not faced adversity in childhood; for instance, they were physically healthier and had stronger marriages. Werner's data revealed that one of the most important factors contributing to long-term resilience in these individuals was authoritative parenting.

Self-esteem and optimism
Studies in several countries have found that children of authoritative parents tend to have higher self-esteem than those of authoritarian parents, other things being equal. This association between authoritative parenting and higher self-esteem holds true both in individualistic Western cultures, like the UK and USA, and in more collectivist Asian cultures such as China. So too does an association between authoritarian parenting and low self-esteem.

The pioneering psychologist William James once defined

self-esteem as 'the ratio of success to pretensions'. He was making a valid point. Children's self-esteem will depend to some extent on what is expected of them. If the hurdles are set too high they will experience mostly disappointment, but if too little is expected they will not be stretched or realise their potential. The ideal, beloved of management consultants and self-help books alike, is to set goals that are challenging but realistic.

Parents obviously play a crucial role in shaping these goals. For example, research has found that parents who regard themselves as poor at maths tend to have lower expectations of their children's achievement in maths, which in turn leads their children to expect less of themselves. Getting the balance right can be hard. Some parents manage to convey a corrosive sense that nothing is ever good enough, leaving their children feeling like failures. On the other hand, low expectations can easily become a self-fulfilling prophecy. Authoritative parents are better placed to strike the right balance because they are keenly interested in their children and monitor their progress.

Optimism is another common characteristic of happy people that turns out to be associated with authoritative parenting. Mothers who display the authoritative parenting style tend to have optimistic children, whereas highly authoritarian mothers are more likely to have children with symptoms of depression.

Outward focus

We saw in chapter 4 that another common characteristic of happy people is outward focus – that is, an active interest in the world and other people. Outward focus contrasts with the introspection or even self-obsession that is often apparent in unhappy people. Becoming preoccupied with your own thoughts, feelings and circumstances is generally a recipe for gloom. Research indicates that children of authoritative parents are less inclined to be introspective or narcissistic.

Probably the simplest and most effective way of fostering an outward focus is to value and help other people. An ancient Chinese proverb put it like this: 'If you want happiness for a year, inherit a fortune; if you want happiness for a lifetime, help someone else.' Most successful religions and philosophies advocate caring about other people, both on moral grounds and because it improves everyone's well-being. To give just one example, the form of Buddhism taught by the Dalai Lama recommends cultivating a deep respect and compassion for other people, regardless of who they are.

Scientific research lends support to this approach as a strategy for building happiness. Various studies have found that individuals who are genuinely interested in the well-being of others tend to be happier than those who are primarily concerned for themselves. Indeed, it has been suggested that one reason why more of us are not happier now, despite our ever-growing material wealth, is that fewer and fewer of us really care about others. The consumerist 'me' culture does not encourage altruism.

Research shows that individuals who take part in community volunteer work are happier, less prone to depression, physically healthier and longer-lived than those who do not, other things being equal. Moreover, volunteer work appears to create a virtuous circle, since research also shows that happy people are more likely to do it in the first place. This may be because happy, healthy people are more inclined to volunteer, or because they are more likely to be sought out by charitable organisations, or both.

Whatever the reason, helping other people makes us happier, and being happy makes us more inclined to help other people. In this case, at least, morality and self-interest point in the same direction.

A less respectable mechanism by which helping others boosts happiness is through exposing the helper to people in a less fortunate position. As we saw in chapter 8, we tend to feel happier when making downward comparisons with people who are less well off than us.

One straightforward way to help children develop an outward focus is by getting them involved with charitable or volunteer activity of some sort. As well as being worthy in its own right, the experience could make them happier. Adults can also encourage outward focus by teaching children to be courteous in their behaviour and attitudes towards other people. Despite its somewhat old-school image, courtesy or politeness is nothing more than a demonstration of basic consideration for others. Individuals who lack respect for other people are seldom happy.

Parents can promote outward focus in their children by steadfastly refusing to give in to sulking. Parents who respond to their children's sulks are simply reinforcing that behaviour. Worse, they are inadvertently teaching their children to get what they want by being unhappy. For the inveterate sulker, the distinction between appearing to be miserable and actually feeling miserable soon evaporates. Sulking is little better than emotional self-abuse. Parents should instead be teaching their children the opposite lesson – namely, that they are more likely to get what they want by being happy.

Playfulness

Playfulness is another important contributor to happiness that thrives under authoritative parenting. As we saw earlier, the authoritative combination of security and autonomy encourages children to explore and play, which in turn helps to develop their social, emotional, physical and thinking skills. (We shall return to play in the next chapter.)

Among the worst enemies of playfulness are overanxious and overprotective parents. There is a growing tendency for parents to try protecting their children from any unpleasantness or risk. The sociologist Frank Furedi has dubbed this 'paranoid parenting'. A common symptom of paranoid parenting is a reluctance to let children play freely with friends. Play, especially of the outdoors or rough-and-tumble varieties, is seen as potentially nasty or even dangerous: the child might be upset, bullied, hit, or worse. The problem here is that while parents understandably want to protect their children, attempting to insulate them from all risks will also deprive them of opportunities for play and social interaction which can be crucial for their development.

Anxieties about physical safety have led many parents to insist on driving their children to and from school rather than letting them walk with their friends. Again, the net effect is to deprive children of valuable opportunities for social interaction and physical exercise. Driving children everywhere contributes more to their expanding waistlines than it does to their social and emotional development. Paradoxically, it also stops them learning how to become safe pedestrians, thereby probably adding to their risk of being knocked over when older.

As we saw earlier, social and emotional competence is another crucial ingredient of happiness and success. And one of the main mechanisms by which children acquire such competence is through playing. Suppressing children's play deprives them of experiences that teach them how to cope with the world. Overprotective parenting can also exacerbate shyness, because it teaches the child that the world is a hostile place.

Today's risk-averse and restrictive approach to children's play is strikingly different from the carefree, laissez-faire world portrayed in Richmal Crompton's *William* books of the 1920s and 30s. William and his young friends, most of whom are only ten or eleven years old, enjoy virtually limitless freedom to range far and wide in unsupervised play, roaming across fields and around the streets. The remarkable degree of autonomy granted to William and co is epitomised by this fairly typical introduction to one of their adventures: 'It was sunny. It was holiday time. They had each other and a dog. Boyhood could not wish for more. The whole world lay before them. "Let's go trespassin'"', said William the lawless.'

Arthur Ransome's *Swallows and Amazons*, which is of similar pre-World War Two vintage, is another children's book that reminds us how risk-averse our society has become. It starts with four children, the youngest of whom is aged seven, seeking their absent father's permission to go on a sailing adventure in their small boat and camp on an island. Back comes their father's answer by telegram: 'BETTER DROWNED THAN DUFFERS. IF NOT DUFFERS WON'T DROWN.' (In other words, 'yes'.) Nowadays a father with such a permissive attitude towards childish adventure would probably be accused of neglect.

Why do some parents succumb to overprotective paranoid parenting? One reason may be that they do not have a proper grasp of risks. Psychological research indicates that we are all inclined to overestimate the likelihood of unusual hazards, such as that of our children being abducted and murdered by a stranger, while underestimating mundane risks that are actually much more common, such as being injured or killed in a domestic accident or a vehicle. The actual risk of a child in the UK being seriously injured or dying in a domestic accident is vastly greater than their risk of being abducted and murdered by a stranger (which, despite the tabloid headlines, has not changed much over the past 30 years). Accidents in the home result in two or three child deaths and about 20,000 children being taken to hospital *every week*, whereas fewer than ten children a year on average are killed by strangers. Parents who understand and think about the reality of different types of risk are better equipped to strike a rational balance; they can allow their children to play and experience the world, while still protecting them from the serious and avoidable hazards.

Sometimes, however, paranoid parenting can have more selfish motives. It may be that some overprotective parents wrap their children in cotton wool because they want to avoid feeling worried themselves. Allowing children the freedom to play, explore and enjoy rich experiences also means having to let go and put up with some anxiety. This is especially true with adolescents, whose alarming behaviour can easily disturb their parents' calm. But suppressing children's playfulness will do them no good in the long run.

Freedom from excessive materialism
Finally, another ingredient of happiness that benefits from authoritative parenting is freedom from excessive materialism. We saw in chapter 8 that accumulating material

wealth contributes remarkably little to the development of enduring happiness, whereas chasing after it causes unhappiness. Highly materialistic people are generally less happy than those with more balanced priorities.

Research indicates that authoritative parents are less likely than authoritarian parents to have children who are highly materialistic. The children of authoritarian parents often develop a strong desire for money as they grow up. Psychologists have suggested that this greater need for external reward and recognition in the form of material wealth could be a response to feelings of insecurity, engendered in childhood by their cold, controlling parents.

In sum, then, authoritative parenting creates fertile conditions for children to become, and remain, happy people. It promotes secure attachment and fosters the development of many personal characteristics that contribute to happiness, including connectedness, freedom from excessive anxiety, a sense of control, outward focus and playfulness. Children of authoritative parents are better placed to grow up regarding the world as a basically friendly and interesting place. They discover that they can have an effect on the world, which helps them to acquire self-confidence and a sense of control. Conversely, children who have experienced the unresponsive discipline of an authoritarian parent, or the erratic indifference of an uninvolved parent, come to see the world as an unpredictable and unfriendly place in which they are not valued, leading them to become anxious, insecure, self-obsessed, untrusting and lacking in self-confidence.

Authoritative parenting is composed of various components, some of which (such as granting autonomy) may not always come easily to parents. But probably the single most fundamental aspect of authoritative parenting is unconditional love and acceptance. If nothing else, parents who want their children to be happy should aim to love their children for who they *are*, not who they would like them to be, nor for what they achieve. Parental love and respect should not be made conditional upon meeting performance targets.

Beyond authoritative parenting

Authoritative parenting creates solid foundations for happiness and success. But there are, of course, other things for parents to think about as well, including their children's physical health and simply spending enough time with them.

The quality and emotional warmth of the relationship between parent and child is obviously pivotal, but the sheer *quantity* of time they spend together can also make a difference. The comforting notion of 'quality time' may have seduced some busy parents into believing they can maintain a rich, nurturing relationship with their children despite spending little time in their presence.

The concept of a trade-off between the quantity of time spent together and the quality of the interactions does contain an obvious grain of truth. However, like any simple idea it can be – and sometimes is – stretched too far. There comes a point in any close relationship when sheer lack of quantity will begin to bite, no matter how superb the quality of the contact time. As someone once said, quantity has a certain quality of its own. For children to flourish, they need a modicum of 'quantity time', as well as 'quality time', with their primary caregivers.

Physical health, exercise and sleep are also important but easily overlooked ingredients of happiness. When contemplating something as cerebral as happiness it is easy to forget the brute physical realities of life. We have bodies as well as minds, and our mental well-being is inexorably intertwined with our physical well-being. A child who is obese, physically unfit and sleep-deprived will be at a big disadvantage when it comes to happiness or success.

No parent would want their child to turn out like Roald Dahl's Augustus Gloop, for example. The greedy nine-year-old is so obese that he looks as though he has been inflated with a giant pump, with folds of fat bulging from every part of his body. In the real world, childhood obesity has become a leading threat to public health. Obese children usually turn into obese adults, and face a substantially heightened risk of developing high blood pressure, coronary heart disease, diabetes, osteoarthritis and various forms of cancer. They also die younger. As long ago as 1998 the World Health Organization declared childhood obesity to be a global epidemic, since when the problem has been growing progressively larger, along with children's waistlines.

We saw in chapter 6 that physical activity and exercise contribute to happiness, and not just because they help to prevent children from getting fat. Regrettably, the trend has been moving in the opposite direction. Since the 1970s, children in the UK have become progressively less active. Far fewer children walk or bicycle to school now than was the case 30 years ago, and parents must bear some of the responsibility. Indulgent parents who allow their children to spend several hours a day slumped in front of the TV, and overprotective parents who refuse to let their children play outdoors, are doing them no favour by restricting their opportunities for physical activity. The advantages of a healthy and physically active lifestyle become increasingly apparent and increasingly important as we grow older. Long-term studies of aging have established that individuals who neglect exercise and become overweight during early adulthood and middle age are much less likely to be happy (or indeed alive) in old age.

Sleep is vital as well. We saw in chapter 6 that something as basic as getting enough sleep can make a big difference to happiness. There is extensive evidence that a substantial proportion of children and adolescents in the UK and other industrialised nations do not get sleep of sufficient quantity or quality. Their mental and physical well-being suffers as a result. It really is difficult to be happy and successful, let alone fulfil your full potential, if you are continually tired, grumpy and unable to concentrate.

Some parents seem to have a blind spot about sleep, and must shoulder at least some of the blame for their children's tiredness. They apparently assume that simply sending a child to their bedroom will ensure they get enough sleep, which obviously is not true. On top of that, many children's bedrooms have become palaces of entertainment rather than places to sleep. TVs and computers in bedrooms are the enemies of sleep.

The simple message here is that children are more likely to be happy people, both in childhood and in adult life, if they develop the habits of a reasonably healthy and active lifestyle. This need not entail anything elaborate or draconian – just the basics of a varied and reasonably balanced diet, plenty of physical activity and sufficient sleep. These will not by themselves ensure happiness, but their absence will certainly erode it.

A final point for parents to consider is the nature of the relationships between their children. A majority of parents (though nowadays only a small and dwindling majority) have more than one child, which means that siblings enter into the happiness equation.

Siblings are often remarkably different from one another in personality and behaviour, despite having the same parents and growing up in the same family. In fact, scientists have discovered that environmental influences on siblings have the opposite effect to what might be expected: they make siblings more *different* from one other, not more similar. One way of thinking about this is to imagine each child unconsciously seeking to occupy their own distinctive identity, or niche, within the family. (Psychologists sometimes refer to this as 'niche-picking'.) The point here is that parents often treat their children very differently because their children really *are* different – and therein can lie a problem.

Children are highly sensitive to how they are treated relative to their siblings. Even very young children compare themselves with their siblings, and they can be surprisingly aware of even subtle differences. Charles Dickens, who was himself the victim of intense sibling rivalry, put it like this: 'In the little world in which children have their existence, whosoever brings them up, there is nothing so finely perceived, and so finely felt, as injustice.' The practical implication is that parents should try to treat their children fairly. But this does not mean trying to treat them *equally*, which is often impossible and not necessarily desirable.

Despite the potential for sibling rivalry, having a brother or sister is usually more of a help than a hindrance in children's development. Siblings provide mental and social stimulation for each other. On the other hand, there is no clear evidence that only children are generally less happy or less healthy than children with one or more siblings. This is just as well, because the long-term trend in the UK and other wealthy nations is for people to have smaller families or no families at all, which obviously means that fewer and fewer children now have a sibling. The average number of children per family in the UK has dropped from 2.0 in 1971 to 1.8 in 2001, and the last time the average British family consisted of the proverbial 2.4 children was in the 1950s. Almost a quarter of all British children are now the only child in their family.

The evidence that being an only child need not diminish the prospects for happiness is also good news for the population of China, where for decades the government has been conducting a vast and unintentional experiment on the psychological consequences of growing up as an only child. In 1979 the Chinese government implemented an official one-child policy, limiting families in cities to just one child each. The result of China's one-child policy has been a whole generation of only children, with another generation following behind. According to some critics, these products of China's one-child policy are overindulged and self-centred brats, who are sometimes referred to as 'Little Emperors'. But several scientific studies have as yet failed to uncover clear evidence that the Chinese are any less happy or healthy than they would have been growing up with siblings – which is probably just as well for the rest of us.

ELEVEN

Education, education

It is forbidden to waste time by playing in the playground.
GILLIAN CROSS, *The Demon Headmaster* (1982)

What is education for?
Education helps to make happy people. During their years at school (and university, if they go there) young people acquire an array of skills, attitudes, knowledge and experience that underpin long-term happiness. They develop social and emotional competence, communication skills and wisdom; they have plentiful opportunities to engage in meaningful activity and to acquire a sense of purpose and meaning in their lives; and of course they form close personal relationships.

The most tangible dividend of education is a passport to satisfying and reasonably well-paid work. But education brings many other, less concrete benefits as well. For instance, it insulates us from the malign consequences of ignorance. The more we understand about the nature of the world and humankind, the less vulnerable we are to irrational fears and disabling superstitions. At the very least, we are better able to appraise the dubious claims of marketers, crooks, pundits and gurus. Education also equips us with the knowledge (if not always the motivation) to live healthier and longer lives. And of course it promotes happiness; as we saw in chapter 6, the more education someone has received, the more likely they are to be a happy person.

The connection between education and happiness is mutually reinforcing: education helps to make happy people, and happy people gain more from their education. Research shows that happy children typically learn and perform better in the classroom than unhappy children, for all sorts of reasons. They are more energetic, more persistent, more creative, more focused, and better able to get on with their classmates and teachers. So, even if exam grades were the sole consideration, parents and teachers should still want children to be happy.

The case for happiness to feature prominently on the educational agenda is compelling. In most countries, however, the reality is rather different. Making happy people is rarely an explicit aim of education, let alone its prime purpose. Schools are geared up to deliver measurable academic achievement, not something fluffy and intangible like happiness. Governments do not set performance targets for schools to produce happier children, nor do they demand year-on-year improvements in children's social skills or emotional literacy. Instead, we have a culture of delivery that focuses on exam grades and other supposedly hard-edged performance indicators. And given the huge effort that goes into raising academic standards, surprisingly little attention is paid to how happiness affects children's performance in the classroom. The implicit belief seems to be that education and happiness have little to do with one another.

Now, I am emphatically *not* implying that pushing up standards in literacy, numeracy and other core competences is a waste of time. Such capabilities are clearly crucial for every child's future success and well-being. But they are not enough. There is much more to education than the specific knowledge and skills that are measured by most formal examinations. Many of the crucial benefits young people acquire from education are intangible assets that exist in their minds, not on bits of paper. But these benefits are not always straightforward to measure, and they rarely appear on the public policy radar screen.

A cynic might say that education has come to be regarded as little more than an economic tool. Parents understandably want schools and universities to furnish their children with qualifications that will enable them to get good jobs. Governments equally want schools and universities to act as the engine room of the economy, turning out citizens with useful skills and qualifications. Young people are encouraged to go to university partly because of the extra money they will later earn; they are assured that the large cost of a university education will more than pay for itself eventually, because having a degree will boost their lifetime earnings by six-figure sums. (In fact, this is true only if they enter certain well-paid professions – as any graduate nurse, schoolteacher, university lecturer, research scientist or charity worker will confirm.[1] UK government statistics reveal that graduates in arts subjects, education or social sciences are little or no better off financially than non-graduates.)

If education really is intended to promote national economic prosperity, a sceptic might wonder why it does not focus more on developing young people's creativity, initiative and capacity for independent thinking.[2] Initiative – the ability to assess and initiate things independently – is an increasingly valuable asset in the knowledge economy, and yet children and adolescents have few opportunities to learn or practise it in school, let alone in common leisure pursuits like watching TV.

What would an education system look like if it had been designed with happiness in mind? If schools were tasked with maximising long-term happiness, they would have to be different places – but not radically different. Making happy people may be a broader goal than raising average exam grades, but the two are not mutually exclusive; promoting happiness certainly does not mean transforming classrooms into playpens full of undisciplined children avoiding all hard work.

The personal qualities of happy people are, by and large, the same ones that are needed to be successful in school, university and the workplace. As we have seen, they include such attributes as social and emotional competence, freedom from excessive anxiety, communication skills, resilience, future-mindedness and wisdom. Happy pupils learn better and achieve more. Nonetheless, an education system that had happiness as one of its key performance indicators would be somewhat different. In particular, happiness-centred education would:

- promote a lifelong love of learning for its own sake
- be less preoccupied with short-term measurable attainment
- place greater emphasis on social and emotional development
- let children play, and
- stop encouraging children to acquire academic qualifications at younger and younger ages

A lifelong love of learning

The world is self-evidently a complex and somewhat unpredictable place. In the UK and other wealthy industrialised nations, most jobs require intellectual and emotional capabilities rather than brute muscle power. To succeed in the knowledge economy, even according to narrow criteria like pay and promotion, workers must perform well in areas such as interpersonal skills, communication and creative thinking. Few young people will do the same job for many years, let alone a whole working lifetime, and the pace of change continues to accelerate. A lifelong capacity to learn and adapt to change will clearly be even more crucial in future than it already is.

A lifelong love of learning is highly desirable for all sorts of other reasons besides earning money and avoiding unemployment. It is central to long-term happiness and health. Most of the key characteristics of happy people, including connectedness, communication skills, a sense of control and wisdom, are fostered by education. Someone who loves learning for its own sake, and therefore continues to learn throughout their life, is much better equipped to be happy, healthy and successful than someone whose learning gland withers the day they leave school.

A love of learning remains central to happiness and health throughout the lifespan, including in old age. Long-term studies of aging have established that individuals who retain an inherent desire to learn when they are elderly are much more likely to be happy and healthy than those whose minds are closed for new business. An appetite for learning in old age is strongly correlated with mental and physical well-being, and helps to counteract the slowing down of mental processes.

In view of all this, the suggestion that education should be designed to promote a lifelong love of learning might seem uncontroversial to the point of being blindingly obvious – that is, until you consider how most children are actually educated and how most adults actually behave.

Governments and parents have become increasingly preoccupied in recent decades with measurable academic attainment, forcing schools and teachers to follow suit. Factual knowledge and academic skills are repeatedly assessed and compared, in a process that sometimes seems to resemble more of an obstacle race than a preparation for life. An intensive regime of competitive testing demotivates some young people, turning them off learning before they even leave school. An excessive concern with grades also undermines a love of learning in a more insidious way, by creating an ethos in which learning is viewed simply as a means of gaining qualifications, rather than as something worthwhile in its own right. To understand why this is so undesirable, even in the short term, we must delve briefly into the nature of human motivation.

Decades ago, psychologists identified a crucial distinction between what are known as intrinsic motivation and extrinsic motivation. You are *in*trinsically motivated when a task is *in*herently rewarding – that is, when you want to do it for its own sake because it is enjoyable or satisfying. Activities that are intrinsically rewarding, such as playing games or engaging in a hobby, do not require external incentives. *Ex*trinsic motivation, on the other hand, depends on some form of *ex*ternal reward or punishment such as money, social status, gold stars, praise or the fear of failure. In the adult world of work, the most obvious extrinsic motivator is money. Many activities, including learning in the classroom, may either be mainly intrinsically motivated or mainly extrinsically motivated, depending on the circumstances.

A nice illustration of the distinction between extrinsic and intrinsic motivation is provided by Mark Twain in *The Adventures of Tom Sawyer*. In punishment for yet another boyish misdeed, Tom Sawyer is forced to spend his Saturday morning whitewashing his aunt's garden fence, which is thirty yards long and nine feet high. Tom really does not want to do this. But he has an inspiration: he will simply transform the tedious task into a game, and thereby trick someone else into doing the job for him. Another boy soon appears and starts to gloat at Tom's predicament, but Tom convinces the boy that whitewashing the fence is actually great fun and a rare opportunity. Before long, the boy has persuaded a seemingly reluctant Tom to hand over his whitewash brush in return for an apple. During the course of the day, several more boys stop to jeer, but all of them end up begging to whitewash the fence and trading prized possessions for the chance to do it. Tom happily idles the day away as the fence accumulates three coats of whitewash. He has exploited the fact that tasks are rendered much more attractive if they are intrinsically motivated.

Mark Twain rounds off the story by noting that work consists of whatever we are obliged to do, and play consists of whatever we are not obliged to do. As he puts it: 'There are wealthy gentlemen in England who drive four-horse passenger-coaches twenty or thirty miles on a daily line, in the summer, because the privilege costs them considerable money; but if they were offered wages for the service, that would turn it into work, then they would resign.' Incidentally, we humans are not alone in our willingness to perform demanding tasks for their own sake. More than half a century ago scientists discovered that monkeys will happily work away at solving mechanical problems on a laboratory puzzle apparatus in the absence of any external rewards or punishments. Monkeys, like people, just enjoy solving puzzles.

There is more. Research has also shown that extrinsic rewards can undermine intrinsic motivation. Someone who is intrinsically motivated to do something may become less motivated and less persistent if an external reward like money is introduced and later withdrawn. The external reward 'buys off' the intrinsic motivation to perform the task for its own sake.

This important principle about the nature of motivation was revealed by a seminal experiment in the 1970s, in which psychologists asked volunteers to perform a problem-solving game. Some subjects were paid to perform the game and some were not paid. The unpaid subjects were generally willing to work away at solving the puzzle for no external reward, and they were usually persistent in their efforts. However, subjects who were paid to perform the same task often gave up trying as soon as the prospect of financial reward was withdrawn. The extrinsic motivation of money undermined their intrinsic motivation to solve the puzzle for its own sake.

More than a hundred scientific studies over the past 30 years have confirmed and extended the general truth of this finding. By and large, people are more persistent when driven by intrinsic motivators like enjoyment or satisfaction than when driven by extrinsic motivators like money or grades. People will often work longer and harder at a task they are doing for its own sake. Of course, extrinsic motivation is not all bad, and the right sorts of external incentives play crucial roles in education, work and other spheres.

Research has further revealed that people tend to feel more energetic and 'alive' when they are intrinsically motivated, and this vitality contributes to their general sense of happiness. You might recognise this feeling if you have a hobby or a job you really love, or if you enjoy taking part in sport. Conversely, people who are strongly motivated by money or social status are found on average to have less energy and vitality. As we saw earlier, pursuing material wealth or celebrity is often a recipe for unhappiness.

The discovery that extrinsic motivation can undermine intrinsic motivation is clearly relevant to education. Children who are intrinsically motivated to learn will typically work harder and be more persistent. However, their intrinsic motivation may be eroded if too much weight is placed on extrinsic rewards like grades or qualifications. Children whose only motivation for learning is extrinsic may stop trying when those external rewards are no longer on offer.

Intrinsically motivated learning is desirable in other ways as well. It is typically deeper and broader than extrinsically motivated learning; someone who is intrinsically motivated to learn will tend to engage more actively with the learning process, range more widely in their studying, dig more deeply into areas that interest them, and end up with a firmer understanding of the underlying concepts. By comparison, extrinsic motivation produces a more superficial form of learning, in which the student focuses on doing only what is necessary to pass the test or achieve the requisite grade.

School is of course not the only influence on children's attitudes towards learning. Parents obviously play a key role as well. Research shows that the extent to which children are intrinsically motivated to learn, both in school and later in life, depends on their home environment as well as their school. Children with a mentally stimulating home background, in which learning is valued, are found to have greater intrinsic motivation in school, even after taking account of other factors such as their parents' socioeconomic status. Parental education has a major bearing on their children's educational attainment. For example, 72 per cent of young people in England and Wales whose parents were university graduates achieved five or more GCSEs grade A*–C in the year 2000, compared to only 39 per cent of young people whose parents had no qualifications.

Intrinsic motivation also promotes creativity, both in school and the adult world of work. Business researchers have found that many companies and organisations inadvertently squash their employees' creativity by suppressing their intrinsic motivation in the pursuit of efficiency and managerial control. Intrinsic motivation and creativity flourish when employees are challenged and stimulated by their work, but not overwhelmed.

The message from psychology, then, is that if we want to foster a lifelong love of learning we should cultivate children's intrinsic motivation by encouraging them to have fun and enjoy what they are doing. We should also avoid undermining their intrinsic motivation by placing too much weight on extrinsic rewards like grades and qualifications. Ideally, children should regard learning as an inherently satisfying process that is worth pursuing for its own sake. In practice, however, their intrinsic motivation is often eroded by a heavy emphasis on measurable academic attainment, which leaves them regarding learning as merely a means to an end.

The proof of the pudding is the marked lack of enthusiasm that many adults display towards learning, despite the increasing pressures from their employers. Government research in 2002 found that more than 80 per cent of employees in the UK had undertaken no work-related learning within the recent past. The most common reason given by employees for their lack of involvement in adult learning was that they preferred to spend their time doing other things; this explanation came above practical constraints such as being unable to take time off work, family pressures, lack of advice, or the cost of course fees. Of those workers who had done no learning within the previous three years, nearly half said that no form of practical support or encouragement would have persuaded them to take part in any learning or training. In other words, this depressingly widespread indifference to lifelong learning was largely down to a basic lack of motivation.

Obsessed with the measurable

Governments and parents have become increasingly preoccupied with short-term, quantitative measures of academic attainment, while paying less attention to personal qualities such as social skills and creativity that are crucial but less straightforward to measure. The testing and assessment regimes that operate in many education systems add a hefty dose of extrinsic motivation to the behaviour of pupils and teachers alike.[3] Obtaining good qualifications is regarded as the main aim of learning, and so that is how children and teachers must approach it. The result can be the displacement of intrinsic motivation by the more fragile extrinsic motivators of exam scores and league tables. The evidence suggests that this is indeed what has been happening in the UK. One recent report concluded that the pressure to excel in exams and league tables has fostered a culture primed to produce a generation of unimaginative grafters who will be ill-equipped for the real world.

The scale and intensity of testing in British (and especially English) schools has grown over the past two decades, and so too has the practical importance attached to their results. The average pupil in an English school takes more than a hundred formal tests between the ages of four and 18, while British schools spend in the region of £250 million a year on running exams. The pressure on young people to perform is relentless – so much so that performance-enhancing drugs have even spread into the educational world. In the USA it is estimated that as many as one in seven university students have taken the stimulant drug methylphenidate (better known under its trade name of Ritalin) for recreational purposes and to help them concentrate.[4] There is a growing unease among parents and teachers that something is amiss.

One person who might have approved of this situation is Thomas Gradgrind, of Charles Dickens's *Hard Times*. Gradgrind is proud of being an 'eminently practical man', and explains his philosophy of education thus: 'Now, what I want is, Facts. Teach these boys and girls nothing but Facts. Facts alone are wanted in life. Plant nothing else, and root out everything else. You can only form the minds of reasoning animals upon Facts: nothing else will ever be of any service to them.' (Gradgrind applies this soulless doctrine to his own children, with tragic consequences: his daughter stumbles into a loveless marriage and his son is revealed to be a hypocrite and thief. Despite wanting his children to be happy, Thomas Gradgrind manages to achieve precisely the opposite.)

Now, there is little doubt that a certain amount of assessment can be highly beneficial. The right sorts of tests help to maintain and raise academic standards, as well as motivating students and teachers to work even harder. There is good evidence, for example, that informal teacher assessment in the classroom, coupled with constructive feedback, boosts children's attainment. But assessment alone will not raise standards. As someone once said, you cannot make a pig fatter simply by weighing it more often. More importantly, excessive testing of the wrong type can turn some children off learning for ever. High-stakes national exams are demotivating for pupils who do not expect to do well, which might explain why more extensive national testing in the UK has had the unintended effect of widening the gap between the best- and worst-performing students.

The wrong kinds of testing and assessment can distort education in other ways too. Schools and teachers are under pressure to improve children's test scores, and they have been quite successful at achieving this. However, one consequence of such pressure is that a larger proportion of teaching time is spent on work relating directly to the tests, leaving less time for activities that promote broader skills and kindle intrinsic motivation. What goes on in the classroom is increasingly shaped by the contents of past exam papers – an effect that education experts refer to as 'measurement-driven teaching'. This narrower style of teaching does not suit all pupils, including some of the brighter ones who prefer to learn in a more active and creative way. In science classes, in particular, pupils experience less of the fun and excitement that made most professional scientists fall in love with science in the first place. This dulling down of science teaching has been exacerbated by zealous health and safety regulators, whose wish to eliminate risks has resulted in fewer children being exposed to the colours, noises and smells that make science so stimulating.

Some experts argue that improvements in national exam results are more a reflection of teachers becoming more skilled in training children to perform in tests than of underlying improvements in children's knowledge and skills. They point to clear evidence that competent teachers can train children to perform better in almost any kind of test – even tests that are supposed to assess higher learning skills and concepts rather than factual knowledge. Intensive testing may produce better test scores, but the extent to which it produces better educated pupils is less certain.

A highly competitive culture of testing can also undermine intrinsic motivation by encouraging comparisons between children. Psychological research suggests that intrinsic motivation is strengthened when the individual can see how his or her own skills have developed over time. Doing your job better than before, or raising your level in a sport, can be positively motivating regardless of how you rate against other people. But frequent reminders that your performance rates poorly against other people's can be as demoralising for children as it is for adults – and of course that will inevitably be the experience of a large proportion of children, no matter how much standards have risen. After all, we do not live in Garrison Keillor's mythical mid-Western town of Lake Wobegon, where *all* the children are above average.

High-stakes testing can certainly have unfortunate consequences for some children's confidence and self-esteem. An eight-year study of primary school children in England found that the national curriculum tests ('SATs') had significantly lowered the self-esteem of those children who performed poorly in them. Research conducted before the national tests were introduced found no systematic connection between children's self-esteem and their performance in tests of maths and reading. But after the national tests were introduced, lower-achieving pupils started to exhibit lower self-esteem than those who performed better. The extensive preparation and practising for the tests made the situation worse.

Findings such as these are bad news, because denting children's self-confidence makes them less inclined to work hard and succeed. Repeatedly exposing low achievers to hard evidence of their failure is as likely to worsen their performance as improve it. Undermining children's self-confidence can also have long-term effects on their life choices. Research has shown, for example, that children who lack confidence in their own ability often rule themselves out of a whole range of potential future careers which they believe, rightly or wrongly, are beyond them. A child who never aspires to success is obviously less likely to succeed. Conversely, children who believe they have the right qualities for high-status or desirable jobs are found to set their career sights higher, work harder at school, and demonstrate greater persistence in their chosen career paths.

To be fair, the current system of testing and assessment in England was not designed to improve children's learning. Instead, its prime purpose was to measure and compare the performance of children, teachers and schools. Some educationalists have advocated a different approach to testing – one that *would* be explicitly intended to improve learning rather than measure performance. Such 'learning-focused assessment' would measure *how* children learn, as well as what they learn, and would encourage

218

them to take more personal control of their own learning. The evidence shows that children (and adults) learn best when they are intrinsically motivated and feel actively involved in the learning process.

Social and emotional development

We have seen that personal relationships are a crucial component of happiness. If nothing else, then, an education system that placed a high value on happiness would work hard to cultivate children's social and emotional competence. Again, though, the reality falls somewhat short.

In recent years, some schools in the UK have been experimenting with new ways to help pupils develop their emotional literacy – for example, by teaching them practical strategies to manage their own anger and cope better with stress. Experience shows that this can improve pupils' motivation, behaviour and performance. But such schools are still in a minority, and their efforts are focused mainly on children with problems. The only other institutions that run specific programmes for improving social and emotional competence are special schools for children with emotional and behavioural difficulties. The implicit assumption seems to be that 'normal' children do not need extra help in this sphere. But this assumption is highly questionable, if only because social and emotional competence is so central to the success of every child's education.

To learn well in school, any child must possess at least a basic level of social and emotional competence. Children who are in continual conflict with their classmates, or who cannot control their own emotions, are unlikely to have high-quality learning experiences. Sadly, this is sometimes the case. Some children's education is disrupted by pointless conflict, which arises when emotionally illiterate individuals fail to control their anger and abuse each other or their teachers. Children with poor emotional literacy behave aggressively because they find it hard to recognise and respond to their own emotions and other people's. The media add fuel to the flames by portraying a fantasy world in which mundane disputes are settled by force rather than reason, and where aggression is admired. In the parallel universe of TV land you do not negotiate or joke your way out of conflict – you shout and swear and kick ass.

Boys are particularly prone to this sort of emotional incontinence. On average, they are less emotionally literate than girls and more inclined to respond aggressively when faced with problems they cannot easily solve. Anger is the emotion that boys find easiest to express, although what appears on the surface to be red-blooded anger is sometimes a mixture of frustration, fear and feelings of inadequacy. Their relatively poor emotional literacy may partly explain why boys perform worse than girls in many tests of academic ability, including national exams. Nonetheless, girls are just as capable of behaving boorishly, and more of them are doing just that.

Children, and the rest of society for that matter, would be better off if schools and parents placed a higher priority on cultivating their social and emotional competence. Every child needs to learn, for example, that just getting angry will seldom solve their problems or even make them feel better. Until such barriers to effective learning are lowered, we cannot expect all children to realise their true educational potential or be happy people.

Letting children play

Probably the single most effective mechanism by which children develop their social and emotional competence does not require schools, teachers or parents (although it can be obstructed by them). That mechanism is called play, and it is a remarkable thing. As well as promoting social skills and emotional literacy, play fosters the development of thinking, communication, creativity, physical skills and independence. On top of that, it is good for physical health and helps to prevent obesity. All in all, play is powerful stuff. But what exactly is it?

Play behaviour is a universal design feature of organisms with large brains. Many species of mammals and birds, and not just humans, spend a significant proportion of their time playing, especially when young. The hallmark of play, as opposed to 'serious' behaviour or work, is that it appears to have no obvious purpose or immediate benefit for the player. However, play does in fact have an under-lying purpose and important long-term benefits. When children are playing, they are actively shaping their own development.

Play is a biological mechanism for acquiring and honing mental and physical skills. Through play, children develop their core capabilities, foremost among which are social skills, emotional literacy and physical coordination. Children playing together are having fun, but they are also learning how to relate to other people, forge new relation-ships, cooperate, deal with aggression and manage their own anger. Children are predisposed to identify with, and learn from, other children of similar age; you might have noticed, for example, that children usually acquire the spoken accent of their peers, not their parents. Individuals who are deprived of play may end up living unhappy and unsuccessful lives because they are less capable of forming close relationships, cooperating or coping with conflict. The sixteenth-century French writer Montaigne was making a profound point when he wrote that 'children at play are not playing about; their games should be seen as their most serious-minded activity'.

Another hallmark of play is its intrinsic motivation. Indeed, play is the archetypal example of intrinsically motivated behaviour. When we play, we play for the sake of playing, not because we have been rewarded or threatened. Commanding a child to be playful is doomed to failure, in much the same way as ordering someone to be amused rarely produces uproarious laughter. The intrinsic motivation to play can be strong and absorbing. Children at play are often deeply engrossed in what they are doing; their attention is focused on the task in hand and their perception of time may speed up or slow down. In fact, play has many of the key characteristics of flow, the form of optimal experience we encountered in chapter 4.

Self-knowledge is another of play's inestimable benefits. You are better placed to be a happy person if you have a realistic view of your own strengths and limitations. As the inscription at the Greek temple of Apollo advised, it is a good idea to *know thyself*. Play is a form of safe simulation which allows children to experiment with their own capabilities in a variety of situations. By doing this, they can discover their individual 'signature strengths', to use the term coined by Martin Seligman. Research by Seligman and colleagues suggests that a good strategy for enhancing happiness in adult life is to identify your own signature strengths, and then try to live your life in a way that enables you to use them to the fullest extent.[5] By supplying this sort of self-knowledge, play enables each individual to shape their own life in the most fulfilling and enjoyable way.

The concept of play applies to patterns of thought as well as physical behaviour. Mental play involves mixing unrelated thoughts or ideas into novel combinations, without initially bothering whether these make sense according to conventional rules. One of the most common forms of mental play behaviour is humour, which generally revolves around combining disparate ideas in incongruous ways. Mental playfulness and humour are key ingredients of creativity, which similarly involves creating novel combinations of ideas. Research confirms that play helps to develop children's creativity.

Bodies as well as minds benefit from play. Physical play, which encompasses games and sports, is an important source of exercise. As such, it contributes to physical health and well-being, and is also a source of pleasure and satisfaction. By the same token, lack of play can have worrying implications for physical health. The current epidemic of childhood obesity is thought to be partly a product of declining physical activity. A rising proportion of school-aged children are driven to and from school every day instead of walking; and once they get home, their parents prefer them to stay indoors rather than run around outside with their friends. Watching TV, which consumes three hours a day of the average child's time, is another major enemy of active play.

Consumerist attitudes towards education place further constraints on children's play. The competitive pressures on children and schools to perform academically have put the squeeze on supposedly unproductive play, leaving children less time just to muck about. Even though most parents and schools would acknowledge that play is valuable, they may nonetheless be inclined to regard it as just another way of boosting educational attainment. But parents who earnestly thrust 'educational' toys into their children's hands, and attempt to choreograph their play for them, are missing the point. Play is quintessentially an informal and intrinsically motivated activity, and you cannot force children to play in particular ways or at particular times. Moreover, the biggest pay-offs of play, such as better social skills, emotional literacy and physical health, may not become apparent for a long time. By chasing after immediate educational dividends, parents risk poisoning the very thing they are trying to foster.

Faster is not better

Society's preoccupation with short-term, measurable attainment has reinforced another highly dubious belief – namely, that it is desirable to accelerate children's learning by teaching them to reach educational milestones at the earliest possible ages. Most parents are pleased if their child is reading some words at the age of three or four, especially if he or she has stolen a march on other children. The American psychologist Steven Pinker commented that parenting has become 'an unforgiving vigil to keep the helpless infant from falling behind in the great race of life'. Similarly, schools are judged by their ability to get pupils performing academically at younger ages.

The desire for precocious attainment can be seen long before children start school, when competitive parents trade statistics about the ages at which their children uttered their first word or took their first step. For similar reasons, many parents shell out money for products that they think will accelerate the intellectual development of their offspring. One of many examples is the Baby Einstein

Company's best-selling *Baby Shakespeare World of Poetry* DVD. Aimed at children from 12 months up to four years of age, it 'develops little ones' by exposing them to the words of '12 master poets' and the music of Ludwig van Beethoven. Or there is the Baby Einstein *Language Nursery* video, aimed at 12–18-month-olds, which exposes the lucky infant to the sounds of various languages, including Spanish, French, German, Hebrew, Russian and Japanese.

Of course, not all forms of precociousness are attractive to parents. They might want their child to be ahead of the pack academically, but sexual precociousness is an altogether different matter. (And they have a point. Research shows that children who reach puberty abnormally early – which is usually defined as before eight years of age for girls and nine for boys – may suffer negative psychological consequences in the longer term.) Sexuality aside, however, the general assumption seems to be that faster means better.

But faster does *not* necessarily mean better – not even in education. A fundamental lesson from biology is that children are not merely small and incompetent versions of adults. Childhood has a biological purpose; it is a crucial period in development when we acquire the knowledge, skills and experience we need to thrive as independent individuals. And because childhood has a purpose, anything that forestalls or distorts it may be storing up problems for the future. In particular, encouraging children to behave as though they were miniature adults may be less than ideal for their longer-term well-being.

Children need time and space to develop – socially, emotionally, intellectually and physically. Pressing young children into reading and writing before they are ready can undermine their motivation to learn. Moreover, the time they spend acquiring these skills is time they do not spend playing. Forcing the pace by academic hothousing might produce short-term gains in measurable performance, but at a long-term cost. Some children would be better off playing more now and learning more later.

Accelerating the pace of intellectual development can produce undesirable outcomes, especially when viewed in the context of the whole lifespan. Many child prodigies turn out to be less spectacularly successful as adults, and some end up with real problems. In one notorious case, an American child genius was proclaimed as 'the cleverest boy on the planet', with an IQ said to be 298. This wunderkind was playing chess at the age of three and enrolled on an Internet course in computer maths at the age of four. The story ended in tears, however, with allegations that his mother had faked his results. The mother was charged with neglect and the boy had a breakdown. He ended up in hospital, suicidal and estranged from his mother, after apparently trying to kill himself. Later evaluations revealed that he was only of average intelligence. Most of his astonishing feats of precocious intellect had been conducted by e-mail, apparently with the help of his mother.

For every Mozart, there are countless other young geniuses who fail to live up to expectations and sink without trace. Who now listens to the music of Mozart's contemporary and rival Antonio Salieri, who was also a child prodigy? (And while we are on the topic of music, research has shown that the most successful musicians tend to be those whose childhood experience of learning music was one of having fun rather than being pushed hard to excel.)

Every year, the media report stories of precocious children acquiring academic qualifications at ever younger ages. For example, in 2001 a five-year-old boy became the youngest person in Britain to be awarded a GCSE (a grade D in maths, as it happens). The boy's father told one newspaper that he believed *every* child could do the same, with the right encouragement. (Even if that were true, you might wonder why they would want to.) The five-year-old acquired his GCSE at a tutorial college which specialised in teaching young children of normal ability to pass GCSEs. One academic expert on maths education commented that 'none of these children will ever amount to anything. They are not really gifted kids or child prodigies, just children who have taken their exams early.'[6]

With the possible exception of a few rare and genuine geniuses, the vast majority of children are unlikely to reap much long-term benefit from acquiring academic qualifications at a freakishly early age. Passing exams intended for 15- or 16-year-olds at the age of five or six will probably not improve a child's chances of excelling in their adult career, forming close personal relationships or being happy. At worst, it might damage their chances of all three, by depriving them of a normal childhood in which they have ample opportunities to play and develop. More than two hundred years ago the great Samuel Johnson hit the nail on the head when he declared that:

> Endeavouring to make children prematurely wise is a useless labour. Suppose they have more knowledge at five or six years old than other children, what use can be made of it? It will be lost before it is wanted, and the waste of so much time and labour of the teacher can never be repaid. Too much is expected from precocity, and too little performed.

As nations go, the UK seems to be more than averagely sold on the notion that faster means better when it comes to education. We are unusual in sending three-year-olds to school. Formal schooling in the UK starts in the year when a child has his or her fifth birthday (i.e., when they are four or five).[7] This is significantly younger than in most Western countries, and the trend is to start formal education even earlier. The proportion of three- and four-year-olds attending schools in the UK has more than tripled since the early 1970s, rising from 21 per cent in 1970–71 to 64 per cent in 2002–3.

Although we start teaching children at a younger age in the UK, there is little convincing evidence that it does them much good – at least, in terms of measurable academic attainment. The standards of literacy and numeracy in the UK are not outstandingly impressive in comparison to several other European countries where children start formal education when they are six or seven. Indeed, the evidence indicates that starting formal education too young, before some individuals are fully ready, can be counterproductive. In particular, it can damage children's prospects of developing a lifelong love of learning.

A major international study which compared secondary school children in England, France and Denmark found that English pupils, who started formal education at the youngest age, were the least enthusiastic about learning. Danish children, who received little formal education until they were six or seven, had the strongest motivation to learn when they were in their teens and displayed the most positive attitudes towards their teachers. Almost 70 per cent of secondary school pupils in Denmark said they enjoyed learning, compared to just over half of English pupils. The same study found that the strong emphasis in

English schools on the delivery of academic performance had reduced the job satisfaction of teachers – and unhappy teachers do not make for the best possible education.

Other British research has revealed that less academically oriented nursery schools tend to produce better outcomes, in terms of children's social skills and later job success, than nursery schools which emphasise more formal teaching. Children who go to less academic nursery schools spend more time playing and, probably as a result, develop better social skills. They are also found to be less anxious, more confident and better disposed towards learning, and in the longer term they are statistically more likely to marry, stay married, vote in elections and stay out of prison. The clear message from this and other research is that few children will benefit in the long term from being taught formal academic skills too young. Some three- and four-year-olds are just not quite ready for formal education, and trying to force-feed them could turn them off education altogether.

In conclusion, education helps children to become happy, healthy and successful people, both in childhood and throughout their lives. But it must be the right sort of education – one that develops children's social and emotional competence, communication skills, resilience and wisdom. The right sort of education should also leave children with a lifelong love of learning. Academic skills can be acquired surprisingly quickly if the teaching is good and the child is ready and motivated to learn. Meanwhile, leave them some time and space to play.

TWELVE

Last things

Our remedies oft in ourselves do lie . . .
WILLIAM SHAKESPEARE, *All's Well that Ends Well* (1603–4)

Happiness is a subtle, multifaceted beast composed of thoughts and feelings, which is why there is no single, golden key to happiness and never will be. For the same reason, advice on how to achieve lasting happiness cannot be reduced to one or two simple maxims. Many different ingredients contribute to the development of happiness, and the same outcome can be reached via many different routes. But . . . if I were ever forced at gunpoint to compile my top ten tips for children and adults alike, my meagre list might look something like this:

- Take a broad, long-term view of happiness: there is much more to it than immediate pleasure.
- Happiness is good for you, good for your children and good for society, so don't be embarrassed about making it a top priority. (Remember too that adults are better able to help children become happy people if they are

230

happy themselves; we should attend to our own happiness as well as our children's.)

- Personal relationships are absolutely central to happiness and health. Be connected.
- Remember the body: get plenty of sleep and exercise.
- Be active and engaged: throw yourself into meaningful pursuits.
- Look outwards not inwards: focus your attention on other people and the world around you rather than dwelling on your own thoughts and feelings.
- Wealth and celebrity do not produce enduring happiness, but chasing after them can cause unhappiness.
- Be an authoritative parent: love your children unconditionally for who they are, keep a close eye on them, give them lots of support, set clear boundaries, and grant them plenty of freedom within those boundaries.
- A good education is one that fosters, among other things, social and emotional competence, communication skills, wisdom, resilience and a lifelong love of learning. There is far more to education than just acquiring qualifications.
- Let children play.

End notes

CHAPTER ONE: *First things*

1. Aristotle said much of what there is to say about happiness, and his work continues to exert a profound influence on Western thinking. But he did not get everything right. For instance, he harboured a deeply dubious belief that neither children nor animals are capable of being happy, because they lack the capacity to contemplate their lives or perform noble acts.

2. In particular, meditation (and happiness) is associated with increased activity in the left prefrontal cortex of the brain.

3. Twentieth-century psychology's overriding emphasis on the negative and pathological was partly a legacy of Sigmund Freud, who was primarily concerned with curing patients rather than understanding what made normal people tick. It was not always so, however. Before World War Two, a number of eminent psychologists did investigate positive aspects of human psychology, including good parenting, happy marriages and the nature of genius. After World War Two, however, psychology descended into what one eminent commentator described as 'victimology'. To be fair, this

disease-oriented approach to psychology proved to be reasonably successful at finding cures or palliatives: since World War Two, more than a dozen mental disorders have become treatable and some are curable. However, psychology and psychiatry have been less successful at preventing mental health problems in the first place. Even though effective treatments are now available for some forms of depression and anxiety disorder, as many people as ever (if not more) are now suffering from them.

CHAPTER TWO: *What is happiness?*

1. According to the World Health Organization definition, health is a state of 'complete physical, mental and social well-being'. Medical practitioners increasingly seek to judge the effectiveness of clinical care in terms of its effects on patients' quality of life. 'Quality of life' can be defined in various ways, but some idea of happiness usually lies at their heart.

2. Psychologists often use the term *positive affect* to refer to what I have called pleasure, and *negative affect* to refer to displeasure.

3. The ancient Greeks developed a concept they called *eudaimonia*. This is often translated simply as 'happiness' but it means something more subtle than the modern colloquial sense of 'happiness'. A more literal translation would be something like 'feelings accompanying behaviour consistent with your *daimon*, or true self'. Your *daimon* is a state of excellence for which you strive and which gives meaning and direction to your life. (Lovers of *His Dark Materials* take note.) *Eudaimonia* is a state in which you are expressing your true self, striving to realise your own potential, and thereby living the most fulfilling life of which you are capable.

4. The Greek philosopher Epicurus, who lived from 341 to 270 BC, is widely – but mistakenly – associated with mindless pleasure-seeking. The modern word 'epicurean', which derives from his name, is usually equated with the hedonistic pursuit of sensual pleasures, especially fine food and wine. In fact, the philosophy championed by Epicurus was very different. To Epicurus, the supreme good lay not with the pursuit of pleasure, but with the absence of displeasure. He wrote that 'When we say that *pleasure* is the goal, we do not mean the pleasures of the profligate or the pleasures of consumption, but rather the lack of pain in the body and disturbance in the soul.' Epicurus was definitely not an epicurean in the modern sense. He taught that all a person requires in order to be happy are the basic necessities of life – food, water, shelter and warmth – plus friendship, freedom and thought. And for Epicurus, the greatest source of happiness was friendship. He advocated a simple life, arguing that even though everyone has the capacity to be happy, many people poison their lives with needless desires, anxieties and fears. He and his followers lived frugally in their community called 'The Garden' on the outskirts of Athens. The Epicureans espoused this 'Four-Part Cure' for anxiety and unhappiness: Do not fear gods; There is no afterlife, so don't worry about death; What we actually need is easy to get; and What makes us suffer is easy to endure.

5. Recent research suggests that dopamine may in fact be more of a 'desire chemical' than a 'pleasure chemical', but the basic point remains the same.

6. To use the psychological terminology, satisfaction is about *cognition* whereas pleasure and displeasure are about *emotion*.

7. The Greek word for pleasure is *hedone*, hence 'hedonism'.

8. Martin Seligman is one of the psychologists who argue that

happiness has a fourth dimension. In addition to the Pleasant Life (composed of pleasure and the absence of displeasure) and the Good Life (composed of satisfaction), Seligman talks about the Meaningful Life – one that has some greater significance beyond experiencing pleasure and achieving personal goals. Someone living a Meaningful Life is serving some cause that is bigger than they are (which, incidentally, is not coded language for God). If you are one of those supremely fortunate people who is living a Pleasant Life and a Good Life and a Meaningful Life, then you have what Seligman calls a Full Life.

9. For example, the Greek philosopher Aristippus of Cyrene, who was a pupil of Socrates, taught that the goal of each person's life should be to maximise the number of pleasurable moments. Aristippus wrote that 'pleasure is the *sole* good'.

10. Brain scanning has revealed that the brain regions which mediate intensely pleasurable emotional responses to music include the ventral striatum, midbrain, amygdala, orbitofrontal cortex and ventral medial prefrontal cortex.

11. Positron emission tomography (PET) uses radioactive tracers to measure the levels of metabolic activity in different regions of the brain.

CHAPTER THREE: *Why does happiness matter?*

1. This study, by the Office for National Statistics, surveyed people in the age range 16–74 who were living in private households in Great Britain.

2. Natural selection might also have an opinion on how happy and sad we should feel. According to one psychological theory, there is an optimal balance between positive and negative thoughts. When this optimal balance is achieved, the mind is most sensitive to threatening, negative events.

The theory, which is supported by some empirical evidence, predicts that the optimal balance between positive and negative thoughts is the 'golden section' ratio of 0.618:0.382, which has been known throughout history as the aesthetic ideal of harmonious proportions. Thus, when 62 per cent of our experiences, thoughts or judgments are positive and 38 per cent are negative, the negative ones have maximum impact. If the balance shifts too far towards the positive, our ability to detect negative events that threaten our well-being is reduced; being excessively positive is not good because it leaves us unprepared for bad events. Undiluted negativity is also undesirable, because if we are immersed in overwhelming gloom our ability to spot new threats is also impaired. Somewhere in between, at the golden section ratio of about 62 per cent positive to 38 per cent negative, the mind is optimally poised to detect potential threats. The idea of an optimal ratio between positive and negative states of mind has parallels with the ancient Chinese idea of harmony between *yin* and *yang*, and the ancient Greek concept of *sophrosyne*, which is when the mind is in harmonious balance.

CHAPTER FOUR: *Where does happiness come from?*
1. Extroverts continue to be happier than introverts when they are on their own, not just when they are with other people. This suggests that there is more to being an extrovert than simply liking company. More recent research suggests that extroverts do not like social situations per se: rather, they are drawn to those social situations which they find pleasant. Their enjoyment depends on whether the situation is pleasant, not whether it involves other people. The implication is that extroverts are more responsive to pleasure than introverts and have learned that social situations are a ready source of pleasure.

2. By analysing data from various published studies, psychologists have confirmed that measures of life satisfaction and measures of self-esteem do indeed describe two distinct, if interrelated, things.

3. The concept of flow is largely associated with the work of the psychologist Mihaly Csikszentmihalyi.

CHAPTER FIVE: *Being connected*

1. The reasoning goes like this. As the number of individuals in a group increases, so the number of different two-way relationships rises extremely rapidly. (With two individuals in a group there is only one possible two-way relationship, with three individuals there are three possible two-way relationships, with four individuals there are six, with five individuals there are ten, and so on.) Keeping a close track of all those different relationships – of who is doing what with whom – requires a bigger brain: specifically, a bigger neocortex. According to the data there is indeed a correlation across species between the average size of their social groups and the size of their neocortex.

2. In the Prisoner's Dilemma game the two players must separately choose between two options, the outcomes of which depend on the other player's choice. The scenario is usually that of two prisoners in separate cells, both accused of a crime for which there is not much evidence. The two prisoners must independently and simultaneously decide whether or not to confess to the crime. If neither confesses, both get off lightly, whereas if both confess they are both punished. However, if A confesses and B does not, then A gets off lightly while B is heavily punished. Collectively, A and B do best if they trust each other and refuse to confess.

3. The term 'social capital' was coined by analogy with the conventional use of the word capital to mean physical or

financial assets. An organisation such as a company will have 'human capital', meaning the knowledge, expertise and relationships of the people working for it. By analogy, social capital refers to the assets that a society has in the form of social relationships and networks.

4. In 2002 the average household size in Great Britain was 2.4 people.

5. In 2002, 25 per cent of working men in the UK were working more than 50 hours a week. The corresponding figure for working women was 11 per cent.

6. The exception was Northern Ireland.

7. Recent figures from the Office for National Statistics show that there was an upturn in 2002, when 2 per cent more marriages took place than in 2001. It remains to be seen whether this marked a real reversal of the 30-year decline or just a temporary blip.

8. To be more precise: in 2001, 55 per cent of men and 52 per cent of women in England and Wales aged 16 or older were married, down from 71 per cent and 65 per cent respectively in 1971.

CHAPTER SIX: *Authentic ingredients*

1. In that sense, 7.5 out of 10, or 75 per cent, may be viewed as the 'gold standard' of happiness.

2. The poll was carried out by ICM, who interviewed 10,000 people in the UK, USA, Israel, Indonesia, India, Mexico, Lebanon, South Korea, Russia and Nigeria. The interviews were carried out in January 2004. The poll was commissioned by the BBC for their programme 'What the World Thinks of God'.

3. A mere 14 per cent of the female fictional TV characters and 24 per cent of the males were overweight or obese. Among real Americans the proportions are more than double.

CHAPTER SEVEN: *Snares and delusions*

1. To give just one example, the Bible has this to say: 'And whatever my eyes desired I did not keep from them; I kept my heart from no pleasure, for my heart found pleasure in all my toil, and this was my reward for all my toil. / Then I considered all that my hands had done and the toil I had spent in doing it, and behold, all was vanity and a striving after wind, and there was nothing to be gained under the sun.' (Ecclesiastes, 2:10–11)

2. Research has confirmed that people are generally more sensitive to losses than gains. One practical strategy, therefore, is to regard losses as costs rather than losses. Another strategy based on psychological research is to aggregate losses and segregate gains: given the choice, you should opt to receive three unwelcome bills on the same day rather than on three separate days, whereas you should choose to receive three bonus payments on three separate days rather than all together.

3. Many different definitions of self-esteem are floating around in the psychological literature, some of which are long and complicated. Researchers in this field do not universally agree about the nature and definition of self-esteem. However, what most definitions have in common is a sense of valuing or liking oneself.

4. Those wonderful people at www.despair.com have this to say on the subject of optimism: 'Every cloud has a silver lining, but lightning kills hundreds of people each year who are trying to find it.'

5. It must be said, however, that many of the published studies in this area have methodological problems, reducing the degree of confidence that can be attached to their conclusions.

End notes

CHAPTER EIGHT: *Wealth and celebrity*

1. The only major exception to the rule that quality of life is lower in poorer countries is the suicide rate, which tends to be higher in wealthier nations.

2. Here, for example, is one of the many things the Bible has to say on wealth: 'He who loves money will not be satisfied with money; nor he who loves wealth, with gain: this also is vanity. / When goods increase, they increase who eat them; and what gain has their owner but to see them with his eyes?' (Ecclesiastes, 5:10–11)

CHAPTER TEN: *The authoritative parent*

1. Psychologists and popular writers on parenting have applied a variety of labels to these same basic categories. For example, some refer to *indulgent* parenting as *permissive-indulgent*, and to *uninvolved* as *permissive-neglectful*. Others lump together *indulgent* and *uninvolved* into a single category, variously called *permissive*, *laissez-faire* or *passive* parenting. But the underlying idea remains more or less the same.

2. Shyness may be regarded as one manifestation of a more general trait called behavioural inhibition, which is a tendency to withdraw from unfamiliar or challenging situations. In the case of shyness, the behavioural inhibition occurs in social situations. Behavioural inhibition has a significant inherited component and tends to remain fairly stable during an individual's childhood.

3. Judging whether an individual child really is shy can be difficult, especially if the only source of data is the child's mother. Studies have found that mothers of securely attached children tend to overestimate their child's shyness, whereas mothers of insecurely attached children do the opposite. The only reliable way of deciding is to observe the child's behaviour in

social situations. Scientists assess shyness (strictly speaking, behavioural inhibition) using a well-tried technique known as the Strange Situation. The mother leaves her child playing in a room, while the researchers observe and record through a one-way mirror. An unfamiliar adult then enters the room. The child's response to the stranger can be very revealing. Outgoing children with low levels of behavioural inhibition usually respond to the stranger in a friendly, open way, whereas shy children with a high level of behavioural inhibition are usually unresponsive and anxious.

4. Psychologists use the term *self-efficacy* to refer to the individual's sense of their own abilities and capacity to deal with the particular conditions of their life.

CHAPTER ELEVEN: *Education, education*

1. The average salary in 2002 of newly qualified teachers working in English secondary schools was £18,030. The corresponding figure for newly qualified teachers in nursery and primary schools was £17,750. Fortunately, teachers' salaries do rise over time: the overall average salary of full-time regular qualified classroom teachers of all ages in maintained schools in England in March 2002 was £25,250 for nursery and primary schools and £28,040 for secondary schools.

2. The tide may be starting to turn in England. In 2003 the government launched a new national strategy for English primary schools called 'Excellence and Enjoyment'. The policy document acknowledged that 'children learn better when they are excited and engaged', and stated that 'the goal is for every primary school to combine excellence in teaching with enjoyment of learning'.

3. The education systems in England, Wales, Scotland and Northern Ireland differ in various respects. For example, there is no statutory national curriculum in Scotland. The

national school performance tables that were introduced across the UK in 1993 were subsequently abolished in Wales and Northern Ireland.

4. Methylphenidate is normally used to treat Attention Deficit/ Hyperactivity Disorder (ADHD) and about 3 per cent of all Americans aged between 5 and 18 take it for that purpose. However, methylphenidate abuse has become increasingly common among adolescents and adults. Studies have found that between 3 per cent and 16 per cent of American undergraduates admit to having taken methylphenidate for recreational or lifestyle purposes within the previous year.

5. You can find out your own signature strengths by completing an online questionnaire at Professor Seligman's website: www.authentichappiness.org

6. A previous holder of the UK record for acquiring maths qualifications when preternaturally young was a girl called Ruth Lawrence, who clearly was a child of rare and genuine talent. She passed A Level maths at the age of nine and graduated with a first-class honours degree in maths from Oxford University at the age of 13. Ruth never went to school and was tutored by her father, who accompanied her to university and was her constant companion at lectures and tutorials. She later became an academic in Israel, and is perhaps better known now for having been a precocious child.

7. In England, Scotland and Wales, parents are required by law to ensure that their children receive a full-time education between the ages of 5 and 16. This means they must enter full-time schooling no later than the start of the term after their fifth birthday. In Northern Ireland children must by law receive a full-time education between the ages of 4 and 16.

References

General

Argyle, Michael. 2001. *The Psychology of Happiness*. 2nd edn. London: Routledge.

Csikszentmihalyi, Mihaly. 1998: *Living Well: the psychology of everyday life*. London: Phoenix.

Eysenck, Michael W. 1990. *Happiness: facts and myths*. Hove, UK: Lawrence Erlbaum.

Lykken, David. 2000. *Happiness: the nature and nurture of joy and contentment*. NY: St Martin's Griffin.

McCready, Stuart (ed.). 2001. *The Discovery of Happiness*. Naperville, Ill: Sourcebooks.

Seligman, Martin. 2003. *Authentic Happiness*. London: Nicholas Brealey.

CHAPTER ONE: *First things*
The biggest issue

Aristotle. 1996. *The Nicomachean Ethics*. Transl. by H. Rackham. Ware, UK: Wordsworth.

Davidson, R. J. 2003. Well-being: perspectives from affective neuroscience. Presentation at the Royal Society, London, 20 November 2003.

Davidson, R. J. et al. 2003. Alterations in brain and immune function produced by mindfulness meditation. *Psychosom. Med.*, 65, 564–70.

Fordyce, M. W. 1977. Development of a program to increase personal happiness. *J. Counsel. Psychol.*, 24, 511–21.

Frayn, Michael. 1991. *A Landing on the Sun*. London: Viking.

King, L. A. & Napa, C. K. 1998. What makes a life good? *J. Pers. Soc. Psychol.*, 75, 156–65.

Lu, L. 1999. Personal or environmental causes of happiness. *J. Soc. Psychol.*, 139, 79–90.

Rachels, S. 1998. Is it good to make happy people? *Bioethics*, 12, 93–110.

Richards, J. M. 1966. Life goals of American college freshmen. *J. Counsel. Psychol.*, 13, 12–20.

Ryan, R. M. & Deci, E. L. 2001. On happiness and human potentials. *Annu. Rev. Psychol.*, 52, 141–66.

About this book

Crocker, A. C. 2000. The happiness in all our lives. *Am. J. Ment. Retard.*, 105, 319–25.

McEwan, Ian. 1987. *The Child in Time*. London: Jonathan Cape.

Myers, D. G. & Diener, E. 1996. The pursuit of happiness. *Sci. Am.*, 274, 54–6.

Seligman, M. E. P. & Csikszentmihalyi, M. 2000. Positive psychology. *Am. Psychol.*, 55, 5–14.

CHAPTER TWO: *What is happiness?*
Heart and head

Brown, G. W. 1993. Life events and affective disorder. *Psychosom. Med.*, 55, 248–59.

References

Cacioppo, J. T. et al. 1999. The affect system has parallel and integrative processing components. *J. Pers. Soc. Psychol.*, *76*, 839–55.

Diener, E. 1984. Subjective well-being. *Psychol. Bull.*, *95*, 542–75.

———. 2000. Subjective well-being. *Am. Psychol.*, *55*, 34–43.

———. et al. 2003. Personality, culture, and subjective well-being. *Annu. Rev. Psychol.*, *54*, 403–25.

———. & Emmons, R. A. 1984. The independence of positive and negative affect. *J. Pers. Soc. Psychol.*, *47*, 1105–17.

Epicurus. 1994. *The Epicurus Reader: selected writings and testimonia.* Transl. & ed. by B. Inwood & L. P. Gerson. Indianapolis: Hackett.

Foot, P. 2000. A new definition. *BMJ*, *321*, 1576.

Hamer, D. 1996. The heritability of happiness. *Nature Genet.*, *14*, 125–6.

Headey, B. W. & Wearing, A. 1992. *Understanding Happiness.* Melbourne: Longman Cheshire.

Larsen, J. S. 1996. The World Health Organization's definition of health. *Soc. Indic. Res.*, *38*, 181–92.

Larsen, J. T. et al. 2001. Can people feel happy and sad at the same time? *J. Pers. Soc. Psychol.*, *81*, 684–96.

Lemke, M. R. et al. 1999. Psychomotor retardation and anhedonia in depression. *Acta Psychiatr. Scand.*, *99*, 252–6.

Lucas, R. E. et al. 1996. Discriminant validity of well-being measures. *J. Pers. Soc. Psychol.*, *71*, 616–28.

McCready, S. 2001. Pleasure, happiness, and the good. In: *The Discovery of Happiness*, ed. S. McCready. Naperville, Ill: Sourcebooks.

McKevitt, C. et al. 2003. Defining and using quality of life. *Clin. Rehabil.*, *17*, 865–70.

Musschenga, A. W. 1997. The relation between concepts of quality-of-life, health and happiness. *J. Med. Philos.*, *22*, 11–28.

Myers, D. G. 2000. The funds, friends, and faith of happy people. *Am. Psychol., 55*, 56–67.

Phillips, H. 2003. The pleasure seekers. *New Scientist*, 11 October 2003.

Ryan, R. M. & Deci, E. L. 2000. Self-determination theory and the facilitation of intrinsic motivation, social development, and well-being. *Am. Psychol., 55*, 68–78.

Ryff, C. D. 1989. Happiness is everything, or is it? *J. Pers. Soc. Psychol., 57*, 1069–81.

Seligman, Martin. 2003. *Authentic Happiness*. London: Nicholas Brealey.

———. 2003. Positive psychology and authentic happiness. Presentation at the Royal Society, London, 19 November 2003.

Veenhoven, Ruut. 1994. *Correlates of Happiness*. Rotterdam: RISBO.

———. 1998. Two state-trait discussions on happiness. *Soc. Indic. Res., 43*, 211–26.

Warr, P. et al. 1983. On the independence of positive and negative affect. *J. Pers. Soc. Psychol., 44*, 644–51.

Waterman, A. S. 1993. Two conceptions of happiness. *J. Pers. Soc. Psychol., 64*, 678–91.

More than pleasure

Blood, A. J. & Zatorre, R. J. 2001. Intensely pleasurable responses to music correlate with activity in brain regions implicated in reward and emotion. *Proc. Natl Acad. Sci. USA, 98*, 11818–23.

Epicurus. 1994. *The Epicurus Reader: selected writings and testimonia*. Transl. & ed. B. Inwood & L. P. Gerson. Indianapolis: Hackett.

Grape, C. et al. 2003. Does singing promote well-being? *Integr. Physiol. Behav. Sci., 38*, 65–74.

James, William. 1902. *The Varieties of Religious Experience.* London: Longmans, Green.

Kagan, J. 1996. Three pleasing ideas. *Am. Psychol., 51,* 901–8.

Khalfa, S. et al. 2002. Event-related skin conductance responses to musical emotions in humans. *Neurosci. Lett., 328,* 145–9.

Porter, R. 2000. Happy hedonists. *BMJ, 321,* 1572–5.

Reich, J. W. & Zautra, A. 1981. Life events and personal causation. *J. Pers. Soc. Psychol., 41,* 1002–12.

Salamon, E. et al. 2003. Sound therapy induced relaxation. *Med. Sci. Monit., 9,* RA96–101.

Scarre, G. 2001. The greatest happiness of the greatest number. In: *The Discovery of Happiness,* ed. S. McCready. Naperville, Ill: Sourcebooks.

Snyder, M. & Chlan, L. 1999. Music therapy. *Annu. Rev. Nurs. Res., 17,* 3–25.

How is happiness measured?

Chen, D. & Haviland-Jones, J. 2000. Human olfactory communication of emotion. *Percept. Mot. Skills, 91,* 771–81.

Damasio, A. R. et al. 2000. Subcortical and cortical brain activity during the feeling of self-generated emotions. *Nat. Neurosci., 3,* 1049–56.

Davidson, R. J. 2003. Well-being: perspectives from affective neuroscience. Presentation at the Royal Society, London, 20 November 2003.

———. et al. 2003. Alterations in brain and immune function produced by mindfulness meditation. *Psychosom. Med., 65,* 564–70.

Diener, E. & Suh, E. M. 2000. Measuring subjective well-being to compare the quality of life of cultures. In: *Culture and Subjective Well-being,* ed. by E. Diener & E. M. Suh. Cambridge Mass: MIT Press.

Ekman, P. et al. 1990. The Duchenne smile: emotional

expression and brain physiology. *J. Pers. Soc. Psychol.*, *58*, 342–53.

George, M. S. et al. 1995. Brain activity during transient sadness and happiness in healthy women. *Am. J. Psychiatry*, *152*, 341–51.

Helm, D. T. 2000. The measurement of happiness. *Am. J. Ment. Retard.*, *105*, 326–35.

Jackson, D. C. et al. 2003. Frontal brain electrical asymmetry and individual differences in emotion regulation. *Psychol. Sci.*, *14*, 612–17.

Lane, R. D. et al. 1997. Neuroanatomical correlates of happiness, sadness, and disgust. *Am. J. Psychiatry*, *154*, 926–33.

Lewis, C. A. et al. 1996. Convergent validity of the depression-happiness scale with the Crown-Crisp experimental index. *Psychol. Rep.*, *78*, 497–8.

Lloyd, G. G. & Lishman, W. A. 1975. Effect of depression on the speed of recall of pleasant and unpleasant experiences. *Psychol. Med.*, *5*, 173–80.

Murphy, F. C. et al. 2003. Functional neuroanatomy of emotions. *Cogn. Affect. Behav. Neurosci.*, *3*, 207–33.

Ng, Y.-K. 1996. Happiness surveys. *Soc. Indic. Res.*, *38*, 1–27.

Schmitt, M. & Jüchtern, J.-C. 2001. The structure of subjective well-being in middle adulthood. *Aging Ment. Health*, *5*, 47–55.

Seidlitz, L. & Diener, E. 1993. Memory for positive versus negative life events. *J. Pers. Soc. Psychol.*, *64*, 654–64.

Seligman, M. 2003. Positive psychology and authentic happiness. Presentation at the Royal Society, London, 19 November 2003.

Tartter, V. C. & Braun, D. 1994. Hearing smiles and frowns in normal and whisper registers. *J. Acoust. Soc. Am.*, *96*, 2101–7.

References

CHAPTER THREE: *Why does happiness matter?*
Happiness breeds success

Adaman, J. E. & Blaney, P. H. 1995. The effects of musical mood induction on creativity. *J. Creat. Behav.*, 29, 95–108.

Berry, D. S. & Hansen, J. S. 1996. Positive affect, negative affect, and social interaction. *J. Pers. Soc. Psychol.*, 71, 796–809.

Bryan, T. & Bryan, J. 1991. Positive mood and math performance. *J. Learn. Disabil.*, 24, 490–94.

Clark, M. S. & Isen, A. M. 1982. Toward understanding the relationship between feeling states and social behavior. In: *Cognitive Social Psychology*, ed. A. Hastorf & A. M. Isen. NY: Elsevier.

Clarke, A. E. 2001. What really matters in a job? *Labour Econ.*, 8, 223–42.

Clegg, C. W. 1983. Psychology of employee lateness, absence, and turnover. *J. Appl. Psychol.*, 68, 88–101.

Cunningham, M. R. 1988. What do you do when you're happy or blue? *Motiv. Emotion*, 12, 309–31.

Field, T. et al. 2001. Adolescent depression and risk factors. *Adolescence*, 36, 491–8.

Fredrickson, B. L. 2001. The role of positive emotions in positive psychology. *Am. Psychol.*, 56, 218–26.

———. & Joiner, T. 2002. Positive emotions trigger upward spirals towards emotional well-being. *Psychol. Sci.*, 13, 172–5.

———. et al. 2003. What good are positive emotions in crises? *J. Pers. Soc. Psychol.*, 84, 365–76.

Furr, R. M. & Funder, D. C. 1998. A multimodal analysis of personal negativity. *J. Pers. Soc. Psychol.*, 74, 1580–91.

Gasper, K. & Clore, G. L. 2002. Attending to the big picture: mood and global versus local processing of visual information. *Psychol. Sci.*, 13, 34–40.

Goleman, Daniel. 1996. *Emotional Intelligence*. London: Bloomsbury.

Hay, I. et al. 1998. Educational characteristics of students with high or low self-concept. *Psychol. Schools, 35*, 391–400.

Howard, B. & Gould, K. E. 2000. Strategic planning for employee happiness. *Am. J. Ment. Retard., 105*, 377–86.

Kobal, D. & Musek, J. 2001. Self-concept and academic achievement. *Pers. Indiv. Diff., 30*, 887–99.

Mehrabian, A. 2000. Beyond IQ. *Genet. Soc. Gen. Psychol. Monogr., 126*, 133–239.

Nash, L. & Stevenson, H. 2004. Success that lasts. *Harv. Bus. Rev., 82*, 102–9.

Pitkanen, T. 1999. Problem drinking and psychological well-being. *Scand. J. Psychol., 40*, 197–207.

Sternberg, R. J. et al. 1995. Testing common sense. *Am. Psychol., 50*, 912–27.

Veenhoven, R. 1988. The utility of happiness. *Soc. Indic. Res., 20*, 333–54.

Watson, D. 1988. Intraindividual and interindividual analyses of positive and negative affect. *J. Pers. Soc. Psychol., 54*, 1020–30.

Wright, T. A. & Cropanzano, R. 2000. Psychological well-being and job satisfaction as predictors of job performance. *J. Occup. Health Psychol., 5*, 84–94.

Happiness is good for your health

Danner, D. et al. 2001. Positive emotions in early life and longevity: findings from the nun study. *J. Pers. Soc. Psychol., 80*, 804–13.

Davidson, R. J. et al. 2003. Alterations in brain and immune function produced by mindfulness meditation. *Psychosom. Med., 65*, 564–70.

Deeg, D. & van Zonneveld, R. 1989. Does happiness lengthen

life? In: *How Harmful is Happiness?* ed. R. Veenhoven. Rotterdam: Rotterdam University Press.

Dillon, K. M. et al. 1985. Positive emotional states and enhancement of the immune system. *Int. J. Psychiatry, 15*, 13–18.

Edwards, J. R. & Cooper, C. L. 1988. The impacts of positive psychological states on physical health. *Soc. Sci. Med., 27*, 1447–59.

James, G. D. et al. 1986. The influence of happiness, anger, and anxiety on the blood pressure of borderline hypertensives. *Psychosom. Med., 48*, 502–8.

Koivumaa-Honkanen H. et al. 2000. Self-reported life satisfaction and 20-year mortality in healthy Finnish adults. *Am. J. Epidemiol., 152*, 983–91.

———. 2001. Life satisfaction and suicide: a 20-year follow-up study. *Am. J. Psychiatry, 158*, 433–9.

———. 2003. Self-reported happiness in life and suicide in ensuing 20 years. *Soc. Psychiatry Psychiatr. Epidemiol., 38*, 244–8.

———. 2004. Life dissatisfaction and subsequent work disability in an 11-year follow-up. *Psychol. Med., 34*, 221–8.

Martin, Paul. 1998. *The Sickening Mind: brain, behaviour, immunity and disease.* London: Flamingo.

Maruta, T. et al. 2000. Optimists vs. pessimists: survival rate among medical patients over a 30-year period. *Mayo Clin. Proc., 75*, 140–43.

Meltzer, H. et al. 2000. *The Mental Health of Children and Adolescents in Great Britain.* London: Office for National Statistics.

———. 2002. *Non-fatal Suicidal Behaviour among Adults Aged 16 to 74 in Great Britain.* London: Office for National Statistics/TSO.

Murray, C. J. & Lopez, A. D. 1997. Alternative projections of mortality and disability by cause, 1990–2020. *Lancet, 349,* 1498–1504.

Office for National Statistics. 2001. *United Kingdom Health Statistics.* London: The Stationery Office.

———. 2002. *Mortality Statistics Injury and Poisoning.* Series DH4 No. 25. London: TSO.

———. 2003. *Better or Worse: a longitudinal study of the mental health of adults living in private households in Great Britain.* London: The Stationery Office.

———. 2003. *Social Trends 33.* London: The Stationery Office.

———. 2003. *UK 2004: the official yearbook of the United Kingdom of Great Britain and Northern Ireland.* London: TSO.

Oswald, A. J. 1997. Happiness and economic performance. *Econ. J., 107,* 1815–31.

Palmore, E. 1969. Physical, mental, and social factors in predicting longevity. *Gerontol., 9,* 103–8.

Rosenkranz, M. A. et al. 2003. Affective style and in vivo immune response. *Proc. Natl. Acad. Sci. USA, 100,* 11148–52.

Salovey, P. et al. 2000. Emotional states and physical health. *Am. Psychol., 55,* 110–21.

Singleton, N. et al. 2001. *Psychiatric Morbidity among Adults Living in Private Households, 2000.* London: TSO.

Veenhoven, R. 1984. *Conditions of Happiness.* Dordrecht: Reidel Publishing.

Wells, K. B. et al. 1988. Psychiatric disorder and limitations in physical functioning in a sample of the Los Angeles general population. *Am. J. Psychiatry, 145,* 712–17.

Zuckerman, D. M. et al. 1984. Psychosocial predictors of mortality among the elderly poor. *Am. J. Epidemiol., 119,* 410–23.

References

Is there anything *bad* about happiness?

Ashton, J. 2000. An elusive concept? *BMJ, 321,* 1575.

Aspinwall, L. G. 1998. Rethinking the role of positive affect in self-regulation. *Motiv. Emotion, 22,* 1–32.

Aspinwall, L. G. & Brunhart, S. M. 1996. Distinguishing optimism from denial. *Pers. Soc. Psychol. Bull., 22,* 993–1003.

Aspinwall, L. G. & Richter, L. 1999. Optimism and self-mastery predict more rapid disengagement from unsolvable tasks in the presence of alternatives. *Motiv. Emotion, 23,* 221–45.

Bentall, R. P. 1992. A proposal to classify happiness as a psychiatric disorder. *J. Med. Ethics, 18,* 94–8.

Diener, E. & Seligman, M. E. 2002. Very happy people. *Psychol. Sci., 13,* 81–4.

Harris, J. et al. 1993. A proposal to classify happiness as a psychiatric disorder. *Br. J. Psychiatry, 162,* 539–42.

Reed, M. B. & Aspinwall, L. G. 1998. Self-affirmation reduces biased processing of health-risk information. *Motiv. Emotion, 22,* 99–132.

Is there anything good about *un*happiness?

Buss, D. M. 2000. The evolution of happiness. *Am. Psychol., 55,* 15–23.

Cacioppo, J. T. et al. 1999. The affect system has parallel and integrative processing components. *J. Pers. Soc. Psychol., 76,* 839–55.

Damasio, Antonio R. 1994. *Descartes' Error: emotion, reason and the human brain.* London: Picador.

Greaves, D. 2000. The obsessive pursuit of health and happiness. *BMJ, 321,* 1576.

Lewis, Gwyneth. 2002. *Sunbathing in the Rain: a cheerful book about depression.* London: HarperCollins.

Melzack, Ronald. 1973. *The Puzzle of Pain.* NY: Basic Books.

Nesse R. 1998. Emotional disorders in evolutionary perspective. *Br. J. Med. Psychol., 71,* 397–415.

Nesse R. M. 1999. The evolution of hope and despair. *Soc. Res., 66,* 429–69.

———. 2000. Is the market on Prozac? *Edge, 64.* www.edge. org.

———. 2000. Is depression an adaptation? *Arch. Gen. Psychiatry, 57,* 14–20.

———. 2003. Natural selection and the elusiveness of wellbeing. Presentation at the Royal Society, London, 20 November 2003.

Oatley, K. & Johnson-Laird, P. N. 1995. The communicative theory of emotions. In: *Goals and Affect,* ed. L. L. Martin & A. Tesser. Hillsdale, NJ: Erlbaum.

Schopenhauer, Arthur. 1966. *The World as Will and Representation. Vol 2.* Transl. E. F. J. Payne. NY: Dover.

Schwartz, R. M. & Garamoni, G. L. 1986. A structural model of positive and negative states of mind. *Adv. Cogn. Behav. Res., 5,* 1–62.

Thomas, Lewis. 1980. *The Medusa and the Snail.* London: Allen Lane.

Zangara, A. et al. 2002. A comparison of the effects of a beta-adrenergic blocker and a benzodiazepine upon the recognition of human facial expressions. *Psychopharmacology (Berl)., 163,* 36–41.

CHAPTER FOUR: *Where does happiness come from?*
Happiness is (mostly) in the mind

Argyle, Michael. 2001. *The Psychology of Happiness.* 2nd edn. London: Routledge.

———. 2001. Personality and happiness. In: *The Discovery of Happiness,* ed. S. McCready. Naperville, Ill: Sourcebooks.

Argyle, M. & Martin, M. 1991. The psychological causes of

happiness. In: *Subjective Well-being*, ed. F. Strack et al. Oxford: Pergamon.

Biswas-Diener, R. & Diener, E. 2001. Making the best of a bad situation: satisfaction in the slums of Calcutta. *Soc. Indic. Res., 55,* 329–52.

Breetvelt, I. S. & Van Dam, F. S. 1991. Underreporting by cancer patients. *Soc. Sci. Med., 32,* 981–7.

Brickman, P. et al. 1978. Lottery winners and accident victims: is happiness relative? *J. Pers. Soc. Psychol., 36,* 917–27.

Cameron, P. et al. 1973. The life satisfaction of nonnormal persons. *J. Counsel. Clin. Psychol., 41,* 207–14.

Costa, P. T. et al. 1987. Environmental and dispositional influences on well-being. *Br. J. Psychol., 78,* 299–306.

DeNeve, K. M. & Cooper, H. 1998. The happy personality: a meta-analysis of 137 personality traits and subjective well-being. *Psychol. Bull., 124,* 197–229.

Diener, E. & Diener, C. 1996. Most people are happy. *Psychol. Sci., 7,* 181–5.

Dijkers, M. 1997. Quality of life after spinal cord injury. *Spinal Cord, 35,* 829–40.

Easterlin, R. A. 2003. Explaining happiness. *Proc. Natl Acad. Sci. USA, 100,* 11176–83.

Epictetus. 1983. *The Handbook*. Transl. N. P. White. Indianapolis: Hackett.

Headey, B. & Wearing, A. 1989. Personality, life events, and subjective well-being. *J. Pers. Soc. Psychol., 57,* 731–9.

Keping, W. 2001. Dao, Confucianism, and Buddhism. In: *The Discovery of Happiness*, ed. S. McCready. Naperville, Ill: Sourcebooks.

Lawton, M. P. 1983. The varieties of wellbeing. *Exp. Aging Res., 9,* 65–72.

Lu, L. 1999. Personal or environmental causes of happiness. *J. Soc. Psychol., 139,* 79–90.

Lyubomirsky, S. 2001. Why are some people happier than others? *Am. Psychol., 56,* 239–49.

Rowe, D. C. 2001. Do people make environments or do environments make people? *Ann. NY Acad. Sci., 935,* 62–74.

Schimmack, U. et al. 2002. Culture, personality, and subjective well-being. *J. Pers. Soc. Psychol., 82,* 582–93.

Schulz, R. & Decker, S. 1985. Long-term adjustment to physical disability. *J. Pers. Soc. Psychol., 48,* 1162–72.

The characteristics of happy people

Ardelt, M. 1997. Wisdom and life satisfaction in old age. *J. Gerontol. B. Psychol. Sci., Soc. Sci., 52B,* P15–27.

Argyle, Michael. 1989. *The Social Psychology of Work.* 2nd edn. London: Penguin.

———. 2001. *The Psychology of Happiness.* 2nd edn. London: Routledge.

Aristotle. 1996. *The Nicomachean Ethics.* Transl. H. Rackham. Ware UK: Wordsworth.

Baltes, P. B. & Staudinger, U. M. 2000. Wisdom. *Am. Psychol., 55,* 122–36.

Bateson, Patrick & Martin, Paul. 2000. *Design for a Life: how behaviour develops.* London: Vintage.

Baumeister, R. F. et al. 1996. Relation of threatened egotism to violence and aggression: the dark side of high self-esteem. *Psychol. Rev., 103,* 5–33.

Bech, P. & Angst, J. 1996. Quality of life in anxiety and social phobia. *Int. Clin. Psychopharmacol., 11 S3,* 97–100.

Berk, L. S. et al. 1989. Neuroendocrine and stress hormone changes during mirthful laughter. *Am. J. Med. Sci., 298,* 390–96.

Berry, D. S. & Hansen, J. S. 1996. Positive affect, negative affect, and social interaction. *J. Pers. Soc. Psychol., 71,* 796–809.

References

Bohnert, A. M. et al. 2003. Emotional competence and aggressive behavior in school-age children. *J. Abnorm. Child Psychol.*, *31*, 79–91.

Boyd-Wilson, B. M. et al. 2002. Present and correct: we kid ourselves less when we live in the moment. *Pers. Individ. Diff.*, *33*, 691–702.

Cammock, T. et al. 1994. Personality correlates of scores on the Depression–Happiness Scale. *Psychol. Rep.*, *75*, 1649–50.

Christiansen, C. H. et al. 1999. Occupations and well-being. *Am. J. Occup. Ther.*, *53*, 91–100.

Clark, A. E. & Oswald, A. J. 1994. Unhappiness and unemployment. *Econ. J.*, *104*, 648–59.

Clarke, S. G. & Haworth, J. T. 1994. Flow experience in the daily lives of 6th-form college-students. *Br. J. Psychol.*, *85*, 511–23.

Cohen, M. 2001. Happiness and humour. *Aust. Fam. Physician*, *30*, 17–19.

Compton, W. C. 2000. Meaningfulness as a mediator of subjective well-being. *Psychol. Rep.*, *87*, 156–60.

Costa, P. T. et al. 1981. Personal adjustment to aging: longitudinal prediction from neuroticism and extraversion. *J. Gerontol.*, *36*, 78–85.

Crandall, J. E. 1984. Social interest as a moderator of life stress. *J. Pers. Soc. Psychol.*, *47*, 164–74.

Csikszentmihalyi, Mihalyi. 1992. *Flow: the psychology of happiness*. London: Rider.

———. 1998: *Living Well: the psychology of everyday life*. London: Phoenix.

———. 1999. If we are so rich, why aren't we happy? *Am. Psychol.*, *54*, 821–7.

Dalai Lama & Cutler, Howard C. 1998. *The Art of Happiness*. London: Coronet.

DeNeve, K. M. & Cooper, H. 1998. The happy personality: a

259

meta-analysis of 137 personality traits and subjective well-being. *Psychol. Bull., 124,* 197–229.

Diener, E. & Diener, C. 1995. The wealth of nations revisited: income and quality of life. *Soc. Indic. Res., 36,* 275–86.

Diener, E. & Diener, M. 1995. Cross-cultural correlates of life satisfaction and self-esteem. *J. Pers. Soc. Psychol., 68,* 653–63.

Dillon, K. M. et al. 1985. Positive emotional states and enhancement of the immune system. *Int. J. Psychiatry, 15,* 13–18.

Ellermann, C. R. & Reed, P. G. 2001. Self-transcendence and depression in middle-age adults. *West. J. Nurs. Res., 23,* 698–713.

Fordham, K. & Stevenson-Hinde, J. 1999. Shyness, friendship quality, and adjustment during middle childhood. *J. Child Psychol. Psychiatry, 40,* 757–68.

Fry, W. F. 1992. The physiologic effects of humor, mirth, and laughter. *JAMA, 267,* 1857–8.

Green, J. D. et al. 2003. Happy mood decreases self-focused attention. *Br. J. Soc. Psychol., 42,* 147–57.

Hallowell, Edward M. 2002. *The Childhood Roots of Adult Happiness.* NY: Ballantine.

Hermans, H. J. 1992. Unhappy self-esteem. *J. Psychol., 126,* 555–70.

Hills, P. & Argyle, M. 2001. Happiness, introversion-extraversion and happy introverts. *Pers. Indiv. Diff., 30,* 595–608.

Jackson, S. A. et al. 1998. Psychological correlates of flow in sport. *J. Sport Exerc. Psychol., 20,* 358–78.

King, L. A. et al. 1998. Daily goals, life goals, and worst fears. *J. Pers., 66,* 713–44.

Kopp, R. G. & Ruzicka, M. F. 1993. Women's multiple roles and psychological well-being. *Psychol. Rep., 72,* 1351–4.

Kwan, V. S. Y. et al. 1997. Pancultural explanations for life satisfaction: adding relationship harmony to self-esteem. *J. Pers. Soc. Psychol., 73*, 1038–51.

Lapierre, S. et al. 1997. Personal goals and subjective well-being in later life. *Int. J. Aging Hum. Dev., 45*, 287–303.

Larson, R. 1989. Is feeling 'in control' related to happiness in daily life? *Psychol. Rep., 64*, 775–84.

Lucas, R. E. & Diener, E. 2001. Understanding extraverts' enjoyment of social situations: the importance of pleasantness. *J. Pers. Soc. Psychol., 81*, 343–56.

Lucas, R. E. et al. 1996. Discriminant validity of well-being measures. *J. Pers. Soc. Psychol., 71*, 616–28.

Magnus, K. et al. 1993. Extraversion and neuroticism as predictors of objective life events. *J. Pers. Soc. Psychol., 65*, 1046–53.

Maruta, T. et al. 2000. Optimists vs pessimists: survival rate among medical patients over a 30-year period. *Mayo Clin. Proc., 75*, 140–43.

Maslow, A. H. 1959. Cognition of being in the peak experiences. *J. Genet. Psychol., 94*, 43–66.

Massimini, F. & Delle Fave, A. 2000. Individual development in a bio-cultural perspective. *Am. Psychol., 55*, 24–33.

Masten, A. S. 2001. Ordinary magic: resilience processes in development. *Am. Psychol., 56*, 227–38.

Maughan, B. 2003. Developmental perspectives on well-being. Presentation at the Royal Society, London, 20 November 2003.

Mischel, W. et al. 1988. The nature of adolescent competencies predicted by preschool delay of gratification. *J. Pers. Soc. Psychol., 54*, 687–96.

———. 1989. Delay of gratification in children. *Science, 244*, 933–8.

Natvig, G. K. et al. 2003. Associations between psychosocial factors and happiness among school adolescents. *Int. J. Nurs. Pract., 9*, 166–75.

Neiss, M. B. et al. 2002. Self-esteem. *Eur. J. Pers., 16*, 351–67.

Neto, F. 2001. Personality predictors of happiness. *Psychol. Rep., 88*, 817–24.

Office for National Statistics. 2003. *UK 2004: the official year-book of the United Kingdom of Great Britain and Northern Ireland*. London: TSO.

Pates, J. et al. 2003. Effects of asynchronous music on flow states and shooting performance among netball players. *Psychol. Sport Exerc., 4*, 415–27.

Peterson, C. 2000. The future of optimism. *Am. Psychol., 55*, 44–55.

Philippot, P. & Feldman, R. S. 1990. Age and social competence in preschoolers' decoding of facial expressions. *Br. J. Soc. Psychol., 29*, 43–54.

Pitkanen, T. 1999. Problem drinking and psychological well-being. *Scand. J. Psychol., 40*, 197–207.

Rathunde, K. 1997. Parent–adolescent interaction and optimal experience. *J. Youth Adolesc., 26*, 669–89.

Riolli, L. & Savicki, V. 2003. Optimism and coping as moderators of the relationship between chronic stress and burnout. *Psychol. Rep., 92*, 1215–26.

Russell, Bertrand. 1930. *The Conquest of Happiness*. London: George Allen & Unwin.

Ryan, R. M. & Deci, E. L. 2001. On happiness and human potentials. *Annu. Rev. Psychol., 52*, 141–66.

Schwartz, S. H. & Melech, G. 2000. National differences in micro and macro worry. In: *Culture and Subjective Well-being*, ed. E. Diener & E. M. Suh. Cambridge, Mass: MIT Press.

Seki, N. 2001. Relationships between walking hours, sleeping hours, meaningfulness of life (*ikigai*) and mortality in the elderly. *Nippon Eiseigaku Zasshi, 56*, 535–40.

Seligman, Martin. 1995. *The Optimistic Child*. NY: Harper Perennial.

References

Stenbacka, M. 2000. The role of competence factors in reducing the future risk of drug use among young Swedish men. *Addiction, 95*, 1573–81.

Storr, Anthony. 1997. *Solitude*. London: HarperCollins.

Suh, E. M. 2000. Self, the hyphen between culture and subjective well-being. In: *Culture and Subjective Well-being*, ed. E. Diener & E. M. Suh. Cambridge, Mass: MIT Press.

Theodossiou, I. 1998. The effects of low pay and unemployment on psychological well-being. *J. Health Econ., 17*, 85–104.

Vitterso, J. & Nilsen, F. 2002. The conceptual and relational structure of subjective well-being, neuroticism, and extraversion. *Soc. Indic. Res., 57*, 89–118.

Weaver, C. N. 2001. Contribution of job satisfaction to happiness of Asian Americans. *Psychol. Rep., 89*, 191–8.

Winkelmann, L. & Winkelmann, R. 1998. Why are the unemployed so unhappy? *Economica, 65*, 1–15.

Wrosch, C. et al. 2000. Primary and secondary control strategies for managing health and financial stress across adulthood. *Psychol. Aging, 15*, 387–99.

Two pictures of happiness

Crompton, Richmal. 1922. *Just – William*. London: George Newnes.

Grahame, Kenneth. 1908. *The Wind in the Willows*. London: Methuen.

The characteristics of very happy people

Diener, E. & Seligman, M. E. 2002. Very happy people. *Psychol. Sci., 13*, 81–4.

CHAPTER FIVE: *Being connected*
Relationships rule, OK?

Aldridge, S. et al. 2002. *Social capital – a discussion paper.* London: Cabinet Office Performance & Innovation Unit.

Altmann, J. 2003. Physiological and behavioural perspectives on well-being in primates. Presentation at the Royal Society, London, 20 November 2003.

Costa, P. T. et al. 1981. Personal adjustment to aging: longitudinal prediction from neuroticism and extraversion. *J. Gerontol., 36,* 78–85.

Demura, S. et al. 2001. Factors related to satisfaction level in daily life for older people. *Nippon Koshu Eisei Zasshi, 48,* 356–66.

Diener, E. & Fujita, F. 1995. Resources, personal strivings, and subjective well-being. *J. Pers. Soc. Psychol., 68,* 926–35.

Dunbar, R. I. M. 1993. Coevolution of neocortical size, group size and language in humans. *Behav. Brain Sci., 16,* 681–735.

House, J. S. 2002. Understanding social factors and inequalities in health. *J. Health Soc. Behav., 43,* 125–42.

Lu, L. 1999. Personal or environmental causes of happiness. *J. Soc. Psychol., 139,* 79–90.

Manusov, E. G. et al. 1995. Dimensions of happiness. *J. Am. Board Fam. Pract., 8,* 367–75.

Natvig, G. K. et al. 2003. Associations between psychosocial factors and happiness among school adolescents. *Int. J. Nurs. Pract., 9,* 166–75.

Neto, F. 2001. Personality predictors of happiness. *Psychol. Rep., 88,* 817–24.

Pinquart, M. & Sorensen, S. 2000. Influences of socioeconomic status, social network, and competence on subjective well-being in later life. *Psychol. Aging, 15,* 187–224.

Putnam, R. D. 2003. The social context of well-being. Presentation at the Royal Society, London, 19 November 2003.

References

Sheldon, K. M. & Bettencourt, B. A. 2002. Psychological need-satisfaction and subjective well-being within social groups. *Br. J. Soc. Psychol., 41*, 25–38.

Watson, D. 1988. Intraindividual and interindividual analyses of positive and negative affect. *J. Pers. Soc. Psychol., 54*, 1020–30.

West, C. G. et al. 1998. Can money buy happiness? *J. Am. Geriatr. Soc., 46*, 49–57.

Trust

Buss, D. M. 2000. The evolution of happiness. *Am. Psychol., 55*, 15–23.

Cialdini, R. B. & Goldstein, N. J. Social influence: compliance and conformity. *Annu. Rev. Psychol., 55*, 591–621.

DeNeve, K. M. & Cooper, H. 1998. The happy personality: a meta-analysis of 137 personality traits and subjective well-being. *Psychol. Bull., 124*, 197–229.

Ekman, P. 1996. Why don't we catch liars? *Soc. Res., 63*, 801–17.

Fehr, E. & Fischbacher, U. 2003. The nature of human altruism. *Nature, 425*, 785–91.

Fehr, E. & Rockenbach, B. 2003. Detrimental effects of sanctions on human altruism. *Nature, 422*, 137–40.

Grimes, K. 2003. To trust is human. *New Scientist*, 10 May 2003.

Laland, Kevin N. & Brown, Gillian R. 2002. *Sense and Nonsense: evolutionary perspectives on human behaviour.* Oxford: Oxford University Press.

Martin, Paul. 1998. *The Sickening Mind: brain, behaviour, immunity and disease.* London: Flamingo.

McCabe, K. et al. 2001. A functional imaging study of co-operation in two-person reciprocal exchange. *Proc. Natl Acad. Sci. USA, 98*, 11832–5.

O'Sullivan, M. 2003. The fundamental attribution error in detecting deception. *Pers. Soc. Psychol. Bull., 29,* 1316–27.

Rilling, J. et al. 2002. A neural basis for social cooperation. *Neuron, 35,* 395–405.

Russell, Bertrand. 1930. *The Conquest of Happiness.* London: George Allen & Unwin.

Sanfey, A. G. et al. 2003. The neural basis of economic decision-making in the Ultimatum Game. *Science, 300,* 1755–8.

Tooby, J. & Cosmides, L. 1996. Friendship and the Banker's Paradox. *Proc. Brit. Acad., 88,* 119–43.

Social capitalism

Cote, S. & Healey, T. 2001. The well-being of nations. In: *The Role of Human and Social Capital.* Paris: OECD.

Haezewindt, P. 2003. Investing in each other and the community: the role of social capital. In: *Social Trends 33.* London: Office for National Statistics/TSO.

Office for National Statistics. 2001. *United Kingdom Health Statistics.* London: TSO.

———. 2002. *Living Next Door: social capital.* London: ONS.

———. 2003. *Social Trends 33.* London: TSO.

Putnam, Robert D. 2000. *Bowling Alone: the collapse and revival of American community.* NY: Touchstone.

———. 2003. The social context of well-being. Presentation at the Royal Society, London, 19 November 2003.

Marriage

Bookwala, J. & Schulz R. 1996. Spousal similarity in subjective well-being. *Psychol. Aging, 11,* 582–90.

Dalgas-Pelish, P. L. 1993. The impact of the first child on marital happiness. *J. Adv. Nurs., 18,* 437–41.

Donnellan, Craig (ed.) 1999. *Separation and Divorce.* Cambridge: Independence.

References

Easterlin, R. A. 2003. Explaining happiness. *Proc. Natl Acad. Sci. USA, 100*, 11176–83.

Forgas, J. P. et al. 1994. Affective influences on the perception of intimate relationships. *Pers. Relatsh., 1*, 165–84.

Hobcraft, J. & Kiernan, K. 2001. Childhood poverty, early motherhood and adult social exclusion. *Br. J. Sociol., 52*, 495–517.

Hughes, M. E. & Waite, L. J. 2002. Health in household context. *J. Health Soc. Behav., 43*, 1–21.

Inglehart, Ronald. F. 1990. *Culture Shift in Advanced Industrial Society.* Princeton, NJ: Princeton University Press.

Lester, D. 1996. Trends in divorce and marriage around the world. *J. Divorce & Remarriage, 25*, 169–71.

Lucas, R. E. et al. 2003. Reexamining adaptation and the set point model of happiness: reactions to changes in marital status. *J. Pers. Soc. Psychol., 84*, 527–39.

Maughan, B. 2003. Developmental perspectives on well-being. Presentation at the Royal Society, London, 20 November 2003.

Murrin, Kristina & Martin, Paul. 2004. *What Worries Parents.* London: Vermilion.

Office for National Statistics. 2001. *United Kingdom Health Statistics.* London: The Stationery Office.

———. 2003. *Divorce Increases.* London: ONS.

———. 2003. *Marriage in Decline.* London: ONS.

———. 2003. *Social Trends 33.* London: TSO.

———. 2003. *UK 2004: the official yearbook of the United Kingdom of Great Britain and Northern Ireland.* London: TSO.

———. 2004. *Marriage Increase.* London: ONS.

Rodgers, Bryan & Pryor, Jan. 1998. *Divorce and Separation: the outcomes for children.* York: Joseph Rowntree Foundation.

Stack, S. & Eshleman, J. R. 1998. Marital status and happiness: a 17-nation study. *J. Marriage Fam., 60,* 527–36.

Storr, Anthony. 1997. *Solitude.* London: HarperCollins.

VanLaningham, J. et al. 2001. Marital happiness, marital duration, and the U-shaped curve. *Social Forces, 79,* 1313–42.

CHAPTER SIX: *Authentic ingredients*

Geography

Cummins, R. A. 1995. On the trail of the gold standard for subjective well-being. *Soc. Indic. Res., 35,* 179–200.

Diener, E. & Diener, C. 1996. Most people are happy. *Psychol. Sci., 7,* 181–5.

Diener, E. et al. 1995. Factors predicting the subjective well-being of nations. *J. Pers. Soc. Psychol., 69,* 851–64.

———. 1995. National differences in subjective well-being. *Soc. Indic. Res., 34,* 7–32.

Frey, B. S. & Stutzer, A. 2000. Happiness, economy and institutions. *Econ. J., 110,* 918–38.

Hagedorn, J. W. 1996. Happiness and self-deception. *Soc. Indic. Res., 38,* 139–60.

Hagerty, M. R. 2000. Social comparisons of income in one's community. *J. Pers. Soc. Psychol., 78,* 764–71.

Headey, B. & Wearing, A. 1988. The sense of relative superiority – central to well-being. *Soc. Indic. Res., 20,* 497–516.

Inglehart, R. & Klingemann, H-D. 2000. Genes, culture, democracy, and happiness. In: *Culture and Subjective Well-being,* ed. E. Diener & E. M. Suh. Cambridge, Mass: MIT Press.

Koivumaa-Honkanen, H. et al. 2003. Self-reported happiness in life and suicide in ensuing 20 years. *Soc. Psychiatry Psychiatr. Epidemiol., 38,* 244–8.

Kwan, V. S. Y. et al. 1997. Pancultural explanations for life satisfaction: adding relationship harmony to self-esteem. *J. Pers. Soc. Psychol., 73,* 1038–51.

Lester, D. 2002. National ratings of happiness, suicide, and homicide. *Psychol. Rep., 91*, 758.

Office for National Statistics. 2002. *Living Next Door: social capital.* London: ONS.

Rask, K. et al. 2002. Adolescent subjective well-being and realized values. *J. Adv. Nurs., 38*, 254–63.

Schimmack, U. et al. 2002. Culture, personality, and subjective well-being. *J. Pers. Soc. Psychol., 82*, 582–93.

Schwartz, R. M. & Garamoni, G. L. 1986. A structural model of positive and negative states of mind. *Adv. Cogn. Behav. Res., 5*, 1–62.

Triandis, H. C. 2000. Cultural syndromes and subjective well-being. In: *Culture and Subjective Well-being*, ed. E. Diener & E. M. Suh. Cambridge, Mass: MIT Press.

Warr, P. & Payne, R. 1982. Experience of strain and pleasure among British adults. *Soc. Sci. Med., 16*, 1691–7.

World Values Study Group. 1994. *World Values Survey, 1981–1984 and 1990–1993.* Ann Arbor: University of Michigan.

Genes

Bandura, A. et al. 2001. Self-efficacy beliefs as shapers of children's aspirations and career trajectories. *Child Dev., 72*, 187–206.

Bateson, P. 2001. Where does our behaviour come from? *J. Biosci., 26*, 561–70.

———. & Martin, P. 2000. Recipes for humans. *Guardian*, 6 September 2000.

Bateson, Patrick & Martin, Paul. 2000. *Design for a Life: how behaviour develops.* London: Vintage.

Cloninger, C. R. 2002. The discovery of susceptibility genes for mental disorders. *Proc. Natl Acad. Sci. USA, 99*, 13365–7.

Costa, P. T. et al. 1987. Environmental and dispositional influences on well-being. *Br. J. Psychol., 78*, 299–306.

Easterlin, R. A. 2003. Explaining happiness. *Proc. Natl Acad. Sci. USA, 100,* 11176–83.

Hamer, D. 1996. The heritability of happiness. *Nature Genet., 14,* 125–6.

Inglehart, R. & Klingemann, H.-D. 2000. Genes, culture, democracy, and happiness. In: *Culture and Subjective Well-being,* ed. E. Diener & E. M. Suh. Cambridge, Mass: MIT Press.

Kozma, A. & Stones, M. J. 1983. Predictors of happiness. *J. Gerontol., 38,* 626–8.

Lykken, D. & Tellegen, A. 1996. Happiness is a stochastic phenomenon. *Psychol. Sci., 7,* 186–9.

Health

DeNeve, K. M. & Cooper, H. 1998. The happy personality: a meta-analysis of 137 personality traits and subjective well-being. *Psychol. Bull., 124,* 197–229.

Diener, E. et al. 1999. Subjective well-being. *Psychol. Bull., 125,* 276–302.

Gill, D. et al. 1998. GP frequent consulters. *Br. J. Gen. Pract., 48,* 1856–7.

Martin, Paul. 1998. *The Sickening Mind: brain, behaviour, immunity and disease.* London: Flamingo.

Mayou, R. & Sharpe, M. 1995. Diagnosis, disease and illness. *Q. J. Med., 88,* 827–31.

Musschenga, A. W. 1997. The relation between concepts of quality-of-life, health and happiness. *J. Med. Philos., 22,* 11–28.

Office for National Statistics. 2001. *United Kingdom Health Statistics.* London: TSO.

Okun, M. A. & George, L. K. 1984. Physician- and self-ratings of health, neuroticism and subjective well-being among men and women. *Pers. Indiv. Diff., 5,* 533–9.

Okun, M. A. et al. 1984. Health and subjective well-being. *Int. J. Aging Hum. Dev., 19*, 111–32.

Perneger, T. V. et al. 2004. Health and happiness in young Swiss adults. *Qual. Life Res., 13*, 171–8.

Roysamb, E. et al. 2003. Happiness and health. *J. Pers. Soc. Psychol., 85*, 1136–46.

Vaillant, George E. 2002. *Aging Well: surprising guideposts to a happier life from the landmark Harvard study of adult development.* NY: Little, Brown.

Sleep and exercise

Bates, J. E. et al. 2002. Sleep and adjustment in preschool children. *Child Dev., 73*, 62–74.

Boivin, D. B. et al. 1997. Complex interaction of the sleep-wake cycle and circadian phase modulates mood in healthy subjects. *Arch. Gen. Psychiatry, 54*, 145–52.

Bonnet, M. H. & Arand, D. L. 1995. We are chronically sleep deprived. *Sleep, 18*, 908–11.

Crews, D. J. & Landers, D. M. 1987. A meta-analytic review of aerobic fitness and reactivity to psychosocial stressors. *Med. Sci. Sports Exerc., 19S*, S114–S120.

Dahl, R. E. & Lewin, D. S. 2002. Pathways to adolescent health sleep regulation and behavior. *J. Adolesc. Health, 31(6S)*, 175–84.

Diener, E. & Seligman, M. E. 2002. Very happy people. *Psychol. Sci., 13*, 81–4.

Hicks, R. A. et al. 2001. The changing sleep habits of university students. *Percept. Mot. Skills, 93*, 648.

Johnson, E. O. & Breslau, N. 2001. Sleep problems and substance abuse in adolescence. *Drug Alcohol Depend., 64*, 1–7.

Koivumaa-Honkanen, H. et al. 2003. Self-reported happiness in life and suicide in ensuing 20 years. *Soc. Psychiatry Psychiatr. Epidemiol., 38*, 244–8.

Lane, A. M. et al. 2002. Mood changes following exercise. *Percept. Mot. Skills, 94*, 732–4.

Martin, Paul. 2003. *Counting Sheep: the science and pleasures of sleep and dreams.* London: Flamingo.

McAuley, E. et al. 2000. Social relations, physical activity, and well-being in older adults. *Prev. Med., 31*, 608–17.

Murrin, Kristina & Martin, Paul. 2004. *What Worries Parents.* London: Vermilion.

Office for National Statistics. 2001. *United Kingdom Health Statistics.* London: The Stationery Office.

Rask, K. et al. 2002. Adolescent subjective well-being and realized values. *J. Adv. Nurs., 38*, 254–63.

Ryff, C. D. 2003. Positive health: the nexus of neurobiology and psychosocial well-being. Presentation at the Royal Society, London, 19 November 2003.

Sadeh, A. et al. 2002. Sleep, neurobehavioral functioning, and behavior problems in school-age children. *Child Dev., 73*, 405–17.

Strauss, R. S. et al. 2001. Psychosocial correlates of physical activity in healthy children. *Arch. Pediatr. Adolesc. Med., 155*, 897–902.

Thayer, R. E. 1989. *The Biopsychology of Mood and Arousal.* NY: Oxford University Press.

Tucker, L. A. 1990. Physical fitness and psychological distress. *Int. J. Sport Psychol., 21*, 185–201.

Valentine, E. & Evans, C. 2001. The effects of solo singing, choral singing and swimming on mood and physiological indices. *Br. J. Med. Psychol., 74*, 115–20.

Wolfson, A. R. & Carskadon, M. A. 1998. Sleep schedules and daytime functioning in adolescents. *Child Dev., 69*, 875–87.

Wood, C. et al. 1990. Measuring vitality. *J. R. Soc. Med., 83*, 486–9.

Education

Easterlin, R. A. 2001. Income and happiness. *Econ. J., 111,* 465–84.

Frey, B. S. & Stutzer, A. 2000. Happiness, economy and institutions. *Econ. J., 110,* 918–38.

Haezewindt, P. 2003. Investing in each other and the community: the role of social capital. In: *Social Trends 33.* London: Office for National Statistics/TSO.

Keyes, C. L. et al. 2002. Optimizing well-being. *J. Pers. Soc. Psychol., 82,* 1007–22.

Kubzansky, L. D. et al. 1998. Is educational attainment associated with shared determinants of health in the elderly? *Psychosom. Med., 60,* 578–85.

Lantz, P. M. et al. 1998. Socioeconomic factors, health behaviors, and mortality. *JAMA, 279,* 1703–8.

Lu, L. 1995. The relationship between subjective well-being and psychosocial variables in Taiwan. *J. Soc. Psychol., 135,* 351–7.

Maughan, B. 2003. Developmental perspectives on well-being. Presentation at the Royal Society, London, 20 November 2003.

Meleis, A. I. 1982. Effect of modernization on Kuwaiti women. *Soc. Sci. Med., 16,* 965–70.

Meltzer, H. et al. 2000. *The Mental Health of Children and Adolescents in Great Britain.* London: Office for National Statistics.

Mookherjee, H. N. 1998. Perception of happiness among elderly persons in metropolitan USA. *Percept. Mot. Skills, 87,* 787–93.

Murrell, S. A. et al. 2003. Educational attainment, positive psychological mediators, and resources for health and vitality in older adults. *J. Aging Health, 15,* 591–615.

Office for National Statistics. 2003. *Social Trends 33.* London: TSO.

Ross, C. E. & Van Willigen, M. 1997. Education and the subjective quality of life. *J. Health Soc. Behav.*, 38, 275–97.

Ryff, C. D. 2003. Positive health: the nexus of neurobiology and psychosocial well-being. Presentation at the Royal Society, London, 19 November 2003.

Vaillant, George E. 2002. *Aging Well: surprising guideposts to a happier life from the landmark Harvard study of adult development.* NY: Little, Brown.

Veenstra, G. 2000. Social capital, SES and health. *Soc. Sci. Med.*, 50, 619–29.

Young T. M. et al. 2001. Internal poverty and teen pregnancy. *Adolescence, 36*, 289–304.

Religion

ABC News. 2004. Religion. www.pollingreport.com/religion. htm.

Argyle, Michael. 2000. *Psychology and Religion: an introduction.* London: Routledge.

BBC. 2004. Nigeria leads in religious belief. http://news.bbc. co.uk.

———. How religion defines America. http://news.bbc.co.uk.

Beit-Hallahmi, B. & Argyle, M. 1997. *The Psychology of Religious Behaviour, Belief and Experience.* London: Routledge.

Cameron, P. 1975. Mood as an indicant of happiness. *J. Gerontol., 30*, 216–24.

Diener, E. & Seligman, M. E. 2002. Very happy people. *Psychol. Sci., 13*, 81–4.

Ellison, C. G. 1991. Religious involvement and subjective well-being. *J. Health Soc. Behav., 32*, 80–99.

Emmons, R. A. & Paloutzian, R. F. 2003. The psychology of religion. *Annu. Rev. Psychol., 54*, 377–402.

Francis, L. J. et al. 2003. Correlation between religion and happiness. *Psychol. Rep., 92*, 51–2.

References

Grom, B. 2000. Religiosity and subjective well-being. *Psychother. Psychosom. Med. Psychol.*, *50*, 187–92.

Hinde, Robert A. 1999. *Why Gods Persist: a scientific approach to religion*. London: Routledge.

Kim, A. E. 2003. Religious influences on personal and societal well-being. *Soc. Indic. Res.*, *62–3*, 149–70.

King, L. A. & Napa, C. K. 1998. What makes a life good? *J. Pers. Soc. Psychol.*, *75*, 156–65.

King, M. et al. 1999. The effect of spiritual beliefs on outcome from illness. *Soc. Sci. Med.*, *48*, 1291–9.

Koenig, Harold G., McCullough, Michael E., & Larson, David B. 2001. *Handbook of Religion and Health*. Oxford: Oxford University Press.

Krause, N. 2003. Religious meaning and subjective well-being in late life. *J. Gerontol. B Psychol. Sci. Soc. Sci.*, *58*, S160–70.

Lester, D. 1999. Zen and happiness. *Psychol. Rep.*, *84*, 650.

Maughan, B. 2003. Developmental perspectives on well-being. Presentation at the Royal Society, London, 20 November 2003.

McCullough, M. E. & Larson, D. B. 1999. Religion and depression. *Twin Res.*, *2*, 126–36.

Myers, D. G. 2000. The funds, friends, and faith of happy people. *Am. Psychol.*, *55*, 56–67.

Park, C. et al. 1990. Intrinsic religiousness and religious coping as life stress moderators for Catholics versus Protestants. *J. Pers. Soc. Psychol.*, *59*, 562–74.

Veenhoven, Ruut. 1994. *Correlates of Happiness*. Rotterdam: RISBO.

Looking good

Bateson, Patrick & Martin, Paul. 2000. *Design for a Life: how behaviour develops*. London: Vintage.

Bruce, Vicki & Young, Andy. 1998. *In the Eye of the Beholder: the science of face perception*. Oxford: Oxford University Press.

Dion, K. K. et al. 1972. What is beautiful is good. *J. Pers. Soc. Psychol., 24*, 285–90.

Erickson, S. J. et al. 2000. Are overweight children unhappy? *Arch. Pediatr. Adolesc. Med., 154*, 931–5.

Greenberg, B. S. et al. Portrayals of overweight and obese individuals on commercial television. *Am. J. Public Health, 93*, 1342–8.

Kasser, T. & Ryan, R. M. 1996. Further examining the American Dream: differential correlates of intrinsic and extrinsic goals. *Pers. Soc. Psychol. Bull., 22*, 2807.

Langlois, J. H. et al. 1990. Infants' different social responses to attractive and unattractive faces. *Dev. Psychol., 26*, 153–9.

———. 2000. Maxims or myths of beauty? *Psychol. Bull., 126*, 390–423.

Molinari, E. et al. 2002. Psychological and emotional development, intellectual capabilities, and body image in short normal children. *J. Endocrinol. Invest., 25*, 321–8.

Newton, J. T. et al. 2003. The impact of dental appearance on the appraisal of personal characteristics. *Int. J. Prosthodont., 16*, 429–34.

Stokes, R. & Frederick-Recascino, C. 2003. Women's perceived body image: relations with personal happiness. *J. Women Aging, 15*, 17–29.

References

CHAPTER SEVEN: *Snares and delusions*
Mindless pleasure

Brickman, P. et al. 1978. Lottery winners and accident victims: is happiness relative? *J. Pers. Soc. Psychol., 36*, 917–27.

Cabanac, M. 1992. Pleasure: the common currency. *J. Theor. Biol., 155*, 173–200.

Diener, E. et al. 1985. Intensity and frequency: dimensions underlying positive and negative affect. *J. Pers. Soc. Psychol., 48*, 1253–65.

———. 1991. The psychic costs of intense positive affect. *J. Pers. Soc. Psychol., 61*, 492–503.

———. 1991. Happiness is the frequency, not the intensity, of positive versus negative affect. In: *Subjective Well-being*, ed. F. Strack et al. Oxford: Pergamon.

Epicurus. 1994. *The Epicurus Reader: selected writings and testimonia.* Transl. & ed. B. Inwood & L. P. Gerson. Indianapolis: Hackett.

Kahneman, D. & Tversky, A. 1984. Choices, values, and frames. *Am. Psychol., 39*, 341–50.

Lucas, R. E. et al. 2004. Unemployment alters the set point for life satisfaction. *Psychol. Sci., 15*, 8–13.

Phillips, H. 2003. The pleasure seekers. *New Scientist*, 11 October 2003.

Reich, J. W. & Zautra, A. 1981. Life events and personal causation. *J. Pers. Soc. Psychol., 41*, 1002–12.

Ryff, C. D. & Heidrich, S. M. 1997. Experience and well-being. *Int. J. Behav. Dev., 20*, 193–206.

Schwartz, R. M. & Garamoni, G. L. 1986. A structural model of positive and negative states of mind. *Adv. Cogn. Behav. Res., 5*, 1–62.

Suh, E. et al. 1996. Events and subjective well-being: only recent events matter. *J. Pers. Soc. Psychol., 70*, 1091–1102.

Tversky, M. & Kahneman, D. 1981. The framing of decisions and the psychology of choice. *Science, 211,* 453–8.

An easy life

Argyle, Michael. 1996. *The Social Psychology of Leisure.* London: Routledge.

———. 2001. *The Psychology of Happiness.* 2nd edn. London: Routledge.

Lu, L. & Argyle, M. 1993. TV watching, soap opera and happiness. *Gaoxiong Yi Xue Ke Xue Za Zhi, 9,* 501–7.

Martin, Paul. 2003. *Counting Sheep: the science and pleasures of sleep and dreams.* London: Flamingo.

Youth and sex

Allain, T. J. et al. 1996. Determinants of happiness and life satisfaction in elderly Zimbabweans. *Cent. Afr. J. Med., 42,* 308–11.

Ardelt, M. 1997. Wisdom and life satisfaction in old age. *J. Gerontol. B Psychol. Sci. Soc. Sci., 52B,* P15–27.

Hagberg, M. et al. 2002. The significance of personality factors for various dimensions of life quality among older people. *Aging Ment. Health, 6,* 178–85.

Haring, M. J. et al. 1984. A research synthesis of gender and social class as correlates of subjective well-being. *Hum. Rel., 37,* 645–57.

King, L. A. & Broyles, S. J. 1997. Wishes, gender, personality, and well-being. *J. Pers., 65,* 50–75.

Lu, L. 1995. The relationship between subjective well-being and psychosocial variables in Taiwan. *J. Soc. Psychol., 135,* 351–7.

Lucas, R. E. & Gohm, C. L. 2000. Age and sex differences in subjective well-being across cultures. In: *Culture and Subjective Well-being,* ed. E. Diener & E. M. Suh. Cambridge, Mass: MIT Press.

Mroczek, D. K. & Kolarz, C. M. 1998. The effect of age on positive and negative affect. *J. Pers. Soc. Psychol., 75,* 1333–49.

Myers, D. G. & Diener, E. 1995. Who is happy? *Psychol. Sci., 6,* 10–19.

Petrie, K. J. et al. 1999. Photographic memory, money, and liposuction: survey of medical students' wish lists. *BMJ, 319,* 1593–5.

Pinquart, M. & Sorensen, S. 2000. Influences of socioeconomic status, social network, and competence on subjective well-being in later life. *Psychol. Aging, 15,* 187–224.

Ryff, C. D. & Heidrich, S. M. 1997. Experience and well-being. *Int. J. Behav. Dev., 20,* 193–206.

Vaillant, George E. 2002. *Aging Well: surprising guideposts to a happier life from the landmark Harvard study of adult development.* NY: Little, Brown.

Warr, P. & Payne, R. 1982. Experience of strain and pleasure among British adults. *Soc. Sci. Med., 16,* 1691–7.

Intelligence

Cohen, David. 2002. *How the Child's Mind Develops.* Hove, UK: Routledge.

DeNeve, K. M. & Cooper, H. 1998. The happy personality: a meta-analysis of 137 personality traits and subjective well-being. *Psychol. Bull., 124,* 197–229.

Kuncel, N. R. et al. 2004. Academic performance, career potential, creativity, and job performance. *J. Pers. Soc. Psychol., 86,* 148–61.

Robinson, R. J. 2000. Learning about happiness from persons with Down Syndrome. *Am. J. Ment. Retard., 105,* 372–6.

Empty self-esteem

Baumeister, R. F. et al. 1996. Relation of threatened egotism to violence and aggression: the dark side of high self-esteem. *Psychol. Rev., 103*, 5–33.

Cole, D. A. et al. 2001. The development of multiple domains of child and adolescent self-concept. *Child Dev., 72*, 1723–46.

Emler, Nicholas. 2001. *Self-esteem: the costs and causes of low self-worth*. York: York Publishing/Joseph Rowntree Foundation.

Furedi, F. 2002. Can self-esteem be bad for your child? *The Times*, 7 January 2002.

Hagedorn, J. W. 1996. Happiness and self-deception. *Soc. Indic. Res., 38*, 139–60.

Hewitt, John P. 1998. *The Myth of Self-esteem: finding happiness and solving problems in America*. NY: St Martin's Press.

Hodge, D. R. et al. 1995. Reciprocal effects of self-concept and academic-achievement in 6th-grade and 7th-grade. *J. Youth Adolesc., 24*, 295–314.

Muijs, R. D. 1997. Predictors of academic achievement and academic self-concept. *Br. J. Educ. Psychol., 67*, 263–77.

Raskin, R. et al. 1991. Narcissism, self-esteem, and defensive self-enhancement. *J. Pers., 59*, 19–38.

Rosenberg, M. et al. 1995. Global self-esteem and specific self-esteem. *Am. Sociol. Rev., 60*, 141–56.

Mindless optimism

Eckersley, R. & Dear, K. 2002. Cultural correlates of youth suicide. *Soc. Sci. Med., 55*, 1891–1904.

Friedman, H. S. et al. 1993. Does childhood personality predict longevity? *J. Pers. Soc. Psychol., 65*, 176–85.

Lovallo, D. & Kahneman, D. 2003. Delusions of success. How optimism undermines executives' decisions. *Harv. Bus. Rev., 81*, 56–63.

Norem, Julie K. 2001. *The Positive Power of Negative Thinking*. Cambridge, Mass: Basic Books.

———. & Chang, E. C. 2002. The positive science of negative thinking. *J. Clin. Psychol., 58*, 993–1001.

Peterson, C. 2000. The future of optimism. *Am. Psychol., 55*, 44–55.

Seligman, Martin. 1995. *The Optimistic Child*. NY: Harper Perennial.

Wrosch, C. & Scheier, M. F. 2003. Personality and quality of life. *Qual. Life Res., 12S1*, 59–72.

Drugs

Baum-Baicker, C. 1985. The psychological benefits of moderate alcohol consumption. *Drug Alcohol Depend., 15*, 305–22.

Boswell, James. 1791. *The Life of Samuel Johnson*.

Courtwright, David T. 2001. *Forces of Habit: drugs and the making of the modern world*. Cambridge, Mass: Harvard University Press.

Nesse, R. M. & Berridge, K. C. 1997. Psychoactive drug use in evolutionary perspective. *Science, 278*, 63–6.

Strickland, S. & Tallack, C. 2002. *Addictive Behaviour: a review of research*. London: Cabinet Office Strategy Unit.

Warburton, D. M. 1995. Effects of caffeine on cognition and mood without caffeine abstinence. *Psychopharmacol. (Berl.), 119*, 66–70.

Quick fixes

Astin, J. A. et al. 2003. Mind-body medicine. *J. Am. Board Fam. Pract., 16*, 131–47.

Canter, P. H. 2003. The therapeutic effects of meditation. *BMJ, 326*, 1049–50.

Dalai Lama & Cutler, Howard C. 1998. *The Art of Happiness*. London: Coronet.

Grayling, A. C. 2003. *What Is Good? The search for the best way to live.* London: Weidenfeld & Nicolson.

King, M. S. et al. 2002. Transcendental meditation, hypertension and heart disease. *Aust. Fam. Physician, 31,* 164–8.

Lester, D. 1999. Zen and happiness. *Psychol. Rep., 84,* 650.

Reibel, D. K. et al. 2001. Mindfulness-based stress reduction and health-related quality of life. *Gen. Hosp. Psychiatry, 23,* 183–92.

Seeman, T. E. et al. 2003. Religiosity/spirituality and health. *Am. Psychol., 58,* 53–63.

Smith, J. C. & Karmin, A. D. 2002. Idiosyncratic reality claims, relaxation dispositions, and ABC relaxation theory. *Percept. Mot. Skills, 95,* 1119–28.

Smith, W. P. et al. 1995. Meditation as an adjunct to a happiness enhancement program. *J. Clin. Psychol., 51,* 269–73.

CHAPTER EIGHT: *Wealth and celebrity*

Money, money, money

Blanchflower, D. G. & Oswald, J. A. 1999. *Well-being over Time in Britain and the USA.* Warwick: University of Warwick.

Brickman, P. et al. 1978. Lottery winners and accident victims: is happiness relative? *J. Pers. Soc. Psychol., 36,* 917–27.

Clark, A. E. & Oswald, A. J. 1996. Satisfaction and comparison income. *J. Public Econ., 61,* 359–381.

———. 2002. A simple statistical method for measuring how life events affect happiness. *Int. J. Epidemiol., 31,* 1144–6.

Csikszentmihalyi, M. 1999. If we are so rich, why aren't we happy? *Am. Psychol., 54,* 821–7.

Diener, E. & Diener, C. 1995. The wealth of nations revisited: income and quality of life. *Soc. Indic. Res., 36,* 275–86.

Diener, E. & Diener, M. 1995. Cross-cultural correlates of life satisfaction and self-esteem. *J. Pers. Soc. Psychol., 68,* 653–63.

Diener E. & Oishi S. 2000. Money and happiness. In: *Cul-*

ture and Subjective Well-being, ed. E. Diener & E. M. Suh. Cambridge, Mass: MIT Press.

Diener, Ed & Suh, Eunkook M. (eds.) 2000. *Culture and Subjective Well-being*. Cambridge, Mass: MIT Press.

Diener, E. et al. 1985. Happiness of the very wealthy. *Soc. Indic. Res., 16*, 263–74.

Donovan, N. & Halpern, D. 2002. *Life Satisfaction: the state of knowledge and implications for government*. London: Cabinet Office Strategy Unit.

Easterlin, R. A. 2001. Income and happiness. *Econ. J., 111*, 465–84.

———. 2003. Explaining happiness. *Proc. Natl. Acad. Sci. USA, 100*, 11176–83.

Emerson, Ralph Waldo. 1860. *The Conduct of Life.*

Hagerty, M. R. 2000. Social comparisons of income in one's community. *J. Pers. Soc. Psychol., 78*, 764–71.

Hobcraft, J. & Kiernan, K. 2001. Childhood poverty, early motherhood and adult social exclusion. *Br. J. Sociol., 52*, 495–517.

Inglehart, Ronald F. 1997. *Modernization and Postmodernization: cultural, economic and political changes in 43 societies*. Princeton, NJ: Princeton University Press.

Inglehart, R. & Klingemann, H.-D. 2000. Genes, culture, democracy, and happiness. In: *Culture and Subjective Well-being*, ed. E. Diener & E. M. Suh. Cambridge, Mass: MIT Press.

Kasser, T. & Ryan, R. M. 1993. A dark side of the American dream: correlates of financial success as a central life aspiration. *J. Pers. Soc. Psychol., 65*, 410–22.

———. 1996. Further examining the American Dream: differential correlates of intrinsic and extrinsic goals. *Pers. Soc. Psychol. Bull., 22*, 2807.

King, L. A. & Napa, C. K. 1998. What makes a life good? *J. Pers. Soc. Psychol., 75*, 156–65.

Lane, Robert E. 2000. *The Loss of Happiness in Market Democracies*. New Haven: Yale University Press.

Loewentstein, G. & Schkade, D. 1999. Wouldn't it be nice? In: *Well-being: the foundations of hedonic psychology*, ed. D. Kahneman et al. NY: Russell Sage Foundation.

Lyubomirsky, S. 2001. Why are some people happier than others? *Am. Psychol., 56*, 239–49.

———. & Ross, L. 1997. Hedonic consequences of social comparison: a contrast of happy and unhappy people. *J. Pers. Soc. Psychol., 73*, 1141–57.

Martin, A. 1995. Can money buy happiness? *Science, 268*, 111–12.

Mayhew, K. P. & Lempers, J. D. 1998. The relation among financial strain, parenting, parent self-esteem, and adolescent self-esteem. *J. Early Adolesc., 18*, 145–72.

Myers, D. G. & Diener, E. 1995. Who is happy? *Psychol. Sci., 6*, 10–19.

Office for National Statistics. 2003. *Social Trends 33*. London: TSO.

Oswald, A. J. 1997. Happiness and economic performance. *Econ. J., 107*, 1815–31.

Schyns, P. 1998. Crossnational differences in happiness. *Soc. Indic. Res., 43*, 3–26.

Sheldon, K. M. et al. 2001. What is satisfying about satisfying events? *J. Pers. Soc. Psychol., 80*, 325–39.

Smith, R. H. et al. 1989. Intrapersonal and social comparison determinants of happiness. *J. Pers. Soc. Psychol., 56*, 317–25.

Solberg, E. C. et al. 2002. Wanting, having, and satisfaction. *J. Pers. Soc. Psychol., 83*, 725–34.

Srivastava, A. et al. 2001. Money and subjective well-being. *J. Pers. Soc. Psychol., 80*, 959–71.

Strack, F. et al. 1990. Salience of comparison standards and the activation of social norms. *Br. J. Soc. Psychol., 29*, 303–14.

Street, H. 2002. Exploring relationships between goal setting, goal pursuit and depression. *Aust. Psychol., 37*, 95–103.

Wills, T. A. 1981. Downward comparison principles in social psychology. *Psychol. Bull., 90*, 245–71.

Worcester, R. M. 1998. More than money. In: *The Good Life*, ed. I. Christie & L. Nash. London: Demos.

The bitch-goddess celebrity

Douglas, K. 2003. When you wish upon a star. *New Scientist*, 16 August 2003.

Henrich, J. & Gil-White, F. J. 2001. The evolution of prestige. *Evol. Hum. Behav., 22*, 165–96.

James, Oliver. 2002. *They F*** You Up*. London: Bloomsbury.

Kasser, T. & Ryan, R. M. 1996. Further examining the American Dream: differential correlates of intrinsic and extrinsic goals. *Pers. Soc. Psychol. Bull., 22*, 2807.

Maltby, J. et al. 2003. A clinical interpretation of attitudes and behaviors associated with celebrity worship. *J. Nerv. Ment. Dis., 191*, 25–9.

McCutcheon, L. E. et al. 2002. Conceptualization and measurement of celebrity worship. *Br. J. Psychol., 93*, 67–87.

———. 2003. A cognitive profile of individuals who tend to worship celebrities. *J. Psychol., 137*, 309–22.

Russell, Bertrand. 1930. *The Conquest of Happiness*. London: George Allen & Unwin.

Street, H. 2002. Exploring relationships between goal setting, goal pursuit and depression. *Aust. Psychol., 37*, 95–103.

———. et al. 2004. Understanding the relationships between well-being, goal-setting and depression in children. *Aust. N. Z. J. Psychiatry, 38*, 155–61.

Why TV and advertising are bad for you

Boynton-Jarrett, R. et al. 2003. Impact of television viewing patterns on fruit and vegetable consumption among adolescents. *Pediatrics, 112,* 1321–6.

Burdette, H. L. et al. 2003. Association of maternal obesity and depressive symptoms with television-viewing in low-income preschool children. *Arch. Pediatr. Adolesc. Med., 157,* 894–9.

Christakis, D. A. et al. 2004. Early television exposure and subsequent attentional problems in children. *Pediatrics, 113,* 708–13.

Coon, K. A. & Tucker, K. L. 2002. Television and children's consumption patterns. *Minerva Pediatr., 54,* 423–36.

Eisenmann, J. C. et al. 2002. Physical activity, TV viewing, and weight in US youth. *Obes. Res., 10,* 379–85.

Epicurus. 1994. *The Epicurus Reader: selected writings and testimonia.* Transl. & ed. B. Inwood & L. P. Gerson. Indianapolis: Hackett.

The Food Commission. 2003. Football sells out to junk food brands. www.foodcomm.org.uk.

Food Standards Agency. 2004. Food promotion and children. www.foodstandards.gov.uk.

Giammattei, J. et al. 2003. Television watching and soft drink consumption. *Arch. Pediatr. Adolesc. Med., 157,* 882–6.

Gutierres, S. E. et al. 2000. Contrast effects in self-assessment reflect gender differences in mate selection. *Pers. Soc. Psychol. Bull., 25,* 1126–34.

Halford, J. C. et al. 2004. Food advertisements induce food consumption in both lean and obese children. *Obes. Res., 12,* 171.

Hastings, G. et al. 2003. *Review of Research on the Effects of Food Promotion to Children.* London: Food Standards Agency.

Johnson, J. G. et al. 2002. Television viewing and aggressive behavior during adolescence and adulthood. *Science, 295,* 2468–71.

Kaur, H. et al. 2003. Duration of television watching is associated with increased body mass index. *J. Pediatr. 143,* 506–11.

Kenrick, D. T. et al. 1989. Influence of erotica on ratings of strangers and mates. *J. Exp. Soc. Psychol., 25,* 159–67.

——. 1994. Contrast effects as a function of sex, dominance, and physical attractiveness. *Pers. Soc. Psychol. Bull., 20,* 210–17.

Lewis, M. K. & Hill, A. J. 1998. Food advertising on British children's television. *Int. J. Obes. Relat. Metab. Disord., 22,* 206–14.

Lu, L. & Argyle, M. 1993. TV watching, soap opera and happiness. *Gaoxiong Yi Xue Ke Xue Za Zhi, 9,* 501–7.

Office for National Statistics. 2003. *Social Trends 33.* London: TSO.

Pine, K. J. & Nash, A. 2003. Preschool children's preference for branded products and evidence for gender-linked differences. *J. Dev. Behav. Pediatr., 24,* 219–24.

Schwartz, Barry. 2004. *The Paradox of Choice: why more is less.* NY: Ecco.

Schwartz, B. et al. 2002. Maximizing versus satisficing. *J. Pers. Soc. Psychol., 83,* 1178–97.

Tiggemann, M. & Slater, A. 2004. Thin ideals in music television. *Int. J. Eat. Disord., 35,* 48–58.

Utter, J. et al. 2003. Couch potatoes or french fries? *J. Am. Diet. Assoc., 103,* 1298–1305.

What governments could do

Bond, M. 2003. The pursuit of happiness. *New Scientist,* 4 October 2003.

Hutton, W. 2003. In pursuit of true happiness. *Observer,* 9 March 2003.

Kasser, Tim. 2002. *The High Price of Materialism*. Cambridge, Mass: MIT Press.

CHAPTER TEN: *The authoritative parent*

Barber, B. K. et al. 1992. Parental behaviors and adolescent self-esteem in the United States and Germany. *J. Marriage Fam.,* 54, 128–41.

Chambers, J. A. et al. 2000. The quality of perceived parenting and its associations with peer relationships and psychological distress. *Int. J. Offender Ther. Comp. Criminol.,* 44, 350–68.

Feinstein, L. & Symons, J. 1999. Attainment in secondary school. *Oxford Econ. Papers – New Series,* 51, 300–321.

Field, T. et al. 2001. Adolescent depression and risk factors. *Adolescence,* 36, 491–8.

Gonzalez-Pienda, J. A. et al. 2002. Parental involvement, motivational and aptitudinal characteristics and academic achievement. *J. Exp. Educ.,* 70, 257–87.

Lau, S. & Kwok, L. K. 2000. Relationship of family environment to adolescents' depression and self-concept. *Soc. Behav. Pers.,* 28, 41–50.

Lopez, M. A. & Heffer, R. W. 1998. Self-concept and social competence of university student victims of childhood physical abuse. *Child Abuse Negl.,* 22, 183–95.

Maughan, B. 2003. Developmental perspectives on well-being. Presentation at the Royal Society, London, 20 November 2003.

Oakleybrowne, M. A. et al. 1995. Adverse parenting and other childhood experience as risk-factors for depression in women aged 18–44 years. *J. Affect. Dis.,* 34, 13–23.

References

All you need (to begin with) is love

Bowlby, J. 1977. The making and breaking of affectional bonds. *Br. J. Psychiatry, 130,* 201–10.

Bowlby, John. 1988. *A Secure Base: the clinical applications of attachment theory.* London: Routledge.

Cassidy, J. 1999. The nature of the child's ties. In: *Handbook of Attachment,* ed. J. Cassidy & P. R. Shaver. NY: Guilford Press.

Denham, S. A. et al. Compromised emotional competence: seeds of violence sown early? *Am. J. Orthopsychiatry, 72,* 70–82.

Dubowitz, H. et al. 2001. Father involvement and children's functioning at age 6 years. *Child Maltreat., 6,* 300–309.

Kaler, S. R. & Freeman, B. J. 1994. Cognitive and social development in Romanian orphans. *J. Child Psychol. Psychiatry, 35,* 769–81.

Kochanska, G. 2001. Emotional development in children with different attachment histories. *Child Dev., 72,* 474–90.

Laible, D. J. & Thompson, R. A. 1998. Attachment and emotional understanding in preschool children. *Dev. Psychol., 34,* 1038–45.

Main, M. 1999. Attachment theory. In: *Handbook of Attachment,* ed. J. Cassidy & P. R. Shaver. NY: Guilford Press.

Rutter, M. & O'Connor, T. 1999. Implications of attachment theory for child care policies. In: *Handbook of Attachment,* ed. J. Cassidy & P. R. Shaver. NY: Guilford Press.

Vaillant, George E. 2002. *Aging Well: surprising guideposts to a happier life from the landmark Harvard study of adult development.* NY: Little, Brown.

Weinfeld, N. S. et al. 1999. The nature of individual differences in infant-caregiver attachment. In: *Handbook of Attachment,* ed. J. Cassidy & P. R. Shaver. NY: Guilford Press.

Style with substance

Aunola, K. et al. 1999. The role of parents' self-esteem, mastery-orientation and social background in their parenting styles. *Scand. J. Psychol.*, *40*, 307–17.

Biddulph, Steve & Biddulph, Shaaron. 1999. *More Secrets of Happy Children*. London: Thorsons.

Gray, M. R. & Steinberg, L. 1999. Unpacking authoritative parenting. *J. Marriage Fam.*, *61*, 574–87.

Miller, Alice. 2001. *The Truth Will Set You Free*. London: Perseus Press.

Steinberg, L. et al. 1992. Impact of parenting practices on adolescent achievement. *Child Dev.*, *63*, 1266–81.

Thompson, M. J. et al. 2002. Parenting behaviour described by mothers in a general population sample. *Child Care Health Dev.*, *28*, 149–55.

The authoritative difference

Aunola, K. et al. 2000. Parenting styles and adolescents' achievement strategies. *J. Adolesc.*, *23*, 205–22.

Bronstein, P. et al. 1996. Family and parenting behaviors predicting middle school adjustment. *Fam. Relat.*, *45*, 415–26.

Bush, K. R. et al. 2002. Adolescents' perceptions of parental behaviors as predictors of adolescent self-esteem in mainland China. *Social. Inq.*, *72*, 503–26.

Chorpita, B. F. & Barlow, D. H. 1998. The development of anxiety. *Psychol. Bull.*, *124*, 3–21.

Crandall, J. E. 1984. Social interest as a moderator of life stress. *J. Pers. Soc. Psychol.*, *47*, 164–74.

Dalai Lama & Cutler, Howard C. 1998. *The Art of Happiness*. London: Coronet.

Dekovic, M. & Meeus, W. 1997. Peer relations in adolescence. *J. Adolesc.*, *20*, 163–76.

Dickens, M. N. & Cornell, D. G. 1993. Parent influences on

the mathematics self-concept of high ability adolescent girls. *J. Educ. Gifted, 17,* 53–73.

Furedi, Frank. 2001. *Paranoid Parenting.* London: Penguin.

Furnham, A. & Cheng, H. 2000. Perceived parental behaviour, self-esteem and happiness. *Soc. Psychiatry Psychiatr. Epidemiol., 35,* 463–70.

Gomez, R. et al. 2001. Perceived maternal control and support. *J. Child Psychol. Psychiatry, 42,* 513–22.

Hasan, N. & Power, T. G. 2002. Optimism and pessimism in children. *Int. J. Behav. Dev., 26,* 185–91.

Herz, L. & Gullone, E. 1999. The relationship between self-esteem and parenting style. *J. Cross Cult. Psychol., 30,* 742–61.

Hickman, G. P. et al. 2000. Influence of parenting styles on the adjustment and academic achievement of college freshmen. *J. Coll. Stud. Dev., 41,* 41–54.

Jackson, C. et al. 1998. The Authoritative Parenting Index: predicting health risk behaviors among children and adolescents. *Health Educ. Behav., 25,* 319–37.

Karavasilis, L. et al. 2003. Associations between parenting style and attachment to mother in middle childhood and adolescence. *Int. J. Behav. Dev., 27,* 153–64.

Kasser, T. et al. 1995. The relations of maternal and social environments to late adolescents' materialistic and prosocial values. *Dev. Psychol., 31,* 907–14.

Kelley, S. A. et al. 2000. Mastery motivation and self-evaluative affect in toddlers. *Child Dev., 71,* 1061–71.

Kremers, S. P. et al. 2003. Parenting style and adolescent fruit consumption. *Appetite, 41,* 43–50.

Lapierre, S. et al. 1997. Personal goals and subjective well-being in later life. *Int. J. Aging Hum. Dev., 45,* 287–303.

McClun, L. A. & Merrell, K. W. 1998. Relationship of perceived parenting styles, locus of control orientation, and self-concept. *Psychol. Schools, 35,* 381–90.

Murrin, Kristina & Martin, Paul. 2004. *What Worries Parents*. London: Vermilion.

Musick, M. A. et al. 1999. Volunteering and mortality among older adults. *J. Gerontol. B Psychol. Sci. Soc. Sci., 54*, S173–80.

Onatsu-Arvilommi, T. et al. 1998. Mothers' and fathers' well-being, parenting styles, and their children's cognitive and behavioural strategies. *Eur. J. Psychol. Educ., 13*, 543–56.

Parker, J. 2003. Raising a smile. *The Times*, 15 November 2003.

Phelps, C. D. 2001. A clue to the paradox of happiness. *J. Econ. Behav. Org., 45*, 293–300.

Raboteg-Saric, Z. et al. 2001. The relation of parental practices and self-conceptions to young adolescent problem behaviors and substance use. *Nord. J. Psychiatry, 55*, 203–9.

Ramsey, A. et al. 1996. Self-reported narcissism and perceived parental permissiveness and authoritarianism. *J. Genet. Psychol., 157*, 227–38.

Simons-Morton, B. et al. 2001. Peer and parent influences on smoking and drinking among early adolescents. *Health Educ. Behav., 28*, 95–107.

Steele, M. et al. 2002. Maternal predictors of children's social cognition. *J. Child Psychol. Psychiatry, 43*, 861–72.

Steinberg, L. et al. 1994. Over-time changes in adjustment and competence among adolescents from authoritative, authoritarian, indulgent, and neglectful families. *Child Dev., 65*, 754–70.

Stevenson-Hinde, J. 2000. Shyness in the context of close relationships. In: *Shyness*, ed. W. R. Crozier. London: Routledge.

Sumer, N. & Gungor, D. 1999. The impact of perceived parenting styles on attachment styles, self-evaluations and close relationships. *Turk Psikoloji Dergisi, 14*, 35–62.

Taris, T. W. & Semin, G. R. 1998. How mothers' parenting

styles affect their children's sexual efficacy and experience. *J. Genet. Psychol., 159*, 68–81.

Thoits, P. A. & Hewitt L. N. 2001. Volunteer work and well-being. *J. Health Soc. Behav., 42*, 115–31.

Werner, E. E. 1993. Risk, resilience, and recovery. *Dev. Psychopathol., 5*, 503–15.

—— 1997. Vulnerable but invincible: high-risk children from birth to adulthood. *Acta Paediatrica, 86*, 103–5, Suppl. 422.

Beyond authoritative parenting

Bateson, Patrick & Martin, Paul. 2000. *Design for a Life: how behaviour develops*. London: Vintage.

Chang, L. et al. 2003. Life satisfaction, self-concept and family relations in Chinese adolescents and children. *Int. J. Behav. Dev., 27*, 182–9.

Dunn, Judy & Plomin, Robert. 1990. *Separate Lives: why siblings are so different*. NY: Basic Books.

Fox, K. R. 2004. Childhood obesity and the role of physical activity. *J. R. Soc. Health, 124*, 34–9.

Hesketh, T. et al. 2003. Health effects of family size. *Arch. Dis. Child., 88*, 467–71.

Jones, G. 2000. China's little emperors. *Independent on Sunday*, 12 November 2000.

Martin, Paul. 2003. *Counting Sheep: the science and pleasures of sleep and dreams*. London: Flamingo.

Murrin, Kristina & Martin, Paul. 2004. *What Worries Parents*. London: Vermilion.

Office for National Statistics. 2003. *Social Trends 33*. London: The Stationery Office.

——. 2003. *UK 2004: the official yearbook of the United Kingdom of Great Britain and Northern Ireland*. London: TSO.

Ogden, C. L. et al. 2003. Epidemiologic trends in overweight and obesity. *Endocrinol. Metab. Clin. North Am., 32,* 741–60.

Rudolf, M. C. et al. 2004. Rising obesity and expanding waist-lines in schoolchildren. *Arch. Dis. Child., 89,* 235–7.

Rugg, K. 2004. Childhood obesity. *Nurs. Times, 100,* 28–30.

Shen, J. & Yuan, B. J. 1999. Moral values of only and sibling children in mainland China. *J. Psychol., 133,* 115–24.

Tao, K. T. 1998. An overview of only child family mental health in China. *Psychiatry Clin. Neurosci., 52S,* S206–11.

Vaillant, George E. 2002. *Aging Well: surprising guideposts to a happier life from the landmark Harvard study of adult development.* NY: Little, Brown.

Veenhoven, R. & Verkuyten, M. 1989. The well-being of only children. *Adolescence, 24,* 155–66.

Wan, C. et al. 1994. Comparison of personality traits of only and sibling school children in Beijing. *J. Genet. Psychol., 155,* 377–88.

Wang, D. et al. 2000. Physical and personality traits of preschool children in Fuzhou, China: only child vs sibling. *Child Care Health Dev., 26,* 49–60.

Witt, L. 2003. Why we're losing the war against obesity. *Am. Demogr., 25,* 27–31.

Yang, B. et al. 1995. Only children and children with siblings in the People's Republic of China: levels of fear, anxiety, and depression. *Child Dev., 66,* 1301–11.

CHAPTER ELEVEN: *Education, education*

What is education for?

Barrow, Robin. 1980. *Happiness.* Oxford: Martin Robertson.

Barton, P. E. 1999. Learn more, earn more? *ETS Policy Notes, 9,* 1–12.

DfES (Department for Education and Skills). 2004. *Statistics of Education: school workforce in England, 2003 edition.* London: TSO.

References

Larson, R. W. 2000. Toward a psychology of positive youth development. *Am. Psychol.*, *55*, 170–83.

Walker, I. & Zhu, Y. 2003. Education, earnings and productivity. *Labour Market Trends*, March 2003. London: Office for National Statistics.

A lifelong love of learning

Amabile, T. M. 1998. How to kill creativity. *Harv. Bus. Rev.*, *76*, 76–87.

Crooks, T. 1988. The impact of classroom evaluation practices on students. *Rev. Educ. Res.*, *58*, 438–81.

Deci, E. L. 1971. Effects of externally mediated rewards on intrinsic motivation. *J. Pers. Soc. Psychol.*, *18*, 105–15.

Deci, E. L. & Ryan, R. M. 1980. The empirical exploration of intrinsic motivational processes. *Adv. Exp. Soc. Psychol.*, *13*, 39–80.

———. 1985. *Intrinsic Motivation and Self-determination in Human Behavior*. NY: Plenum Press.

Deci, E. L. et al. 1999. A meta-analytic review of experiments examining the effects of extrinsic rewards on intrinsic motivation. *Psychol. Bull.*, *125*, 627–68.

Fillit, H. M. et al. 2002. Achieving and maintaining cognitive vitality with aging. *Mayo Clin. Proc.*, *77*, 681–96.

Gottfried, A. E. et al. 1998. Role of cognitively stimulating home environment in children's academic intrinsic motivation. *Child Dev.*, *69*, 1448–60.

Harlen, W. & Deakin Crick, R. 2002. A systematic review of the impact of summative assessment and tests on students' motivation for learning. *Research Evidence in Education Library*. London: Institute of Education, EPPI-Centre.

Harlow, H. F. et al. 1950. Learning motivated by a manipulation drive. *J. Exp. Psychol.*, *40*, 228–34.

Kasser, T. & Ryan, R. M. 1993. A dark side of the American

dream: correlates of financial success as a central life aspiration. *J. Pers. Soc. Psychol.*, 65, 410–22.

———. 1996. Further examining the American Dream: differential correlates of intrinsic and extrinsic goals. *Pers. Soc. Psychol. Bull.*, 22, 2807.

Kellaghan, T. et al. 1996. *The Use of External Examinations to Improve Student Motivation*. Washington, DC: AERA.

Kohn, A. 1993. *Punished by Rewards*. Boston: Houghton Mifflin.

Office for National Statistics. 2003. *Social Trends 33*. London: The Stationery Office.

Runco, M. A. 2004. Creativity. *Annu. Rev. Psychol.*, 55, 657–87.

Ryan, R. M. & Deci, E. L. 2000. Intrinsic and extrinsic motivations. *Contemp. Educ. Psychol.*, 25, 54–67.

Ryan, R. M. & Frederick, C. 1997. On energy, personality, and health. *J. Pers.*, 65, 529–65.

Vaillant, George E. 2002. *Aging Well: surprising guideposts to a happier life from the landmark Harvard study of adult development*. NY: Little, Brown.

Wolf, Alison. 2002. *Does Education Matter? Myths about education and economic growth*. London: Penguin.

Obsessed with the measurable

Assessment Reform Group. 1999. *Assessment for Learning: beyond the black box*. Cambridge: University of Cambridge School of Education.

Babcock, Q. & Byrne, T. 2000. Student perceptions of methylphenidate abuse at a public liberal arts college. *J. Am. Coll. Health*, 49, 143–5.

Bandura, A. et al. 2001. Self-efficacy beliefs as shapers of children's aspirations and career trajectories. *Child Dev.*, 72, 187–206.

Davies, J. & Brember, I. 1998. National curriculum testing and self-esteem. *Educ. Psychol.*, 18, 365–75.

————. 1999. Reading and mathematics attainments and self-esteem. *Educ. Stud., 25*, 145–57.

Foley, R. et al. 2000. A profile of methylphenidate exposures. *J. Toxicol. Clin. Toxicol., 38*, 625–30.

Gordon, S. & Reese, M. 1997. High stakes testing: worth the price? *J. School Leadership, 7*, 345–68.

Harlen, W. & Deakin Crick, R. 2002. A systematic review of the impact of summative assessment and tests on students' motivation for learning. *Research Evidence in Education Library*. London: Institute of Education, EPPI-Centre.

Kellaghan, T. et al. 1996. *The Use of External Examinations to Improve Student Motivation*. Washington, DC: AERA.

Kohn, A. 2000. *The Case Against Standardized Testing*. Portsmouth, NH: Heinemann.

Leonard, M. & Davey, C. 2001. *Thoughts on the 11 Plus*. Belfast: Save the Children Fund.

Linn, R. 2000. Assessments and accountability. *Educ. Res., 29*, 4–16.

McDonald, A. 2001. The prevalence and effects of test anxiety in school children. *Educ. Psychol., 21*, 89–101.

McNeil, L. & Valenzuela, A. 2000. *The Harmful Impact of the TAAS System of Testing in Texas: beneath the accountability rhetoric*. Houston: Rice University.

OECD. 2001. *Knowledge and Skills for Life: first results from PISA 2000*. Paris: OECD.

Office for National Statistics. 2003. *UK 2004: the official yearbook of the United Kingdom of Great Britain and Northern Ireland*. London: TSO.

Pollard, A. et al. 2000. *What Pupils Say: changing policy and practice in primary education*. London: Continuum.

Teter, C. J. et al. 2003. Illicit methylphenidate use in an undergraduate student sample. *Pharmacotherapy, 23*, 609–17.

Social and emotional development

Blum, Paul. 2001. *A Teacher's Guide to Anger Management.* London: RoutledgeFalmer.

Bohnert, A. M. et al. 2003. Emotional competence and aggressive behavior in school age children. *J. Abnorm. Child Psychol., 31*, 79–91.

Rutter, Michael & Rutter, Marjorie. 1993. *Developing Minds: challenge and continuity across the lifespan.* NY: Basic Books.

Letting children play

Bateson, P. & Martin, P. 2000. Why all work and no play can be bad for business. *Financial Times*, 8 April 2000.

———. 2000. *Design for a Life: how behaviour develops.* London: Vintage.

Feinstein, L. & Symons, J. 1999. Attainment in secondary school. *Oxford Econ. Papers – New Series, 51*, 300–321.

Seligman, Martin. 2003. *Authentic Happiness.* London: Nicholas Brealey.

———. 2003. Positive psychology and authentic happiness. Presentation at the Royal Society, London, 19 November 2003.

Faster is not better

Addley, E. 2001. Are the kids all right? *Guardian*, 24 August 2001.

BBC News. 1999. Young, gifted and a right handful. http://news.bbc.co.uk.

———. 2004. On this day: 1985: teenage genius gets a first. http://news.bbc.co.uk.

McNess, E. et al. 2003. Is the effective compromising the affective? *Br. Educ. Res. J., 29*, 243–57.

Office for National Statistics. 2003. *UK 2004: the official year-*

book of the United Kingdom of Great Britain and Northern Ireland. London: TSO.

Osborn, M. 2001. Comparing learners in England, France and Denmark. *Comp. Educ.*, *37*, 267–78.

Owen, G. 2001. Too much school too soon spoils the child. *The Times*, 12 January 2001.

Pinker, Steven. 1994. *The Language Instinct*. NY: Morrow.

Ritzen, E. M. 2003. Early puberty: what is normal and when is treatment indicated? *Horm. Res.*, *60S3*, 31–4.

Sloboda, J. 1994. What makes a musician? *EGTA Guitar J.*, *5*, 18–22.

Sylva, K. 1997. Critical periods in childhood learning. *Br. Med. Bull.*, *53*, 185–97.

Vulliamy, E. 2002. Shattered life and mind of brightest boy on the planet. *Observer*, 3 March 2002.

Index